THE ENTIRE CHRISTIAN YEAR

DAILY
CONTEMPLATIONS
for
MISFIT
CHRISTIANS

Elane O'Rourke & Benton Stokes

ISBN: 978-1-957181-04-2

Dear Misfit Christian Readers and Friends,

Back at the beginning of 2021, nearly a year into the Covid-19 pandemic, I felt emotionally drained, unsure about the future, and creatively restless. I'd been writing and producing music for months, trying to put as much hope and positivity into the world as I could muster. Along with my ministry partner and best friend Elane I had used Facebook Live and Zoom to consistently connect with our *School For Seekers* students and friends.

I wanted to do more.

So that January, I wrote a made-for-Instagram reflection centered on Job 11:17-19 and coupled it with a photo of hazy sunlight filtering through some tall evergreens. It felt good to lean on Scripture and to share an observation or two. I decided to write a few more, and Elane started writing some too.

Writing and posting became a spiritual practice for me throughout 2021. I felt drawn to the Bible in a way I hadn't in many years. And the prayerful writing challenged me in all the best ways.

Those Instagram posts were the beginnings of the book you hold in your hands. In these daily entries Elane and I draw from our personal experiences as queer people of faith to write entries that are thoughtful, affirming, and most of all, Spirit-inspired.

If you're a misfit Christian, like we are, we believe you'll find both hope and God here.

Loosely based on the three-year cycle of the Daily Lectionary, these contemplations follow the rhythms of the church calendar in which Advent begins the new year. They are meant to be read in sequence, but feel totally free to start wherever you happen to be.

I hope these reading these daily contemplations add a little light to your days, as writing them has mine.

With love and faith,

—Benton

A NOTE ABOUT THE NUMBERING OF DAYS

Daily Contemplations for Misfit Christians is based on the historical Christian calendar, Western version, which is based on the Jewish lunar calendar.

Here's where it gets complicated.

The standard secular calendar (imposed by Pope Gregory XIII in 1582) arranges the solar year into 12 months of 28, 29, 30, or 31 days. The lunar Jewish calendar has 13 months.

The Christian calendar has 5 Big Holy Days. Pentecost is lifted from Jewish tradition. Easter is determined by the lunar calendar. Once you know when Easter will be then Pentecost is 50 days later. Maundy Thursday, Good Friday, and Holy Saturday immediately precede Easter Sunday.

The Christian calendar also has 2 Big Holy Days that have fixed dates on the Western secular calendar—Christmas (December 25th) and Epiphany (January 6th).

There are 6 seasons: Advent, Christmas, Epiphany, Lent, Easter, and Pentecost. Some of the seasons are marked by Sundays (4 in Advent, 7 in Lent); some by numerical days (12 in Christmas, 50 in Easter). The rest are included in Epiphany or Pentecost.

Basically, the Christian year is a mutt of the moon, the Big Holy Days, and the Gregorian calendar.

We find this fascinating but confusing.

So, we're giving you a chart for the years Advent 1 2022 through the Last Saturday of The Year 2027.

All those days that aren't officially part of the seasons of Advent, Christmas, Lent, and Easter—that is, most of the year—we are calling *Common Time* and numbering them sequentially, e.g. *Common 1, Common 2 …. Common 233,* and *The Last Saturday Before Advent.*

We guarantee that in this volume you have at least 52 Sundays to draw from. The rest is up to you, Pope Gregory, and the moon.

—EOR + BKS

CHART OF DAYS

Liturgical Year	Season	Beginning Date	Contemplations
2022-2023	Advent	11/27/2022	Sunday, Advent 1 through Christmas Eve
	Christmas	12/25/2022	Christmas Day through the 12th Day of Christmas
	Epiphany	1/6/2023	Epiphany Day, then Common 1-46
	Lent	2/22/2023	Ash Wednesday through Holy Saturday
	Easter	4/9/2023	Easter Sunday through Saturday of the 7th Week of Easter
	Pentecost	5/28/2023	Pentecost Sunday, then Common 47-233, then The Last Saturday Before Advent
2023-2024	Advent	12/3/2023	Sunday, Advent 1 through Saturday— Advent Week 3, then Christmas Eve
	Christmas	12/25/2023	Christmas Day through the 12th Day of Christmas
	Epiphany	1/6/2024	Epiphany Day, then Common 1-38
	Lent	2/14/2024	Ash Wednesday through Holy Saturday
	Easter	3/31/2024	Easter Sunday through Saturday of the 7th Week of Easter
	Pentecost	5/19/2024	Pentecost Sunday, then Common 39-232, then The Last Saturday Before Advent
2024-2025	Advent	12/1/2024	Sunday, Advent 1 through Christmas Eve
	Christmas	12/25/2024	Christmas Day through the 12th Day of Christmas
	Epiphany	1/6/2025	Epiphany Day, then Common 1-57
	Lent	3/5/2025	Ash Wednesday through Holy Saturday
	Easter	4/20/2025	Easter Sunday through Saturday of the 7th Week of Easter

CHART OF DAYS

Liturgical Year	Season	Beginning Date	Contemplations
	Pentecost	6/8/2025	Pentecost Sunday, then Common 58-230, then The Last Saturday Before Advent
2025-2026	Advent	11/30/2025	Sunday, Advent 1 through Christmas Eve
	Christmas	12/25/2025	Christmas Day through the 12th Day of Christmas
	Epiphany	1/6/2026	Epiphany Day, then Common 1-42
	Lent	2/18/2026	Ash Wednesday through Holy Saturday
	Easter	4/5/2026	Easter Sunday through Saturday of the 7th Week of Easter
	Pentecost	5/24/2026	Pentecost Sunday, then Common 43-229, then The Last Saturday Before Advent
2026-2027	Advent	11/29/2026	Sunday, Advent 1 through Christmas Eve
	Christmas	12/25/2026	Christmas Day through the 12th Day of Christmas
	Epiphany	1/6/2027	Epiphany Day, then Common 1-34
	Lent	2/10/2027	Ash Wednesday through Holy Saturday
	Easter	3/28/2027	Easter Sunday through Saturday of the 7th Week of Easter
	Pentecost	5/16/2027	Pentecost Sunday, then Common 35-228, then The Last Saturday Before Advent

A NOTE ABOUT PRAYING

If you grew up in church, you've gotten lots of direction on how to pray, much of it unhelpful.

If you've been told there is one right way to pray, let it go. If you think you can't pray correctly (whatever that means), let that go too.

Here's the long and short of it. God wants to spend time with you, and prayer is a life-giving act of trust for you that reminds you that God is God and you are (beloved child of God) you.

Prayer is not as hard as you think. Like any relationship-building activity, the important thing is that you do it. The more consistently you do, the more habitual it becomes.

Here are a few options for prayer practice:

1. Pray morning, noon, and night. Set an alarm. Start by acknowledging the greatness and goodness of God, then

    a. The 1st time pray for others who could use some Divine intervention.

    b. The 2nd time pray for the state of the world you live in.

    c. The 3rd time pray for yourself, specifically for your eyes to be opened, heart to be softened, and hands to be used for the purposes of Providence.

2. Pick one time that works for you to practice both pre-written and personal prayer. If you integrate prayer into your daily rhythm it's easier to keep up.

3. Write your conversation with God in a prayer journal, which is a great tool for working through thoughts, ideas, emotions, and desires and then bringing them to God.

4. Utilize *Lectio Divina* (aka Divine Reading) which is a meditative way to read Scripture: one read-through is for knowledge, another is for understanding, and once more is for Spiritual enlightenment—all while praying that God would use the Word to speak to your mind and spirit. (We used *Lectio Divina* in the writing of this book.)

The bottom line: God always wants to hear from you.

If you can manage a rundown of bullet points while you're in line or a barely coherent monologue as you're falling asleep, that's fine with God.

And: just as you would rather have conversations with your spouse/partner/kids/parents/friends that give you a real sense of how they're doing, God would prefer to have that with you too. The way to do that is to set aside time, be intentional, and minimize distractions.

So: no guilt, no shame. Just talk and listen. Find a practice that works for you. Praying in conjunction with this book—the verses and perspectives it presents—could be a great jumping-off place if prayer is new or weird for you.

Here are some prayers to pray when you can't find words or to include in your repertoire.

I. Prayer of Trust

My Lord God,
I have no idea where I am going. I do not see the road ahead of me.
I cannot know for certain where it will end, nor do I really know myself, and the fact that I think I am following your will does not mean that I am actually doing so.
But I believe that the desire to please you does in fact please you.
And I hope I have that desire in all that I am doing.
I hope that I will never do anything apart from that desire.
And I know that if I do this you will lead me by the right road, though I may know nothing about it.
Therefore will I trust you always though I may seem to be lost and in the shadow of death. I will not fear, for you are ever with me,
and you will never leave me to face my perils alone.

Thomas Merton, Thoughts In Solitude © 1956, 1958 The Abbey of Our Lady of Gethsemani

II. The Jesus Prayer

Our Father in heaven, hallowed be your name.
May your kingdom come.
May your will be done on earth as it is in heaven.
Give us today enough for today.
Forgive us our sins as we forgive those who sin against us.
Save us from the time of trial and deliver us from evil.
For the kingdom, and the power, and the glory are yours,
now and forever.
Amen.

III. An Advent prayer

Mysterious God, thank you for coming, and staying. In this Advent season, when we prepare for your arrival, may we make a suitable place in our hearts for you to dwell, now and forever. Amen.

IV. For when you're overwhelmed by tasks

Holy One, as I enter these last hours of Advent, help me to give up my perfectionism and my hustle. Quiet my guilt or worry or sadness or disappointment—anything that separates me from myself and from you. Guide me into doing the one thing that truly matters: accepting and giving love. Amen.

V. For when words don't come easily

Oh, lover of my soul, teach me to long for your companionship. Help me to crave your presence as I do the company of a lover. You are my rock and my refuge in times of trouble; be my hope and joy in times of celebration as well.

VI. A prayer for God's love:

Hopeful, peaceful, joyous, impossibly loving God: there is no one who gives so freely as you. I know that you chose to be human to show me exactly what real love is like. As I continue my Advent journey, and in the days and weeks and years ahead, please keep forming me to be like Jesus, recklessly loving all who pass my way. Amen.

VII. A prayer for accepting and sharing love

Creating and loving God, there is nothing good that does not come from you, and the greatest thing that comes from you is love. You emanate love. All love comes from you. Help me to accept your love fully. Help me to live each day trusting you completely so that I am free to love others well, just as you do. Amen.

VIII. A prayer for getting through anxiety

Oh, God who graciously waits and listens, you are trustworthy. You do not lie or make false promises. I'm struggling. My mind is overwhelmed with details and decisions. I'm worrying, and fearful, and feel like I'm going to burst from my skin. Help me to find a quiet place where I can be alone, and safe, and hear your sweet gentle voice giving me peace. Amen.

IX. A prayer to the Spirit

Holy Spirit, when I become too caught up in material things, guide my eyes back to all that you are doing, for it is through you that I find life and peace. Amen.

X. A prayer of thanks

Great artist, singer of happy melodies, my God: thank you, thank you. Fill me with your joy so that I can shout and sing with the meadows and the valleys, all those happy little trees and me.

XI. A prayer for the dark nights

Loving God, I know you have not forgotten me but everything is dark and my spirit is restless. I cannot see you. Come to me as I cry out for you. I am lonely and scared and I need you. Have compassion and comfort me. I want to sing for joy again, joining my voice with the mountains and the seas and all of creation.

XII. A prayer for when you feel unworthy

Oh Mama God! Oh Papa! How you love me! I don't know what to do with that. I don't think I can even take it in. I'm afraid you're going to want something in return that I can't do. I'm afraid of disappointing you. Be patient with me (like you always are) while I try to soak up your love. Help me to pour it out as extravagantly as you do, for the sake of your world. Amen.

XIII. A prayer for imitating God well

Thank you, Mama (*Papa*) for liking me and loving me, and forgiving me when I mess up. Thank you for lifting me when I fall, and for showing me kindness when I haven't been very kind myself. Help me to be more like you today: compassionate, tender, and joyful with others as you are with me. Amen.

1ST WEEK OF ADVENT: HOPE

SUNDAY—1ST WEEK OF ADVENT

In the beginning was the Word, and the Word was with God, and the Word was God. He was in the beginning with God. All things came into being through him, and without him not one thing came into being. What has come into being in him was life, and the life was the light of all people. The light shines in the darkness, and the darkness did not overcome it. —John 1:1-5

If you're in the northern hemisphere, the hours of light are growing fewer and dimmer. Night begins earlier and ends later, with darkness that is thick and dense.

Today begins the season of Advent. It makes sense that these four weeks before Christmas would be shrouded in darkness (so if you're in Australia you might want to flip your Christian calendar around to start at the end of May...). The season is about waiting and preparing for the coming of the light of the world. It is so much easier to recognize our spiritual darkness when the material world is dark too.

The traditional symbol of this season is the ring of Advent candles, symbolizing the cycle of the year and the neverendingness of eternity. On the first Sunday (and every night after if we remember) we light one candle. As the nights get progressively longer and the Advent weeks pass we light more. Their light increases each week, expanding into the darker-and-darker-still.

Tonight's tiny flame will pierce the gloom, including the gloom in our hearts, if we let it. The name of the first candle is Hope, because it is the coming of the Light of the World that provides us mortals the hope of the Eternal One.

—EOR

What simple action can you take each day of Advent to summon light and hope, for yourself or others?

MONDAY—1ST WEEK OF ADVENT

> A king is not saved by his great army; a warrior is not delivered by his great strength... Truly the eye of the Lord is on those who are in awe of him, on those who hope in his steadfast love, to deliver their soul from death, and to keep them alive in famine. Our soul waits for the Lord... Let your steadfast love, O Lord, be upon us, even as we hope in you. —Psalm 33:13-22, *excerpted*

There are days, even months and years, when having hope can be difficult.

Maybe you've suffered a loss: lost your job, said goodbye to your partner or spouse, watched a child die.

Maybe you've been reading the news, or listening to your permanently pessimistic sibling, and the world seems irrevocably broken.

Maybe you're ill, suffering from a condition or waiting for a diagnosis. *Nov 26 2022*

Or maybe you're facing a decision that terrifies you, even though you know it needs to be made.

We all have times when hope seems farther away than the limits of the universe. Reaching for hope can seem like a waste of time and energy.

Here's the thing: if your hope depends upon specific people, or on your circumstances, or on an election or choice or system, you will lose hope, because people will let you down at some point, your circumstances will be bad sometimes, and you will be disappointed.

The only reason hope can "spring eternal" is because God is eternal, and it is from trusting God that we can gain hope.

Hope is possible because it is grounded on the unbreaking, never-ending, always and forever love of God.

The eye of God is on those who are in awe of him, the Psalmist tells us. Their hearts are glad, even in the midst of sorrow, because they trust in God's steadfast love.

When hope seems far away, write down seven good things that have happened in your life. Then meditate on the fact that all that good is a window into God's impossibly permanent love for you.

—EOR

13

When you have lost hope, even for a moment, what was the disappointment that prompted that loss?

Nov 26 2022 My Neuro Dr. wants me to go a psych Dr. Nov 2022

TUESDAY—1ST WEEK OF ADVENT

For God alone my soul waits in silence, for my hope is from God. —Psalm 62:5

Some ancient Greeks speculated that the original model for humans had been divided into two persons, each seeking the other to unite their souls and once again become whole.

I grew up thinking that somewhere out there was my soulmate—my other half—and when I found them "the two shall become one" (to use the biblical phrase). Usually when we use the term "soulmate" we are talking about the object of our romantic affection. While I've had lovers and spouses and good friends with whom I felt fully at ease and known, I can't say I've ever noticed the other half of myself across the table, or shopping at Target.

If your hope for wholeness relies upon the right romantic partner, listen up: you are already whole. And: even the very best humans will fail from time to time, no matter how special they seem in that first flush of hormonal happiness.

Your soul *is* reaching out for connection. If you're looking for a human being, your soul's hope will be pinned to that person. Being a soulmate is a lot of responsibility to put on a mere mortal.

 When you come to *know* God, and not just know *about* God, then you have met the true mate of your soul.

Knowing God is about intimacy, the kind of relationship you get through lots of talking, listening, and just hanging out with someone.

Practice pouring out your heart to God and inviting God into your holiday preparations. Let God be your companion as well as your refuge. Your soul will be fully at ease and known when it is in the presence of its true soulmate, our beloved God.

—EOR

WEDNESDAY—1ˢᵀ WEEK OF ADVENT

Gone is my glory, and all that I had hoped for from the Lord…. My soul continually thinks of it and is bowed down within me. But this I call to mind, and therefore I have hope: The steadfast love of the Lord never ceases, God's mercies never come to an end… The Lord is my portion, says my soul, therefore I will hope in God.
—Lamentations 3:17-21

Do you always get the credit and the recognition you deserve? How about all the benefits to which you feel entitled?

Are you treated with equity and respect? Or does your gender, race, age, ableness or some other marker expose you to ill treatment?

Even if you receive social privileges and don't have to deal with injustice, just living among other people means your feelings will be hurt.

That isn't trivial: we are emotional creatures and hurt feelings matter. The Psalmist puts it this way: Gone is my glory, and all that I had hoped for from the Lord.

It takes mental and physical effort to lift our souls when they are bowed down. It's not easy to rouse ourselves and to regain hope. And if you face systemic challenges, you can feel there are no safe where can simply rest and be at home.

When your emotions are afflicted, and you feel spiritually (or physically) homeless, you might call this to mind: God's active care for you renews itself continually.

When you feel put down or shoved away, remind yourself: God is always faithful. God never rejects me, never undervalues me.

Tell your soul that it's going to be okay. Literally speak back to the deeply hidden self inside you: I see you. You are hurting. You will be okay. Though you don't believe it now, you already are okay, because you are cherished and appreciated by the One who knows you best. Not just loved by me, but by God, whose love never ceases.

—EOR

What does your soul need to hear from you today?

I will not be dismissed, my seizures are real. Nov 2022

seizures

THURSDAY—1ST WEEK OF ADVENT

Here is my servant, whom I have chosen, my beloved, with whom my soul is well pleased. I will put my Spirit upon him and he will proclaim justice to the nations.
—Matthew 12:15-18a

What pleases a soul? Your soul is a hungry thing. It seeks sustenance, but it latches onto whatever it is given.

For a while your soul may settle for trashy tv or the closest body available. If you've ever depended on "casual" sex or struggled with compulsive eating, you know what a starving soul feels like, and just how short a time physical panaceas last.

Just as your body prefers nutritious food to junk, so does your soul prefer nourishment over quick fixes and cynical triumphs. Your soul may get a thrill from drama, but it thrives when it is fed consistent gentleness and kindness.

You can give it some of that by treating yourself with curiosity and care, but your soul is eternal, and only an eternal connection will satisfy your soul.

Your soul is hungry for deep connection with God, and God wants to nourish your soul. Intimacy between you and God is soul food, for you and for God, if Isaiah got that right.

Did you notice that in the scripture? God's soul was pleased. God gets something out of intimacy with you.

When you draw close to a person and build a relationship, that person can trust you with more of themselves.

When God trusts another person, God can give them more Spirit-power. We can see that with Jesus.

With God empowering you through the Spirit, you can do more of what Jesus did, like heal (yourself and others), proclaim justice, love kindness, serve well, and please your own soul.

—EOR

When have you felt strength to do something you could not have otherwise done? How did you feel?

FRIDAY—1ST WEEK OF ADVENT

We boast in our sufferings, knowing that suffering produces endurance, and endurance produces character, and character produces hope, and hope does not disappoint us. —Romans 5:3-5

I've always been physically strong, so when my back finally succumbed to years of abuse it was a hard blow to both my habits and my ego. I'd leave chiro sore and tired and so emotionally drained that I had to take a minute before I drove. Self-image and fatigue and ancient fears and demon voices tortured me in ways the pain itself never could.

The pain was in my body but the suffering was in my head.

So I got help from therapy (both physical and mental) and from other people. Asking others for help is hard, even when I'm paying, but I'm learning to do it.

I handle it better now than I would have when I was younger, when every weakness was humiliating. Years of living through loss, and choosing how to respond, have turned humiliation into humility, and humility into hope.

Humility is the ability to claim both your strengths and weaknesses without judgment. Hope is knowing, from experience, that this moment of suffering will pass, and anticipating the better that is next.

I'm not great at humility yet. Some days I'm ashamed of needing help and afraid of losing love.

Shame and fear will destroy you if you let them.

I can't always avoid shame and fear, but I can consistently acknowledge that God keeps pulling me through. God responds to my pleas even when I don't know I'm praying them. Choosing to recognize that reality shores up my hope, even on the bad days.

The Apostle Paul went so far as to say he boasted—took pride in—his suffering, because through suffering he gained endurance, character, and hope.

I think he goes a little overboard there. I'm not spiritually advanced enough to take pride in how much I've suffered. I think I'd happily give up suffering, tossing it into the dumpster along with the spoiled milk, even if I had to give up a little endurance too.

I wouldn't hand over hope.

When your heart is hurting and shame and fear are not far away, how do you re-find hope?

When I want to give up somehow I begin to Hope I will get better with the help of others including myself.

Nov 2022

SATURDAY—1ST. WEEK OF ADVENT

God gave me, to present to you, the word of God in its fullness—the mystery that has been kept hidden for ages and generations... Christ in you, the hope of glory.
—Colossians 1:25-27

This season of the Christian calendar is about expectation. For four weeks, today is less real than tomorrow, since today is spent preparing for another day: the feast of the Incarnation, aka Christmas.

"Christmas" is something we understand. It's a baby born to a young girl in a strange town. There's a star involved, and some shepherds. Maybe gifts and a tree. We expect to feel a certain way, and whether we wind up feeling that way or not, we understand what it is we are expecting.

Add in that the girl was a virgin, and that a king was ticked off. Throw in prophecies and angels, and still we understand what we're all talking about.

Does anyone truly understand the Incarnation? Take out the girl and the carols, the ornaments and the sheep. What's left is in no way understandable: God came to the earth in flesh and blood, yet never left eternity. When God departed, God remained present to us. And not only to us, but in us.

Every Christmas we hear the story and we nod agreeably, knowing how it turns out. But beyond the story is God's great mystery: the glorious hope for Jews and Gentiles, for all of creation, is Christ in us.

Our hope is not in the life after this one. Our hope is that in this life, Christ chooses to abide in and among us.

—EOR

What would it look like for you to live with hope, in expectation of what is already so, that God is here, in you?

I wouldn't feel I have no hope, I just feel so sad. Nov 2022

2ND WEEK OF ADVENT: PEACE

SUNDAY—2ND WEEK OF ADVENT

And let the peace of Christ rule in your hearts, to which indeed you were called in the one body. And be thankful. —Colossians 3:15

A few weeks before he died, a deeply loved teacher of mine stood before the hundreds who had come to hear him speak and pronounced a blessing. I had heard it a thousand times, and spoken it myself dozens more, but that day I heard it for the first time because he said it over us.

We don't bless each other much. There's "bless you" when someone sneezes. People will say they're blessed when they want to attribute their good fortune to someone other than themselves. But lovingly, tenderly, invoke God's grace and mercy upon someone else, in their presence? Not so often.

When my teacher, who knew he would die soon, blessed us, he was thanking God and trusting God to grant us peace.

The world is not a peaceful place. The holiday season is often filled with noise and hurry, with forgotten tasks and obligations crowding out life-giving thoughts. Even our souls, which are meant to enjoy the presence of God that is promised by the season, can be terribly restless.

God intends us to be at peace when the world is in tumult. We gain peace through blessing and effort. The effort is choosing where to put our time and attention, selecting how we respond to the world's challenges. The blessing? Christ, who lives in our hearts and who promised peace.

Suppose you faced someone you love, put your hands on their shoulders, and said, "may the peace of Christ rule in your heart," Suppose you trusted God to do what God has promised to do: to provide presence and peace.

With his last breath my teacher is reported to have said "thank you." Sounds like peace to me.

—EOR

Who will you bless in this season? Upon whom will you call forth God's peace?

Laura Walling, Cindy Brown, Deborah Jackson, Lynn Spruiel, my blood family, Nov 2022

MONDAY—2ND WEEK OF ADVENT

> "Answer me when I call, O God of my right! You gave me room when I was in distress. Be gracious to me, and hear my prayer".... When you are disturbed, do not sin; ponder it on your beds, and be silent. —Psalm 4:1, 4

God has good manners. When invited, God shows up, and on time. When we turn and close the door behind us, God does not pound on it, shouting, "you'd better let me in!"

God knows that sometimes even a loving companion is more than we can handle. Sometimes our thoughts are so loud that adding even a sweet voice to the clamor will send us over the edge. In those times, God waits; patience doesn't seem to be a problem for God.

To gain internal peace, humans need silence and solitude. That doesn't mean we're all introverts, or that silence and solitude are necessarily comfortable. Being alone with your thoughts can be terrifying, until their unruly voices hear your "hush!"

When you want sympathetic company with other people, including God, that's great. But many times—especially when you're anxious and want to be seen and noticed by someone—what our souls and minds truly need is to have room. *Nov 2022*

When we have chosen to be alone and silent, we create room for our minds to wander until they finally quiet down and stand still. When your soul is disturbed, your first instinct may be to act, to just do something—anything—to make yourself feel better.

It may be that what your soul needs is for you to go to your room and be still, allowing the anxiety to peak in safety, and to pass. *Nov 2022*

When we give ourselves a little space, and some quiet, it's much easier to trust in God. When we deeply trust in God, we can rest and sleep in peace. *Nov 2022*

—EOR

Do you live with others? How do you claim the time you need?
If you live alone, how do you find the companionship you crave?

I go to my room and journal. 2022

TUESDAY—2ND WEEK OF ADVENT

Let me hear what God the Lord will speak, for he will speak peace...to those who turn to him in their hearts... Steadfast love and faithfulness will meet; righteousness and peace will kiss each other. —Psalm 85:8, 10

When I was around 8 I was spending my long school break with family friends who lived in Texas. He was a Pentecostal preacher with a cheerful face and piercing eyes. She was always dressed simply and appropriately, her hair pulled up into a bun. Except for Sundays, when she attached extra hair—a "fall" it was called then—to plump up the bun and add curls. They were warm and welcoming people. Unlike my tiny family, they and their four children were loud.

One night the preacher and his wife got into a disagreement in the kitchen. The girls' room, where I was staying, was just down the hall. I wasn't used to voices in the night, much less to bickering voices breaking the peace, so the sound woke me and sent me into the kitchen where I commanded my host and hostess to lower their voices because people were trying to sleep.

"Cheeky" is the word you're looking for. Two days later I went to stay with a different family friend.

If I was seeking a peaceful night I went about it the wrong way.

The voice of peace does not shout. It does not chide, or threaten, or draw undue attention to itself. The voice of peace is never pushy, nor is it anxious. And it definitely doesn't insult its hosts or condescend to anyone.

If you ever hear a voice doing those things, whether it's outside or inside your head, trust me: it's not the voice of peace. If you hear people shouting for peace, it's not peace they're looking for but justice or vindication or some other thing worth having.

The voice of peace is peace itself. The voice of peace is Christ's own voice. It is a whisper of love heard through the effort of faith.

Perhaps salvation is less an eternity in heaven than it is the experience of Christ's peace in this life. Perhaps the way to that eternal life is less about religious rightness and more about turning back toward the voice of peace, over and over again.

From the other side of Christmas, Peace whispers sweetly: I am here.

—EOR

How can you turn your attention away from the noise of daily living? What do you need today in order to hear Christ's voice?

To be still, to listen, to shut up. Nov 2022

WEDNESDAY—2ND WEEK OF ADVENT

The people who walked in darkness have seen a great light; those who lived in a land of deep darkness—on them light has shined... For all the boots of the tramping warriors and all the garments rolled in blood shall be burned as fuel for the fire. For a child has been born for us, a son given to us; authority rests upon his shoulders; and he is named Wonderful Counselor, Mighty God, Everlasting Father, Prince of Peace.
—Isaiah 9:2, 5-6

Christmas celebrations differ widely even among churches. Some listen to choirs and share the Eucharist at midnight Christmas Eve. Others sing along to carols two weeks early so members can stay home on the big day.

Two traditions seem close to universal. One is the four-year-old wearing angel wings who stares blankly at the captive audience while the children's minister prompts loudly from the front row. The other is this reading from Isaiah 9.

Isaiah is proclaiming liberation, a literal release from the yoke of oppression. The child to whom he refers is Hezekiah, who restored the temple after its destruction and invited the scattered tribes of Israel to come back to Jerusalem for Passover.

I don't think there's ever been a people who haven't walked in darkness. Internal. External. The demons within. The oppressors without.

Has there ever been a person who hasn't longed for peace? For enough? For the quieting of self-comparison? Or, simply, a tiny bit of pleasant predictability?

Each Advent we read these words from the prophet Isaiah telling us that the child born to us will be called the prince of peace, and that he has the authority to reign righteously and forever.

Each Advent, the passage also reminds us that true peace must travel from our joyful hearts into the painful world. True peace from the One Sovereign becomes real when people are set free, and we live at war no more. Inside or out.

The promise of a wonderful counselor, someone to stand by us, comfort and guide, is fulfilled by our practiced, vulnerable, relationship with God.

And: we need people who step in, stand by, point, and wait.

Where is your lack of peace this week? What deep need can only God (and counseling) begin to address?

I want something done about my horrible experiece at the ER. I know I need peace to handle the problem. Nov 2022

THURSDAY—2ND WEEK OF ADVENT

As Jesus was now approaching the path down from the Mount of Olives, the whole multitude of the disciples began to praise God joyfully with a loud voice for all the deeds of power that they had seen, saying, "Blessed is the king who comes in the name of the Lord! Peace in heaven, and glory in the highest heaven!" As he came near and saw the city, he wept over it, saying, "If you, even you, had only recognized on this day the things that make for peace!" —Luke 19:37-38, 41-42

Today's meditation and prayer is an excerpt from Longfellow's poem, *I Heard the Bells on Christmas Day*.

> I heard the bells on Christmas Day
> Their old, familiar carols play,
> And wild and sweet
> The words repeat
> Of peace on earth, good-will to men!
>
> Then from each black, accursed mouth
> The cannon thundered in the South,
> And with the sound
> The carols drowned
> Of peace on earth, good-will to men!
>
> It was as if an earthquake rent
> The hearth-stones of a continent,
> And made forlorn
> The households born
> Of peace on earth, good-will to men!
>
> And in despair I bowed my head;
> "There is no peace on earth," I said:
> "For hate is strong,
> And mocks the song
> Of peace on earth, good-will to men!"
>
> Then pealed the bells more loud and deep:
> "God is not dead; nor doth he sleep!
> The Wrong shall fail,
> The Right prevail,
> With peace on earth, good-will to men!"

FRIDAY—2ND WEEK OF ADVENT

The Advocate, the Holy Spirit, whom the Father will send in my name, will teach you everything, and remind you of all that I have said to you. Peace I leave with you; my peace I give to you. I do not give to you as the world gives. Do not let your hearts be troubled, and do not let them be afraid. —John 14:26-27

What did his disciples feel when Jesus died, returned, and then left them again?

Angry. Afraid. Abandoned.

Babies cling to their mothers (or other primary caretakers) for a reason. It's not affection: we need that adult in order to survive. The wailing only infants can manage is a biological and emotional expression of fear and abandonment. Babies don't have words; their cries emerge like a siren proclaiming danger.

Over time we gain independence, but that primal need never goes away. When a loving parent is present, besides getting our physical needs met, we feel safely connected. We can sleep,

When people we depend upon leave us, the infant inside us cries and reaches out, grasping the empty space they were in. We feel deep pain and sorrow and fear, as if both love and survival are out of reach. We feel the opposite of peace.

Our souls are the spiritual infants of ourselves. They reach out constantly, grabbing whatever they can, nursing on whatever we give them. What they want is their Mother: God.

When your soul is clinging to God, it rests and thrives.

I imagine the souls of Jesus' disciples were bereft. Until the Holy Spirit came, their inner infants must have grieved. They must have been confused, abandoned, and anything but peaceful.

Jesus's promise of peace is fulfilled by the presence of the Spirit. When you are aware of the Spirit's presence it is much easier to quiet your troubled mind and to release your fears.

God will not leave you alone, ever. Let that knowledge be a source of peace.

—EOR

When have you known the ache of abandonment? How have you begun to heal?

I feel that God has abandon me, Nov 2022

SATURDAY—2ND WEEK OF ADVENT

Those who live according to the flesh set their minds on the things of the flesh, but those who live according to the Spirit set their minds on the things of the Spirit. To set the mind on the flesh is death, but to set the mind on the Spirit is life and peace.
—Romans 8:5-6

If you've been buying presents, making lists, eating the next cookie, you may be extra aware of the physical side of mortal life. Presents, lists, cookies are all material things, and they are all good. (I am more fond of cookies than presents, myself, but a checked-off task list is a thing of beauty.)

It's a fleshly focused season, to use the Apostle Paul's word, this lead-up to Christmas. When Paul warns against the things of the flesh he's not talking about your body, or anyone else's body. Paul doesn't mean that bodies are bad, or desiring is bad, or sex/eating/drinking/dancing are bad. He would have been just fine with cookies if he'd known about them, and the Christian Bible is full of human-given gifts.

The problem with flesh is not that it's material or the object of physical desires. It's that flesh decays. It passes away, yet demands attention. The flesh distracts our eyes away from the things of the Spirit.

Television takes time away from reading. Rushed meals become a mainstay. Weighing our value by our income, rather than by our care for others, is a foundation for our society,

That doesn't mean TV and fast food and having money (or not having it) are immoral. It does mean that they are powerful seducers of our minds, and our sticky souls latch onto them with a death grip.

You are not merely matter, not a pile of chemicals or potential energy.

You are an immortal being living a material life. Both the physical and the spiritual can be life-giving, but the physical is a lot noisier, shouting "me, me, want me! Look at me!" The spiritual is quieter, whispering "Come."

If you set your mind on the material, it will take all your time and attention.

If you set your mind on the spiritual, you'll fill up on peace but still have plenty of room for the tinsel and the tree.

Enjoy the cookie. Make the great present. Just be sure that they do not become the point of the season, or the meaning of your life.

—EOR

What "of the flesh" do you not actually enjoy, but use as an escape?

My imagination. Nov 2022

3RD WEEK OF ADVENT: JOY

SUNDAY—3RD WEEK OF ADVENT

Splendor and majesty flow from and surround God; strength and joy are in God's dwelling place. —1 Chronicles 16:27

Imagine you're looking at a photo of God in the heavens. What do you see?

Clouds, check. Grey beard, sure.

Is God dancing? Is God laughing? Is God the perfect portrayal of pure contentment? Joyful?

Sing your favorite song about God. What words does it use to describe God? My favorite today has these words: immortal, invisible, wise, mighty, victorious, hidden. Not a single word about God enjoying a good joke, or smiling at a kitten's Instagram antics.

We are taught to honor God by saying how big and glorious God is. We are taught to thank God for answered prayers or provision given. God is big, for sure, and able to do anything, so it's easy to picture the Divine Countenance as serious, even taciturn or grumpy. Does God's immensity and power that mean that God has to be a stick in the mud?

Scripture tells us that God enjoys the work of His hands. God enjoys His creation. God enjoys you.

With all that enjoying going on, God is surely joyful Himself. When you think about a time when you were joyful, didn't God seem just a little closer than usual?

We get tired and angry, cynical and jaded. The labor of daily living can yank the joy right out of us.

But when you notice a flower springing from a sidewalk crack, that's God's joy you feel. When you finish a difficult project and step back to enjoy your completion, that's God's joy in which you're participating. When a friend texts you out of the blue just to say hello, God's joy runs from celltower to celltower between you.

For God, existence itself is a joy. No wonder God is the source of our deepest joy. Joy simply overflows from God into us.

—EOR

Try this practice this week: Look for your moments of joy or contentment, and notice God in the midst.

MONDAY—3RD WEEK OF ADVENT

I said in my prosperity, I shall never be moved... You had established me as a strong mountain. Then you hid your face; I was dismayed. To you, O Lord, I cried... Hear, O Lord, and be gracious to me, O Lord, be my helper! You have turned my mourning into dancing; you have taken off my sackcloth and clothed me with joy, so that my soul may praise you and not be silent. — Psalm 30

We've all been there, right? Riding along on your high horse, horizon in sight, plenty of green grass (for the horse) and caviar dreams (for you). And then: thud; oof. You hit the ground hard, wind's knocked out of you, the horse sees his chance and takes off.

Your losses didn't start with a horse, you say? Even so, you know what the Psalmist was going through. He was feeling strong, successful, solid in his position, when suddenly everything fell apart. And because his life came crashing down he felt as though God's favoritism had vanished, taking everything good away too.

One of those times stands out for me. I had left my pastoring job, the farewell party was months behind me, and I was in Ohio for my doctoral program. I got a call from my denominational representative: I was to immediately cut contact with every person in my former church (i.e. remove them from my Facebook friends, cut them off my Twitter feed, disappear from social media) because the interim pastor felt threatened by me.

The call got uglier and increasingly bizarre and when I hung up I was alone, distraught, and tasked with cutting off others without a word.

I was in such a state that I accidentally threw away my grandmother's diamond earrings, which I had worn 24/7 for 20 years but had taken off because I'd lost the back of one.

Thud. Oof. Bye bye, horsey.

It took me years to stop crying out to God. But at some point I started experiencing joy again (mostly through singing) and in those moments when the hurt fell away and nothing stood between me and the Holy Spirit, all that mourning turned into dancing (or what passes for dancing when you're singing next to someone far better than you who doesn't dance).

That's how it is with joy and God. As Jesuit priest Pierre Teilhard de Chardin wrote "Joy is the infallible sign of the presence of God." As the Psalmist discovered, if you are joyful, God must be with you.

And when you are not joyful, and sorrow holds you fast, God is with you too. But it's easier to believe when you're content and at peace.

—EOR

When has your sorrow turned into joy? How long did it take you to realize that had happened?

TUESDAY—3RD WEEK OF ADVENT

The pastures of the wilderness overflow, the hills gird themselves with joy, the meadows clothe themselves with flocks, the valleys deck themselves with grain, they shout and sing together for joy. —Psalm 65:12-13

Remember Bob Ross? The fellow with the big fluffy hair who taught painting on PBS for a decade? Bob Ross is remembered for many things, but mostly for being very quiet and soothing, and for his "happy little trees." He'd be painting a landscape—a landscape in 30 minutes!—when he'd dab a different green paint onto the canvas, add some brown, and coo "let's build some happy little trees."

Ross's pleasure in creating shined through the tv screen, brighter than any LED or LCD or tube could show. When he added trees and clouds to a painting, the oils themselves seemed cheerful. (Don't think tubes of thick oil paint seem cheerful? You've been hanging with the wrong painters.)

More importantly, Ross created a safe space for creating. His gentleness invited participation: "You can do anything you want. This is your world."

I imagine Bob Ross had more than a dab of God in him. Creating, inviting others to create too, finding beauty in the mundane: sounds like God to me. And you know how divine DNA is: can't really hide it when you are made in God's image.

Like Ross's, God's joy is contagious. God's joy is so captivating that the entire creation is filled with it. The hills gird themselves with joy. The meadows and valleys sing together for joy.

In God's world, joy is everywhere, from the happy little trees to the big fluffy clouds to meadows that clothe themselves with flocks and valleys that deck themselves with grain.

Flora and fauna become party clothes when God whips out a brush.

Today, see if you can slow down, just a bit. Notice how God's creation—the winds, the sky, the flowers, the snow—seem to dance and sing for joy. Then see if you can do the same. You are one of God's creations, after all.

—EOR

How does it feel when you en-joy? how can you do more of that?

WEDNESDAY—3ʳᴰ WEEK OF ADVENT

The wilderness and the dry land shall be glad, the desert shall rejoice and blossom; like the crocus it shall blossom abundantly, and rejoice with joy and singing... Strengthen the weak hands, and make firm the feeble knees, Say to those who are of a fearful heart, Be strong, do not fear! Here is your God. —Isaiah 35:1-4

Did you grow up with the idea that Jesus's second coming was scary? Or that God's showing up at the end of time was more of a threat than a promise?

That's not the way you're supposed to see it. Read through the Hebrew Bible and most of the Christian texts and you'll find a completely different view of the coming of the King. God shows up, causing happiness in the desert as it blossoms. The land itself rejoices, and God's people have plenty and peace.

God's coming is a promise of restoration and healing, the abundance of a Spirit-overflowing life.

That doesn't mean that we live fearlessly now, does it?

If you are growing older—and if you're reading this, you Are growing older—you have probably noticed changes in your body. Curves where they didn't used to be. New textures and colors, Greater skills but lesser strength.

Mortal things come into being, grow, age, and die, and because what's on the other side of bodily life isn't fully knowable we are deeply (if unconsciously) afraid of what death may bring. Meanwhile, our sight grows dimmer (or at least less accurate) and we don't heal as quickly, so living also becomes a bit more tenuous, a shade more dangerous.

So when Isaiah evokes the splendor of creation upon the arrival of the coming King, he also counsels the people to "strengthen the weak hands, and make firm the feeble knees." He urges them to speak to their elders, as well as to others whose hearts are afraid, to be hopeful, to draw on their strength and speak back to their fear.

How can they be strong and not fear? A simple answer: Here is your God.

God's coming at Christmas scared King Herod enough that he murdered all the boy babies. Fear can make us foolish, or ugly.

If we are living well—reflectively, lovingly—we gain wisdom along with wrinkles. Joy sneaks stealthily into our lives as we mature spiritually. Joy rarely shouts its presence, but becomes part of who we are as we are filled with God and gratitude.

What <u>can</u> prevent the presence of joy is fear, for fear will fill every dark crevice of your mind if you allow it.

Fight fear if you would have joy.

—EOR

What fear stands in the way of your joy, or prevents you from seeing the glory of God, who is here?

THURSDAY—3RD WEEK OF ADVENT

Sing for joy, O heavens, and exult, O earth; break forth, O mountains, into singing! For the Lord has comforted his people, and will have compassion on his suffering ones. But Zion said, The Lord has forsaken me, my Lord has forgotten me. Can a woman forget her nursing child, or show no compassion for the child of her womb? Even these may forget, yet I will not forget you. —Isaiah 49:13-15

If you're anything like me, the worst part of hard times is the terrible alliance between sorrow and abandonment. Your closest friend may be far, far away. Your own soul may seem to have withered with grief or pain.

You may feel alone and forgotten, even if people who love you are right there with you. Despair can grab hold of your heart, squeezing out sobs or draining it dry.

Your feelings are legitimate. That doesn't mean they accurately describe the whole of reality.

God is here, even now.

God never forgets. God's thoughts never wander. God's eyes are on you, and God's arms are always open to you. Like the perfect mother, God cherishes God's children, you among them, and wants nothing more than to draw them to Her divine bosom, holding them safe and warm.

That is the truth. It doesn't mean you're going to believe it. If you cannot act on it, you don't really believe it. That says nothing about your faith or your relationship with God; it says everything about the power of despair.

You may not feel like God is near, so remind yourself of the truth: your closest friend is not the one at a distance. Your divine Friend is inside you and around you.

Remind yourself that no matter how you feel, your soul is cradled gently by a compassionate and loving God. You are not alone. In your darkest moments, when the night sky fills every room, remember that the Light has come. The worst darkness may hide light at times, but cannot overcome it.

—EOR

Write down one concrete action you can take to remember God adores you.

FRIDAY—3RD WEEK OF ADVENT

Though the fig tree does not blossom, and no fruit is on the vines; though the produce of the olive fails, and the fields yield no food; though the flock is cut off from the fold, and there is no herd in the stalls yet I will rejoice in the Lord; I will exult in the God of my salvation. —Habakkuk 3:17-18

It's easier to be happy when things are going your way. You have disposable income. Your friends text regularly. No troubling health issues. All you need is a bowl of ice cream and life feels good.

Happiness is a feeling, a fleeting emotion like all the others, dependent upon your environment, your body chemistry, and your momentary attitude. Happiness is not trustworthy. It's good, and you can enjoy it while it lasts, but don't aim for it. Chasing happiness is like looking for the next high: the chase itself is addictive and the crash on the other side devastates.

God is joyful—full of joy—because God cherishes and rejoices. God can see through the storms and fires and find satisfaction. God hears the mountains and the deserts singing, notices the one crocus peeking through snow, and smiles at the old people line dancing.

Joy is the result of the decision to notice the glorious around you, however small. Joy comes when you take full advantage of your capacity for wonder. Joy is inevitable when you hush your inclination to embarrassment and give in to your urge to dance in the grocery store.

I'm not saying it's easy. As someone who still gets embarrassed when I mispronounce a word or trip in the street: it's not easy.

You can choose joy. That's what gratitude journaling is about: turning your attention toward goodness and beauty. God is the source of all goodness and beauty, so rejoicing in God is a good place to start.

Rejoice in the Lord today. Not because you have a roof over your head, if you do. Not because you have enough to eat, if you have. Not because your Christmas shopping is done, if it is.

Rejoice in the Lord today because when nothing is going your way, God is, and God will always give you strength to get through.

—EOR

How will you notice the glorious today?

SATURDAY—3RD WEEK OF ADVENT

Abide in me as I abide in you… As the Father has loved me, so I have loved you; abide in my love. If you keep my commandments, you will abide in my love, just as I have kept my Father's commandments and abide in his love. I have said these things to you so that my joy may be in you, and that your joy may be complete. And this is my commandment, that you love one another as I have loved you. —John 15, *excerpted*

I'm not very good at distinguishing between a demand and a desire. If my child says, "Would you bring me a glass of water?" it feels like a demand, even though I know she's just hoping I'll say yes.

I truly believe—and, to be completely honest, I hope you do too—that God invites us, woos us, hangs out with us just because God wants to be with us and desires that we want to be with God too.

Have you ever had a friend or lover who surprises you by just hanging out with you for no obvious reason? I'm the one who thinks "hmmm….what does this person need or want from me right now?" rather than thinking (for example) "oh yay! This person wants to be with me!!!"

Yes, I do hear what I'm saying about myself. And maybe you.

So when Jesus says, "Abide in me… and your joy may be complete" I used to read that as "you'd better spend more time with Me and then maybe I'll give you some shred of happiness." Or perhaps, "Here's what I demand: spend time with Me or else!!"

Those are my demon voices yelling falsehoods. Those voices sound so much like me that I take them seriously. Maybe you do too.

Jesus isn't laying down the law. Jesus is giving us guidance for living in deep and life-giving relationship with God, his Father and ours.

Here's Jesus' guidance: I love you exactly as my Papa loves you, and if you're wise you'll stick close to Papa and to me, because it's a safe and loving place to be.

Invitation. No demand.

The only commandment Jesus gives here is this: love each other as deeply and thoroughly as I have loved you. Which is a pretty high standard, but way more do-able than "spend more and more time with Me or go to hell forever."

Jesus isn't demanding. He's just like the One he called Father. He wants to be with you, as does God. God desires relationship with you because God loves you and not because God's looking for an excuse to smite you.

Have you looked at what you get when you hang out with Jesus and his Father on a regular basis (what Jesus called "abiding")?

You get the experience of being loved.

There's no demand in anything Jesus says. There's only this: you can have with my Papa what I have; here's how.

And what does Jesus have? Joy that is complete.

Sounds like a good trade to me.

—EOR

What's one thing you could do today to love just a little bit more?

4TH WEEK OF ADVENT: LOVE

SUNDAY—4TH WEEK OF ADVENT

The Lord and his disciples entered the home of Martha. She had a sister named Mary, who sat down in front of the Lord and was listening to what he said. Martha was worried about all that had to be done. Finally, she went to Jesus and said, Lord, doesn't it bother you that my sister has left me to do all the work by myself? Tell her to come and help me! Jesus answered, Martha, Martha! You are worried and upset about so many things, but only one thing is necessary. Mary has chosen what is best.
—Luke 10:38-42

As a recovering Martha it's taken me years to understand Jesus' point. After all, if you're the one who usually cleans and usually cooks and always remembers that medicine needs to be picked up at the pharmacy, Martha is your patron saint. If you're on her side of the mop, you know: Jesus gets to hang out in the living room chatting with his boys because someone's making sure he gets fed. And it's sure not Mary.

Jesus' problem with Martha isn't that she's finding food for the sudden arrival of a passel of men (one of whom is rumored to be the Messiah) instead of chilling at his feet.

Jesus may not like getting pulled into a sisterly squabble but he's managed siblings before (I'm looking at you, James and John).

Jesus gently chides Martha because he notices how she's feeling. Martha is worried, upset, anxious and overwhelmed and crabby. She could be lovingly preparing a very simple meal; she's not.

Hurry and multitasking are enemies of love.

The "best thing" Mary has chosen isn't listening to Jesus, and it isn't shirking work. Mary has chosen love. (And yes, it would have been awesome if she'd chosen love and set the table.)

We cannot love when we do not pay attention. We cannot love if worry and fear crowd our hearts.

In a season bent on showing people just how much you care about them through gifts and food, it's good to remember this:

Your beloveds want your presence more than your presents.

If you are feeling stressed over getting eighteen more details perfected by midnight on Christmas Eve, ask yourself: am I doing this to earn others' love (an impossible task, by the way)? Am I doing this for approval?

If it's either one, you're not doing it out of love.

Today: Stop. Breathe. Listen. Notice. Pray. Pay attention. And love, well.

—EOR

Where can you find balance in this season, whether it's balance between busy and bored, or peopling and solitude, or work and play, or…?

MONDAY—4TH WEEK OF ADVENT

For God so loved the world that he gave his only Son, so that everyone who believes in him may not perish but may have eternal life. Indeed, God did not send the Son into the world to condemn the world, but in order that the world might be saved through him. —John 3:16-17

There is just one way to save the world.

The only way to save the world is through love.

Not sentimental love. Not hearts and lace and happy endings.

The only way to save the world is through love: God's love for each of us, and our God-enabled persistent choosing to act for the good of others.

That's what love is: willing the good of someone else and choosing to act for that good, even when it does not seem to benefit you.

God's love is like that: unwavering, unconditional, affection and care for every one of God's creatures, every atom of God's creation.

God's love is unwavering, unconditional, affection and care for you.

God acts on love by showing up, over and over again, with care and compassion, and selflessness, again and again.

Because you are worthy of rescue.

You. Are. Worthy.

And so is everyone else.

As you wait these last days for the child of God's love to show up, remember:

God loved you so much that God showed up in the flesh, knowing that anyone who trusts God's love will experience eternal living, now, in this material life.

—EOR

Write this down and post it where you can see it: I am worthy.

TUESDAY—4TH WEEK OF ADVENT

My Father is glorified by this, that you bear much fruit and become my disciples. As the Father has loved me, so I have loved you; abide in my love...I have said these things to you so that my joy may be in you, and that your joy may be complete.
—John 15:8-10

When God deals kindly with you, it's not because you do all the right things. You cannot do enough right things, or do things perfectly enough, to earn love. Anyone's love, but especially not God's.

Love isn't like that. Love cannot be earned. Love cannot be demanded.

You have no control over someone else's love.

That means that when someone loves you—truly wills your good and acts on it—it's because of who <u>they</u> are, not because of who you are.

When God loves you, it's because of who <u>God</u> is.

At the same time you cannot be enough to earn God's love there is also a great mystery hovering over you:

You are enough for God.

With all your flaws, all your demon voices reminding you just how weak you are, with all your broken promises and failed project: you are enough for God.

You.

More mystery: When we are loved, and we accept that we are loved (which may be the hardest part), loving others is easier.

Your practice for today? Accept that you are loved.

And then live in that love, for love begets love. Just like God begat Jesus, love following love.

—EOR

When do you feel like enough?

WEDNESDAY—4TH WEEK OF ADVENT

See what love the Father has given us, that we should be called children of God; and that is what we are... We know love by this, that he laid down his life for us—and we ought to lay down our lives for one another. How does God's love abide in anyone who has the world's goods and sees a brother or sister in need and yet refuses help? Little children, let us love, not in word or speech, but in truth and action.
—1 John 3:1, 16-18

What does it mean to lay down your life for another person?

It's not about being a martyr. Have you ever known someone who didn't do what they wanted to do and always did what someone else wanted them to do? Not pretty, and not loving.

Laying down your life isn't about giving someone else what they want.

It's also not about dying in someone's place, no matter what you've been told.

Laying down your life means choosing to live in a different way than the way you are in the habit of living. You pick up your life as you know it and put it aside.

Laying down your life for another person means choosing to do things that aren't your favorites because doing them is good for someone else.

If you have ever had an infant living in your home, you have a sense of what laying down your life means.

The life you had before that baby came along was probably quite different than the one that included the child. You lay down your former life when the child showed up.

God could have remained on a lofty throne, doing what God does, risking nothing. That's not who God is. God chose to change what God was doing and get into the muck with us.

That is the kind of love that God has for us: a laying-down-the-life-you-expected kind of love.

That's the kind of love God wants us to have for others: a laying-down-the-life-you-expected-when-needed kind of love. And we're not expected to love only our own children, but God's children too.

Which is everybody. Including you, beloved child of God.

If you think of Jesus in that way—God laying down God's usual way of living so that we'd get to know God—he stops being a martyr we're supposed to emulate, and starts being a friend we get to appreciate.

—EOR

How are you loving in truth and action these days? What of your life are you willing to lay down if needed?

THURSDAY—4TH WEEK OF ADVENT

Beloved, let us love one another, because love is from God; everyone who loves is born of God and knows God...for God is love...and those who abide in love abide in God, and God abides in them... There is no fear in love, but perfect love casts out fear; for fear has to do with consequences, and whoever fears has not reached perfection in love.
—1 John 4, *excerpted*

Are you afraid of love? If we are honest with ourselves most of us discover that we are afraid of being loved or of loving, or both.

Loving requires us to act, to do things we don't want to do.

Being loved can make us feel like we are in perpetual debt that cannot be paid.

Being loved forces us to accept that we are worthy of care, and to admit that we need care more often than we would like to admit.

Thinking about doing things we don't want to do, or admitting that we need help, can lead us to be afraid of what might happen next.

We get scared of being disappointed, or of disappointing others.

We get worried that if we do *this* loving action we'll be committing ourselves to a hundred more, and then what?

But when we are actually doing love—not thinking about it, but doing it—fear goes away, because God is in the actual loving.

We can love recklessly and indiscriminately because God loves us so very very much.

God lived in this material, hurting world as an infant, a child, an adolescent, an adult, and a martyr for just one reason: God loves and cherishes you.

God took on the pains and deprivations and joys and attractions and disappointments and learnings of humanity, just to show you how love is done.

Don't be afraid to love.

Try this: Spend two minutes in contemplation, eyes closed, mentally looking around for those people who truly love you. Not just the ones who say they love you, and not necessarily those who are the objects of your romantic affections.

Notice the people in your life who are willing to do what they would not prefer to do, just because you are you.

Let the depth of their love touch your soul. If tears come, let them. If you get nervous, ride it out. Try to accept that in their eyes, you are beautiful and worthy of care.

And in God's eyes, you are even better than that.

—EOR

Who enjoys you? Don't be shy, and don't exclude people who maybe you don't enjoy so much. (Pssst: there's at least one Person who fits the bill.)

FRIDAY—4TH WEEK OF ADVENT

Hope does not disappoint us, because God's love has been poured into our hearts through the Holy Spirit that has been given to us. —Romans 5:5

Old Christmas movies are glutted with hope. Hope that Santa will come. Hope that she'll get the date with the guy. Hope that he'll have a tree that's more satisfying than a stick. Hope for a Red Rider BB Gun.

Those very same movies are also rife with disappointment as something hoped for goes wrong. No Santa, wrong guy, wrong present, until the lead character decides that hope and disappointment are too closely linked and so gives up hope.

An older British-ish saying, known to the fans of John Cleese and Welsh soccer, is this: It's the hope that kills you.

Yet there's the Apostle Paul, writing to the persecuted Christians in Rome: Hope does not disappoint us.

Are these simply conflicting points of view? Paul the optimist vs. every Christmas movie ever made? I don't think so. I think Paul knew something about hope that we tend to forget: hoping is not the same as wishing,

You can wish for anything, whether likely or outlandish. But actual hoping involves anticipating something you trust to happen, based on experience and reason.

You wish for a Red Ryder BB gun. You hope for a good breakfast after the opening of gifts.

Hope doesn't disappoint because it's based on trust and experience,

For Paul that experience includes God's love having proved trustworthy across generations and miles, and his own personal experience of God's love in his own heart.

We can hope without fear because we can trust Love.

Think you can't trust God's love? Ponder all the times you weren't hit by the car that ran the red light, including all the times you didn't even notice. Remember the food and shelter you *have* had, rather than fixating on what you haven't.

If Christmas passes without the gift you wanted or the guy you longed for or the tree that brushed the ceiling, remember that wishes don't always come true.

Love remains.

—EOR

Which of your hopes is really a wish?

SATURDAY—4TH WEEK OF ADVENT

If I give all I possess to the poor and give over my body to hardship...but do not have love, I gain nothing. —1 Corinthians 13:3

Long before I was a pastor I worked at a church with massive and committed outreach to the poor and homeless in the city. From Thanksgiving through Christmas people who had more than we needed would bring blankets, clothes, coats, and sleeping bags, along with fanciful presents, to the church for distribution to thousands of people living in want or need.

There was a single rule about what could be given: The gifts had to be new. New blankets. New coats. New toys and books. Nothing used; only new.

At first I didn't understand this. "Look at how much more we could give if we accepted used things!" I wasn't alone in my puzzlement. Plenty of the organizations that took old things and redistributed them shook their heads.

One day I overheard the church's pastor explaining this policy to a potential donor. "Poor people always get used things. Hand-me-downs that don't really fit or have a small stain. Blankets that someone else didn't want. Even if what they hand down is in good shape, don't poor people deserve new things too?"

And then, "Don't you want to show them that they're loved as well as pitied?"

He wasn't saying that the used coat given out of love was worthless. If I had passed someone who needed a coat and I had one I wanted to give, he'd have been all for my handing it over.

The point was this: You can give everything to someone without really seeing them, without actually loving them.

You can work in the soup kitchen every week, give everything to Goodwill, hand out money to every guy standing on a traffic island, and do it all without any actual love, affection, attention, or kindness involved.

While it may bolster your pride and self-righteousness, and serve a good purpose, without love all your good works, all your carefully chosen presents, are as empty as your heart.

For God so loved the world...

Perhaps this Christmas, we can too.

—EOR

Who needs to experience your love today? How will you show it?

CHRISTMAS EVE

What has come into being in him was life, and the life was the light of all people. The light shines in the darkness, and the darkness did not overcome it.... To all who did receive him, to those who believed in his name, he gave the right to become children of God—children born not of natural descent, nor of human decision or a man's will, but born of God. The Word became flesh and made his dwelling among us. We have seen his glory, as of a father's only son, full of grace and truth. —John 1

Reading the news reminds us that the world is a tragedy.

Starvation, military force, brutality, natural disaster, cruelty—all these seem intractable, as if ugliness were lodged in the very nature of human existence.

This is true: Darkness lodges itself in hearts, as well as in clouds of dust, shrapnel, and death.

This too is true: The light shines in the darkness, and the darkness has not overcome it. Over two thousand years ago someone we call John wrote down those three great truths: there is darkness, there is light, and the light is God in the world.

And, still, two thousand years later, the darkness has not, and can never, overcome the light.

During Advent we look toward tomorrow, both the calendar Christmas and tomorrow's promise of hope, peace, joy, and love.

Tonight let us remember that "the true light that gives light to everyone was coming into the world." And is, still.

—EOR

A prayer for Christmas Eve:
Oh, Lord, how you must love us! Why else would leave your throne, give up power, eschew money, and become so vulnerable? Why else would you entrust yourself to our care? Only for love does anyone give up so much. Tonight, as we discover again the Christ child in the manger, let us also see the depth of your love in his face, and in all the other faces we encounter.
Amen.

CHRISTMAS

CHRISTMAS DAY

And Mary brought forth her firstborn son, and wrapped him in swaddling clothes, and laid him in a manger; because there was no room for them in the inn.

And there were in the same country shepherds abiding in the field, keeping watch over their flock by night. And, lo, the angel of the Lord came upon them, and the glory of the Lord shone round about them: and they were sore afraid.

And the angel said unto them, Fear not: for, behold, I bring you good tidings of great joy, which shall be to all people. For unto you is born this day in the city of David a Savior, which is Christ the Lord. And this shall be a sign unto you; You shall find the babe wrapped in swaddling clothes, lying in a manger.

And suddenly there was with the angel a multitude of the heavenly host praising God, and saying, "Glory to God in the highest, and on earth peace, good will toward men."
—Luke 2:7-14 (KJV)

You know it, but it bears repeating. The meaning of Christmas is simply this:

God with us: Emmanuel.

May your heart be gladdened and your day bright with hope, peace, joy, and love.

CHRISTMAS 2

But Mary treasured up all these things and pondered them in her heart. —Luke 2:19

I love the day after Christmas. It's when my (now-grown) kids and I wear our jammies all day, watch Marvel movies, eat leftovers and Xmas treats, and basically enjoy the afterglow of our favorite day of the year.

It comes after the long anticipation of Advent, the Christ-child's blessed arrival on Christmas Eve, and the joyous gift-swapping, overeating, and over-peopling of Christmas Day.

It's like a holiday from the holidays.

It's also the day when, if I'm quiet, I can feel the mystery of Christmas and the realness of real-life come together like no other day of the year.

I mean, even Mary stopped to reflect on all that had happened. Sometimes you just need a minute.

Fact is, the Jesus we celebrate ate leftovers. He spent time with those he loved doing nothing important. He liked a party. He probably would've enjoyed Black Panther.

The buildup to Christmas can be stressful, even exhausting. Even (especially) for those of us in ministry. So, if I may, let me encourage you today to rest, laugh, eat, nap, eat some more, watch a movie, read a book, enjoy your presents, or do whatever brings you joy.

Make December 26 a day you look forward to every year. Your post-Xmas routine—and all that goes along with it—will find you soon enough.

—BKS

What will you do today to rest your body, soul, mind, and spirit?

CHRISTMAS 3

For the grace of God has appeared, bringing salvation to all, training us to renounce impiety and worldly passions, and in the present age to live lives that are self-controlled, upright, and godly, while we wait for the blessed hope and the manifestation of the glory of our great God and Savior, Jesus Christ. He it is who gave himself for us that he might redeem us from all iniquity and purify for himself a people of his own who are zealous for good deeds. —Titus 2:11-14

"Self-control is the ability to regulate one's emotions, thoughts, and behaviors in the face of temptations and impulses." (Thanks, *Psychology Today.*)

As a teen, I chose to avoid secular (not-Christian) music, movies in theaters, and most parties and dances. My church said those things were bad for me, and I was a compliant kid who didn't question authority.

Every day I would read my Bible, practice piano (2 hrs), do 75 push-ups before bed, and keep my room tidy. I was self-disciplined at 16.

I was also afraid. And fear is a mighty strong motivator.

I wasn't afraid of my parents. And I wasn't afraid of my church. But I was afraid of God. Afraid that I'd make a misstep, fall into the enemy's snare, and be doomed to hell. That's a difficult tightrope to walk at any age.

Thankfully, I eventually outgrew those ideas about God—the petty, punitive God that I was afraid of.

But I'm not mad about all the self-discipline. It made me a more grounded, responsible teen—who could play a Joplin rag like nobody's business—and a more mindful, God-aware adult.

My motivations for living a self-controlled life now come from a desire to make life-giving choices rather than life-destroying ones. And I recognize that it takes more than just my will to do it.

I have to practice being patient, generous, others-centered, and the rest. But if I'm intentional about it, over time, I do become more like Jesus— "zealous for good deeds" as Paul puts it.

—BKS

How do you practice being like Jesus? What does self-control look like to you?

CHRISTMAS 4

Simeon took him in his arms and praised God, saying, "Master, now you are dismissing your servant in peace, according to your word; for my eyes have seen your salvation..."
—Luke 2:28-30

Simeon was old—like, really old—and the Holy Spirit promised him he wouldn't die until he saw the Messiah in the flesh. So this day, like most, he was at the Temple, eyes peeled, anticipating a Visitor. A king who would set Israel to right.

I don't know if Simeon expected the Promised One to show up as an infant. Certainly, the Jews weren't expecting their Messiah to arrive in swaddling clothes.

But when Mary and Joseph walked in carrying 40-day-old Jesus, the Holy Spirit tapped on Simeon's shoulder.

"This is him."

Simeon didn't miss a beat. He took the infant Emmanuel into his arms and gushed with praise for God. It was the culmination of his prayers, a fitting end to his (long) life's work, and the keeping of God's promise to him.

I'm sure there wasn't a dry eye in the place. Even Mary and Joseph were taken aback.

Not surprisingly, the Holy Spirit makes Jesus known to us too.

When we're hurting.

When we're tempted.

When we're lonely.

When we're broken.

Because Jesus came as a crying, messy Baby—and grew up to become a Man of sorrows—he can relate to the things we suffer. Even a conquering King couldn't have done that.

—BKS

Where are you encountering Jesus?

CHRISTMAS 5

I will greatly rejoice in the Lord, my whole being shall exult in my God; for he has clothed me with the garments of salvation, he has covered me with the robe of righteousness, as a bridegroom decks himself with a garland, and as a bride adorns herself with her jewels. —Isaiah 61:10

Several years ago, I wrote a song called "Unreal." In it, I admitted to feeling like I was the sum of my mistakes, like a consequence of my past choices, woefully missing the mark of God's expectations time and again.

I was nearing 40 at the time, beginning to come to terms with my sexuality, struggling with being a faithful husband, unsure of where I stood with God, and deeply depressed.

Being a successful Christian songwriter, an upstanding deacon in my Southern Baptist church, a proud Republican, and a super-nice guy were not enough to quiet what was going on in my head and heart. I might've fooled some, but God and I knew what was really happening.

When I looked in the mirror, I didn't see salvation or righteousness. I didn't have the confident swagger of a groom or the radiant beauty of a bride.

What I saw was brokenness, ugliness, and gut-level fear.

I wrestled with that lyric for weeks before arriving at a chorus that held out hope for me and for everyone who struggles with feeling unworthy:

> You're so unreal, too good to be true
> You and only You could bring me back to life
> It's so unreal how Your unrelenting grace
> Flies into the face of everything I feel
> The way You love is just unreal

I still feel unworthy sometimes. But the truth is God loves and treasures me, clothing me in salvation and righteousness. I don't always see it, or feel it, but it's still true.

—BKS

If you feel unworthy of God's love and acceptance, why do you think that is? What are the ideas about God you have that would need to change for you to feel worthy?

CHRISTMAS 6

The Lord is not slow in keeping his promise, as some understand slowness. Instead he is patient with you, not wanting anyone to perish, but everyone to come to repentance.
—2 Peter 3:9

There was a time when I was struggling in what felt like every area of my life. Nothing was working, and I didn't think I was making a difference anywhere, to anyone. I used to earnestly pray that God would give my life meaning.

I longed to know that I mattered, in that Kingdom kind of way.

That trying season continued for the longest time. I wondered why God wasn't opening a door somewhere, providing relief for my financial frustrations and giving me clear direction for my future.

I never stopped believing that God desired good things for me. But it seemed like God was moving at a glacial pace, if at all.

Meanwhile, I stewed and pouted and complained. Like a petulant kid waiting on his Parent to make everything better.

Somewhere in the midst of my mess, I read Jesus' words in John 16:33: "In this world you will have trouble. But take heart! I have overcome the world."

I began to understand that God didn't promise a life without trouble. God promised to be bigger than my trouble.

It isn't God's job to save me from the outcome of my choices. It is up to me to make different choices. I have to participate in my own overcoming.

A few years removed, I can look back and see that, even when I didn't realize it, God was working in and through my life for the good of the Kingdom, and for my good too.

—BKS

Have you been waiting for God to rescue you from your own choices? What could you be doing instead?

CHRISTMAS 7 (NEW YEAR'S EVE)

The Lord bless you and keep you; the Lord make his face to shine upon you, and be gracious to you; the Lord lift up his countenance upon you, and give you peace.
—Numbers 6:24-26

On New Year's Eve, most of us fall into one of two categories—those who feel the need to grieve what's passed, and those who need to celebrate and welcome what's coming.

This year, I'd like to propose that we be both.

Last year at my house, we wrote down things we wanted to say goodbye to before the clock struck twelve and burned them. I felt lighter after watching my breakup and COVID and various other pain-points go up in flames.

Did they go away? No.

Did it feel good to say "so long" to them before the ball dropped? Heck yes, it did.

Then we drank champagne and went to bed.

My point is this: there is room for both grieving and celebrating. We need both. Solomon knew that when he wrote in Ecclesiastes, "for everything there is a season." (3:1).

It's important to pay our respects—or at least attention—to the things that we're leaving behind. It's also important to say hello to the new that awaits with proper fanfare.

So...

Light a candle for someone, or something, you lost this year.

Say a prayer of thanks for lessons learned.

Acknowledge the healing that hasn't happened yet.

Call or write someone and make peace.

Forgive what—or who—you can.

All of it matters. A lot. Then...

Put on some funky music.

Pull out your party dress or cowboy hat or whatever makes you feel festive.

66

Dance in the kitchen.

Toast to possibilities.

Eat junk food.

Hug the people in the room, even if the only one there is you.

Then share the blessing God gave Moses to share with the Israelites with everyone you know. (It's at the top of the page.)

—BKS

What will you bid farewell this year, and what will you welcome?

CHRISTMAS 8 (NEW YEAR'S DAY)

For everything there is a season, and a time for every matter under heaven.
—Ecclesiastes 3:1

"Happy New Year!!! Time to get to work! I want to lose ten pounds! I want $10K in my savings account! I'm gonna volunteer at the homeless shelter twice a month! I want to read a book a month! I'll call my mom twice a week! I'm gonna learn Mandarin, and winemaking, and sign language!"

—A Misguided, Overzealous Resolution-Maker

Yes, it's a new year. It's a time for restarts, refreshed motivations, and renewed perspectives. Something about turning the calendar year gets many of us really energized to accomplish and achieve. Nothing wrong with that.

But in my experience, New Year's resolutions—deciding to make a change or two (or twelve) in your life as the clock strikes midnight—result in more setbacks than successes.

Here's why: Just because I'm in a new year doesn't mean I haven't brought the old me along for the ride.

Changing those habits and behaviors takes a lot of difficult work. It requires a retraining of my mind—getting rid of negative attitudes and speaking back to demon voices of guilt and shame.

It demands a reshaping of my environment—adjusting what I watch, what I listen to, where I hang out and with whom.

And it means drawing close to God so that my sticky soul isn't drawn to the things I say I'd like to get away from.

I can't change anything significant about myself by an act of my will alone. The will just isn't strong enough.

So achieving a goal of $10K in the bank means looking at how I spend my money and why, as well as what I gain from saving—not just in material ways, but also how it benefits my emotional, mental, and spiritual health.

And that's before I do the work of creating a budget, living within it, and actually saving a buck or two.

In Ecclesiastes, we read that there is a season for everything. Building, tearing down, dancing, weeping, feasting, fasting.

—BKS

Maybe this year, instead of making resolutions, start with the question, "What season am I in? What do I want the rest of this season to look like?"

CHRISTMAS 9

Who is wise and understanding among you? Let them show it by their good life, by deeds done in the humility that comes from wisdom. But if you harbor bitter envy and selfish ambition in your hearts, do not boast about it or deny the truth. Such 'wisdom' does not come down from heaven but is earthly, unspiritual, demonic. For where you have envy and selfish ambition, there you find disorder and every evil practice.
—James 3:13-16

I used to have a successful career in the Christian music industry. I wore a lot of hats back then—publisher, record producer, studio musician—but the role that fit me best was always songwriter.

I was part of a tight-knit songwriting community in Nashville. My friends and I wrote many of the hits played on Christian radio back then. We celebrated one another's accomplishments. We made an impact on gospel music.

It felt good.

When I ostensibly left Christian music nearly 20 years ago, I also left behind that close camaraderie. I shed all the roles I'd played and shifted my creative focus to writing songs for me to sing. Songs that reflected my changing views on God, myself, and the world around me.

While I'm usually happy with the choice I made, I occasionally see where someone from my former peer group has had some success—a number-one single, a Dove Award nomination, or some other accolade—and I feel a twinge of "that used to be me."

I sometimes wonder, "What if I'd just kept writing those songs and nurturing those relationships? Am I not as talented as most of the Christian songwriters who are successful today?"

But then I remember a few important things.

I outgrew what I was writing. Those songs no longer felt honest or true to my experience of God.

If I'd let my career, ambition, or envy of others' success keep me there, it would've held me back from becoming who I am now.

Being a part of the Christian music status quo was not God's best for my life.

So I'd say I did the wise thing.

—BKS

When have you made a wise choice that ran against "earthly" wisdom, and what happened?

CHRISTMAS 10

He was in the world, and the world came into being through him; yet the world did not know him. He came to what was his own, and his own people did not accept him.
—John 1:10-11

Jesus was always a little...different.

Stands to reason. But Jesus's differences didn't lead most people to believe he was the promised Son of God. Instead, he came off to most as odd, to some as delusional, and to everyone as, well, different.

His own people didn't see who he was. He didn't look or act like they thought a Messiah would. Instead of being a conquering hero, he was a thorn in the side of their leaders. He was controversial, counter-cultural. Some would say subversive.

And yet, there he was—God dwelling among them. Both human and divine.

I'd like to think I would recognize Jesus. But then, I suppose I rub elbows with him all the time.

That's because Jesus said that when we care for the poor, the sick, the beaten-down, the forgotten, the lonely, that we are, in fact, loving him.

So if we're looking for Jesus, we might just be looking in the wrong places. Like some of the Jews were then.

—BKS

Would you recognize Jesus? How?

CHRISTMAS 11

Now listen, you who say, "Today or tomorrow we will go to this or that city, spend a year there, carry on business and make money." Why, you do not even know what will happen tomorrow. What is your life? You are a mist that appears for a little while and then vanishes. Instead, you ought to say, "If it is the Lord's will, we will live and do this or that." —James 4:13-15

When I was young, I had a Sunday school teacher, Mrs. Worrell, who would always add "If it be Thy will" to every prayer she prayed with us.

"Heal Sheryl of her allergies, if it be Thy will."

"Give safety to Dewayne Gill and his family as they travel to Florida, if it be Thy will."

I don't believe for a second that God wanted Sheryl to suffer with sniffles. Or for the Gills to break down on the interstate en route to Panama City. I don't think Mrs. Worrell believed that either. Still, in her prayers, she was offering deference to God, in the event that God wanted something different.

I want to defer to the will of God too—when I'm making plans, and when I'm asking God for something, for myself or for someone else.

But I don't believe God has a stake in whether or not I plan a trip to Hawaii in February, I assume that if it isn't to be, obstacles will start popping up and I'll change (or cancel) my plans accordingly.

Same goes for bigger things, like changing careers, starting a business, and moving across the country—all of which I did, not knowing for certain if it's what God desired for me at the time.

I used to be terrified of making a misstep that would result in God washing Their hands of me. But now I know that God is not that petty.

Instead of wringing my hands and worrying that God will be displeased with my choices, I spend time with God so that I have a pretty good sense of what They want for (and from) me. Then I do my best to act accordingly.

—BKS

Think about your life right now. What do you think God expects from you, and desires for you?

CHRISTMAS 12

Do to others as you would have them do to you. —Luke 6:31b

I remember when I was in kindergarten, my teachers would tell us to follow the Golden Rule. All the other rules—don't pull each other's hair, don't call each other names, don't take someone else's toy—all led back to that one Rule.

"Treat others the way you want to be treated."

What would our society be like if we all held up the Golden Rule as the standard—the expectation—for all our behavior?

I suppose if that were the case, and I were to encounter a houseless man on the street begging for money, I'd give him all the cash I had. I'd ask him if he was hungry and offer to provide him a meal. If he didn't have a safe place to sleep, I'd find him shelter, or offer him a bed at my house.

Because that's what I would hope someone would do for me.

If someone disagreed with me about the COVID vaccine, the climate crisis, women's rights, LGBTQ+ rights, immigration, or pretty much anything, I'd listen to their point-of-view. I'd approach their opinions with curiosity rather than judgment, and I wouldn't assume they were stupid or evil because their views differed from mine.

Because that's how I would hope someone would engage with me.

Following the Golden Rule is simple, but it isn't easy. Kindergarteners get it. Grownups get it too—we just add a bunch of caveats to it like it's a peace treaty or a bill stuck in Congress. Probably because it's just easier to put ourselves first.

But if we love our neighbors as we love ourselves, it makes for a way better time at the playground.

—BKS

Why do you think following the Golden Rule is so hard? What is one way you could practice loving your neighbor as yourself?

EPIPHANY

EPIPHANY DAY (JANUARY 6)

On entering the house, the magi saw the child with Mary his mother; and they knelt down and paid him homage. Then, opening their treasure chests, they offered him gifts of gold, frankincense, and myrrh. And having been warned in a dream not to return to Herod, they left for their own country by another road. —Luke 2:11-12

"We three kings of Orient are..." the song goes. Poetic license, since the visitors who followed a star weren't kings, and were probably more than three. They were courtiers, priests and astronomers, adherents of Zoroastrianism (a religion that was ancient even in Jesus' time), who looked to the heavens for truth. When they discerned a particular star in the dark Persian sky, they left home on a journey to find that truth.

I can't help but wonder: Did they know that their trip would take them 1100 miles and two years? Would they have gone if they knew? And what all did they have to leave behind in order to make that journey toward God?

Journeys to God are never easy. Every single one of them takes a lifetime. And if you really want to see God, to live in the divine Presence in this material world, you will leave parts of life as you knew it behind.

Every time you make the choice to turn toward God, even if it's something as simple as saying a prayer over your meal, you turn away from something else you *could* be doing.

Strewn over the course of a lifetime, that's a lot of leaving behind.

Most people don't make that journey, or don't make it consistently. I don't. I get distracted by work or family or the latest movie. I decide that *just this once* I'm going to do something other than give to the poor or crack open my Bible. Except it's not just this once, is it?

And: had I never experienced the Presence of God, had I never heard the Divine Whisper, had I never looked at all the times I *should* have been dead or hungry or shattered and *seen* God's hand guiding me away from destruction, I might never have kept on this one-step-at-a-time journey at all.

Once you've experienced God, it changes you. You can't go back to exactly who you were.

When the magi left the place where toddler Jesus was, they went home "by another road." What else could they do? They had found what they were looking for.

—EOR

Would you travel 1100 miles by mule or camel to find God? How would such a journey change you?

For the rest of the season of Epiphany, start with Common 1, and continue until Lent begins.

See the Chart of Days on pages 5-6 for help.

LENT

ASH WEDNESDAY

As for mortals, their days are like grass; they flourish like a flower of the field; for the wind passes over it, and it is gone, and its place knows it no more.
—Psalm 103:15-16

One day, I will die and so will you. Those who love us will mourn as we go on to whatever life looks like after death.

I don't spend a lot of time thinking about the afterlife. I believe the days I'm given are meant to be lived with purpose, going about the work of the Kingdom. I also believe they are to be lived fully—savoring moments, finding joy, and spreading light.

Psalm 103 and other Scripture passages (I'm looking at you, Ecclesiastes!) point to how life begins and ends without fanfare. Most of us don't end wars, cure cancer, or save the planet singlehandedly. Most of us live quietly, exhaling when we can, parenting the best we know how, gambling on big and small decisions, and managing our sometimes-meager resources.

We may do this without much introspection. We may count survival as success. And when we're going about the business of life, that may be all we can manage.

But during Lent, we are invited to ask the hard questions. How do my choices impact my kids? How am I making the world better? What do I do with my one gone-like-grass life?

Truth is, our days are full of ellipses and question marks. Few answers are as pat as we'd like them to be.

So for these next six weeks, my attention goes to the unresolved.

What are your hard questions? Let's ask them together.

—BKS

THURSDAY—1ST WEEK OF LENT

By the sweat of your face you shall eat bread until you return to the ground, for out of it you were taken; you are dust, and to dust you shall return. —Genesis 3:19

Adam had it made in the Garden. He was in close communion with God, who loved him dearly and entrusted him with caring for Eden. God had given him a life without pain or disappointment— essentially heaven on earth.

But in a moment, all that changed. Adam did not trust that God would care for Eve and him, and chose instead to trust the serpent. From that moment forward, Adam would eat only if he worked hard. Like digging-ditches-in-Mississippi-in-August hard. Then one day, he would die and return to the dust from which he was made. The end.

Things we do, and think, and think about doing, basically fall into two categories—life-giving and life-destroying. Sins are the acts and attitudes that destroy life—ours or someone else's—and breach relationships.

What Adam did was life-destroying. When I choose the fruit of the forbidden tree, and I have, I am choosing sin. And sin has consequences in this life, not just when I die. My relationships suffer because I put myself first. My hope dries up and the faith life I show the world is smoke and mirrors. Sin is bad.

Now I'm not a legalist. I'm not going to define what sin is for you, even though I think we could agree on some of the big ones. The most dangerous sins are the insidious ones that creep into our behaviors with barely a notice.

During Lent, one of the things we are called to do is deal with the sin in our lives that we brush aside, or pretend isn't there, or wish wasn't there.

—BKS

What is the sin in your life you aren't calling out?

FRIDAY—1ST WEEK OF LENT

Many times he delivered them, but they were rebellious in their purposes, and were brought low through their iniquity. Nevertheless he regarded their distress when he heard their cry. For their sake he remembered his covenant, and showed compassion according to the abundance of his steadfast love. —Psalm 106:43-45

Sin has consequences.

I know that sentence by itself is something you'd see lit up on a billboard beside an interstate in south Alabama. But it's true. (And I'm not talking about hell. That's a subject for another day.)

What I mean to say is this: when we choose to act in ways that are life-destroying, life is destroyed. Joy is traded for sorrow. Peace for unrest and conflict. Love for self-worship.

God has saved us from ourselves more times than we can count. When our actions have brought us low, God has heard our cries for help and has shown us compassion. Why? Because God has an abundant, steadfast love.

God does not give up on us, even when we act in life-destroying ways.

I've felt the elephant of guilt sitting on my chest because of sin. I've lied to cover up or excuse what I've done. I've avoided the calls and texts from concerned friends.

But I've never had God turn away from me, even when I've turned away from God and everyone else. It isn't in God's nature to do that to me, or to you.

—BKS

**What are the consequences of sin you're living with?
Why haven't you cried out to God? Or, if you have, what have you heard back?**

SATURDAY—1ST WEEK OF LENT

Nathan said to David, "You are the man! Thus says the Lord, the God of Israel"
—2 Samuel 12:7a

Nathan was King David's advisor and trusted friend. He was also a prophet, which means he was a truth teller.

In 2 Samuel 12, Nathan came to share a story with David about a rich man with many herds and a poor man who had nothing but a cherished lamb. When a traveler came to the rich man's home, instead of taking one of his countless sheep to feed his guest, the rich man took the poor man's beloved lamb.

Upon hearing this, David was outraged, saying the rich man should repay the poor man fourfold and be sentenced to die for this injustice. But Nathan was quick to point out that David was the rich man in the story, taking Bathsheba from her husband, Uriah, and then ordering Uriah killed (see 2 Samuel 11).

God had blessed David beyond measure, but David still took what wasn't his to take.

We take things that don't belong to us. When we gossip, we take someone's good reputation. When we cheat to win, we take someone else's victory. When we lie, we take away the ability of others to recognize truth.

Why do we do it? We take because we think that what we have isn't enough. Instead of celebrating God's many blessings with life-giving joy, we diminish what we have and desire what others have with life-destroying envy.

Do you have a Nathan in your life? You know. That friend who can tell you the truth, even when you don't want to hear it? David was able to hear the hard truth from Nathan because he knew Nathan loved him.

God uses those people in our lives to show us where we've mis-stepped, what we need to do to make it right, and how to avoid those life-destroying actions and attitudes going forward.

—BKS

Do you have someone who's willing to tell you the truth...and from whom you can hear it?

SUNDAY—1ST WEEK OF LENT

Other seeds fell on good soil and brought forth grain, some a hundredfold, some sixty, some thirty. —Matthew 13:8

The Parable of the Sower paints a simple picture. A man drops seeds in his planting area. Some land on the path and get eaten by birds. Some land in shallow soil, take root quickly, then burn up in the day's heat. Some land in thorns, where their growth is strangled. And some land in fertile soil and grow to produce lots of grain.

The important takeaway for us in this parable from Jesus is how important it is that we prepare the soil of our souls and spirits.

That's what spiritual disciplines are for. It's why we make a practice of praying, reading the Bible, choosing the longest line at the grocery store, letting someone else have the final word, and so on.

Tending to our spiritual soil takes attention and lots of work. But all the effort that we (and Jesus, as we will see later in Lent) put into preparing our soul-soil is worth it because of the connection it builds between us and God. And once our soil is fertile, we aren't usually even aware when God sows a seed.

—BKS

What are you doing during Lent to prepare your soil for the seed God wants to sow?

MONDAY—1ST WEEK OF LENT

For I do not do the good I want, but the evil I do not want is what I do. Now if I do what I do not want, it is no longer I that do it, but sin that dwells within me.
—Romans 7:19-20

Old habits are hard to break. That's because they get into our muscles if not our bones. Habits so completely take over our bodies that our minds don't even notice we have them. That's why willpower doesn't work: most of the time we do something we aren't even aware we're doing it.

So when we want to change something about ourselves, we have to start by noticing our troublesome habits and then work to form new, healthier ones.

That's what spiritual practices help us do. The life-destroying actions and attitudes we form over time don't change just because we will them to. The inner back-and-forth of Romans 7 is the internal struggle we all face: we want to do good and refrain from what's not good, but longstanding habits pull us right back.

There's the kind of person I want to be—patient, self-denying, kind, and compassionate. And then there's the person I am. But I can retrain my mind and body by taking on a spiritual practice, like choosing to drive in the slow lane in order to become more patient, or fasting from something I typically am quick to indulge in to practice self-denial. Spiritual practices use our bodies to change our minds.

During Lent, one of the things we do is follow Jesus into the desert, where he fasted, prayed, and faced his own temptations. Yes, even Jesus had to be intentional about focusing his mind and body on God. That's why he practiced solitude, and self-denial, and spent time with God: he was retraining his body to change his mind.

In the same way, we build our own spiritual stamina through practice and prayer, becoming more and more like Jesus as we do.

—BKS

What spiritual practice(s) are you taking on during Lent to retrain your body and mind?

TUESDAY—1ST WEEK OF LENT

The righteousness of the righteous shall be his own, and the wickedness of the wicked shall be his own. —Ezekiel 18:20b

By the time of the prophet Ezekiel, the Israelites already knew that the consequences of failing to follow God's commands was death. In this passage, God speaks through Ezekiel, detailing the actions that are considered righteous—things like being just, caring for the poor, and not worshiping idols. No surprises there: the Israelites had heard all of it before.

But before that moment, fathers and sons were punished for one another's sins. If a father committed a wrong act, his sons and their sons could also be punished. In Ezekiel 18, God says something startling: No one would be penalized for sins committed by someone else.

And then, God goes on to say this, When the wicked turn away from the wickedness they have committed and do what is lawful and right, they shall save their life (18:27). God offers the Israelites a chance to commute any death sentence they've earned, by changing their ways.

When we acknowledge our life-destroying behaviors and attitudes and then choose a different path, God offers us abundant life. Making different choices means forming new, life-giving habits. Forming those habits requires spiritual exercise, just like learning a new physical skill requires physical exercise.

Spiritual practices shape habits over time, and turn us from our old, life-destroying ways that affect far more people than just ourselves.

—BKS

What life-destroying actions and intentions do you see in yourself? What spiritual practices might help you form new life-giving behaviors instead?

WEDNESDAY—2ND WEEK OF LENT

Create in me a clean heart, O God, and put a new and right spirit within me.
—Psalm 51:10

In the living of our lives, we pick up stains: the marks of harm we experience and inflict.

Without thinking we retreat into ourselves and away from God.

We get used to destructive opinions and ways of speaking, things like sarcasm, unkindness, and conspiracy-chasing. They shape our thoughts so subtly we don't see it happening.

We destroy others and ourselves in little ways, through neglect, or shame, or arrogance, bit by bit.

Over time all those small errors and lapses take us off course, and sometimes we don't even realize by how far.

"Create in me a clean heart," David prays, after his friend Nathan makes him aware of how he has wronged God and others by taking Bathsheba for himself. Over time, his attitudes and actions had shaped him into a man who would steal another man's wife. His heart had been stained by thoughts and habits he hadn't even realized he had.

David goes to God, pleading for mercy, confessing what he has done, and asking to be restored. In fact, the word create that David uses in verse 10, is the same word used in Genesis 1. David is asking God to literally create his heart all over again.

Maybe you've been shaken by the shoulders after a season of self-absorbed behavior.

I know I have.

Our stained hearts keep us from the closeness we were always meant to have with God. When we move away from God, it's rarely a single, decisive act. It happens one small choice at a time. That's why it is up to us to change what we're doing, to act decisively and consistently to restore the closeness we long for.

—BKS

What life-destroying behaviors have crept into your life?
How will you address them so that you can draw closer to God?

THURSDAY—2ND WEEK OF LENT

Where can I go from your spirit? Or where can I flee from your presence?
—Psalm 139:7

I knew from an early age that God was always around.

As a teenager, I understood that to mean God was watching. Closely. And taking notes. That God was the kind of Father you can run from, but you can't hide from.

Later, as I discovered God outside the church of my youth, I came to see God as present … but also kind of detached, like there were more important matters to tend to than me.

Then when my internal conflicts around faith and sexuality became too big to keep burying, I began to experience God's presence as a source of security and peace. Even when my world was unfamiliar and uncomfortable, God was familiar and close. Despite what I'd been taught, and even what I was feeling, I knew that I was truly seen, fully known, and wonderfully made.

The Psalmist David says God knit me together in my mother's womb and that in God's book were written all the days that were formed for me, when none of them as yet existed.

God knows our thoughts, our ways, and the words we don't speak.

That's why trying to hide from God is fruitless, frustrating, and life-destroying. God sees and knows everything about us, and yet continues to cherish us and desire our company.

We can't flee from God's presence—and why would we want to?

—BKS

Recall a time when you tried to hide from God. What did you discover about yourself and about God?

FRIDAY—2ND WEEK OF LENT

And I heard a loud voice from the throne saying, "See, the home of God is among mortals. He will dwell with them; they will be his peoples, and God himself will be with them." —Revelation 21:3

Do you like the *Lord Of The Rings* books of JRR Tolkien? Read Revelation. It's full of wild, cryptic imagery and apocalyptic weirdness. In this passage, Revelation's writer (John) sees an actual city dropping out of the sky—and that's one of the less shocking events he describes.

Many people read this passage as John predicting the future arrival of a new Jerusalem. But that's not what was happening: John was seeing it happen in real time and recording what he saw as best he could. What he is describing is already there, then. And here, now.

The truth is the kingdom of God has coexisted with our own personal kingdoms, albeit uncomfortably, since Eden. The kingdom is here now, and much of the time we feel it as a threat to what we want. We've stood up to the Almighty over and over again, beating our chests and demanding our way.

As a result, our world isn't free from mourning, crying, pain, and death. Instead we have a climate crisis, crippling poverty, deep racial divides... you get the picture. Nevertheless, the home of God—the new Jerusalem—is and has been with us all along. God lives among us, dries our tears, makes things new.

The reconciliation John saw is already at work. The question we face is whether we will make the lifegiving choice to be a part of it.

As people of God, we can stay safe and comfortable in God's steadiness while the problems of humanity rock our planet. Or we can seek out a life in God's kingdom now, working to bring hope, peace, and light to the darkness around us.

—BKS

What are you doing to help bring reconciliation to your world?

SATURDAY—2ND WEEK OF LENT

For in him all the fullness of God was pleased to dwell, and through him God was pleased to reconcile to himself all things, whether on earth or in heaven, by making peace through the blood of his cross. —Colossians 1:19-20

Want to know how God would treat a woman with a regrettable reputation who was being harassed and humiliated by religious men? Look at how Jesus treated her (John 8:7).

Ever wonder how God feels about the poor, the meek, and the powerful? Jesus talked about that (Matthew 5:3).

The point is, we know God, at least in part, because we know Jesus.

In Jesus' actions, we see God's character, compassion, and heart for humanity.

In Jesus' words, we hear what is most important to God, and how God would say it.

In Jesus' life, we see modeled for us the kind of life God desires us to live.

God's fullness dwelled in Jesus.

But we also believe that Jesus was fully human, so we must accept that he was as capable as we are of making mistakes, choosing wrongly, and even abandoning his calling.

I mean, I've not always been faithful to God. Have you? But because Jesus was, I believe I can be. The fact that I can see both myself and God in Jesus gives me tremendous hope. I am reconciled to God through Jesus.

—BKS

What do you believe about Jesus' divinity? His humanity?
How do your views affect the way you live your Christian life?

SUNDAY—2ND WEEK OF LENT

And the Word became flesh and lived among us, and we have seen his glory, the glory as of a father's only son, full of grace and truth. —John 1:14

I'm a songwriter. I love crafting a new lyric from bits of experience, knowledge, and perspective that I've acquired here, there, and everywhere, and then finding a way to make the words sing. I know it's one of the things God made me to do.

I also know that God is creative too. In John 1, we read "All things came into being through him, and without him not one thing came into being" (1:3). So when I read verse 14, I find it both bizarre and wonderful that God would become one of us, a product of God's own imagination.

It would be like me becoming a song I'd written. Might be fun to be in somebody's *Spiritual But Not Crazy* playlist. Still … seriously weird. I think God knew it was weird too, but that's the mystery of intimacy between God and us.

Here's something else: the word for lived used here means pitched a tent. Imagine being at Coachella and God pitches a tent next to yours, offers you an IPA, and recalls a favorite Led Zeppelin concert where Jimmy Page first played that solo in *Stairway To Heaven*. Sounds ridiculous, but that is pretty much what God did. And does.

As we start recognizing the voice of God in Jesus' words, and seeing the heart of God in Jesus' actions, God become less abstract and less untouchable. More like us.

—BKS

Where do you notice God in your present circumstances?

MONDAY—2ND WEEK OF LENT

And have them make me a sanctuary, so that I may dwell among them. —Exodus 25:8

I enjoy home renovation shows. You know, where a less-than-desirable house gets a makeover, and then there's a big reveal for the homeowners. There's typically minimal drama (It's the wrong shower head!), and everyone is happy in the end.

My current favorite home-reno show is called *Home Town*. The interior designer and her woodworker husband bring old bungalows and farmhouses back to life, adding in awww-inspiring family photos, meaningful heirlooms, and lots of Southern charm. They seem to understand that it takes more than thoughtfully placed pretty things to create a home where someone can live happily ever after.

In Exodus 25, God asks Moses to collect precious things from the Israelites to use in the building of a sanctuary for God. Things like gemstones, leather and skins, precious metals, acacia wood, oils, and incense from all whose hearts prompt them to give (25:2).

None of these items would've been hiding forgotten in a box in the attic. These were things of value, handled with great care and displayed proudly. To part with them would be like giving up your Action Comics #1, or the keys to your 1965 Camaro, or your grandmother's diamond earrings.

Truth is, God doesn't want our precious things. And God doesn't need a nice place to come home to.

What God wants is to dwell with us, and in us. We give God a home when we offer ourselves. And we make that home beautiful by becoming the people God desires us to be.

—BKS

What of yourself—mind, body, soul, spirit, will, environment—are you willing to give to God?

TUESDAY—2ND WEEK OF LENT

Let no foreigner who is bound to the Lord say, "The Lord will surely exclude me from his people." And let no eunuch complain, "I am only a dry tree." For this is what the Lord says: "To the eunuchs who keep my Sabbaths, who choose what pleases me and hold fast to my covenant—to them I will give within my temple and its walls a memorial and a name better than sons and daughters; I will give them an everlasting name that will endure forever." —Isaiah 56:3-5

I got my first worship director job when I was going through a divorce while trying to reconcile my faith with my sexuality. Seems like a great time to start a new church gig, right? I felt unqualified to lead worship. I felt unworthy of a church home. Though the pastor who hired me understood my circumstances, I wasn't 100% sure that God and I were okay.

I was a Christian learning how to accept that I was gay.

I soon came to understand what a soft spot God has for outsiders. One example of this is in Isaiah 56, where God upends the status quo, essentially saying there are no foreigners and that a faithful eunuch is a celebrated child of God, not just a dry tree.

Eunuchs were differently gendered and, according to Jewish law, unclean and unwelcome in the temple.

They would fit under the LGBTQ+ umbrella for sure.

That's why I think there is some comfort in this passage for all of us, but especially those who experience themselves as inherently different. God's kingdom opens its arms to all of us, even though many churches would lead us to believe otherwise. We may feel unworthy, shameful, or built wrongly to accept God's invitation. But God assures us that we do, in fact, belong.

—BKS

How will you confront the shame that tells you that you're unworthy of God's acceptance and love?

WEDNESDAY—3RD WEEK OF LENT

The child grew and became strong, filled with wisdom; and the favor of God was upon him. —Luke 2:40

When I was a teenager, I formed a habit of spending two hours a day at the piano, working on scales, practicing pieces, and writing melodies. Those were hours I could've spent riding my bike or playing Atari games, and there were times I wanted to. But because I didn't, piano and songwriting became second nature to me.

A few years down the road, I began to understand music as my calling from God—something I might not have recognized and would not have been prepared for if I hadn't made music a daily practice. Teenage Me didn't know it, but I was soul training.

Jesus was a precocious twelve-year-old whose parents were good, observant Jews. Given what we know about Jesus as an adult, it's not too surprising that he would stay behind after Passover to sit with the temple teachers. Of course, Mary and Joseph were not happy about it when they discovered he wasn't with their caravan. When they found him, prepared to grab him by the collar and drag him back to Nazareth, he was perplexed, asking them, "Didn't you know I'd be in my Father's house?" He was soul training.

The rhythms and rituals of our youth don't just follow us into adulthood—they shape us as adults.

Soul training is the sum of those habits we form that help us recognize God and understand ourselves better.

Practicing piano can be a spiritual exercise. So can training for a marathon, photographing nature, or volunteering at an animal shelter. Jesus hanging out in the temple as a kid shaped him into the teacher he would become. He didn't come out of the womb with all this wisdom. He asked questions, listened closely, and became… well… Jesus.

—BKS

It's never too late to begin soul training. What interest or passion do you have that could serve as a spiritual exercise for you?

THURSDAY—3RD WEEK OF LENT

During the high priesthood of Annas and Caiaphas, the word of God came to John son of Zechariah in the wilderness. —Luke 3:2

My history professor was short, fat, and unkempt, with an oily combover and a stained tie, who smoked during class. Dr. B's style, along with his harsh grading, made him unpopular among those scrambling for social status, but his course was required and I couldn't afford to be snobby.

By the end of that course I was hooked. Dr. B was always prepared, knew his stuff, and tied history to art and language, as well as redeemed any convoluted thought I babbled.

The last course I took from him probably saved my life.

At the end of my junior year I had decided to drop out of college. For months I had been repeatedly and publicly abused by a powerful faculty member. Exhausted, broken, and deeply ashamed, I couldn't imagine surviving another round. Showing up at Dr. B's office, I begged him to sign the paper that would set me free from my obligations if not my demons.

I don't remember what he said. But he turned me around, literally and academically, acting as light until I could see it myself.

I realize now that God had called him to his work and guided me to his care.

In Luke 3:1-3, Luke lists powerful rulers and then has John wander into the scene. John is the son of a priest of some stature, but a wild man who has been in the desert to fast and pray and learn, tilling the soil of his soul. When he hears God's word, John's prepared. God tells John to call people to repentance, a fancy way of saying to turn back toward God. John does.

While we don't know how many people John taught and saved through baptism, we know of at least one, Jesus, and that one is enough.

Not every weirdo is John the Baptizer and not every unkempt prof is Dr. B. To be the men they were, they had to prepare, listen when God spoke, and obey. That takes discipline of mind, body, and spirit, along with the ability to ignore the name-calling that comes when you aren't what others expect.

I don't know whether Dr. B ever got the respect he deserved, or how many people he rescued. But I know of at least one, and that one is enough for me.

—EOR

When has an unlikely rescuer shined light for you? What did that look like?

FRIDAY—3RD WEEK OF LENT

Then Jesus was led up by the Spirit into the wilderness to be tempted by the devil. He fasted forty days and forty nights, and afterwards he was famished. —Matthew 4:1-2

We can't possibly be prepared for everything life throws at us, but we can prepare for some things. Like starting in save for a family vacation in June. Or studying (a lot) before you take the bar exam.

Sometimes we can brace ourselves for what we see coming—the declining health of our aging parents, the arrival of a new baby, or a job transfer to a new town. But even then, we cannot fully know how we'll be impacted, emotionally or otherwise.

Similarly, there are ways to prepare spiritually for things we are sure to face. Like Jesus did in the wilderness.

In Matthew 3, Jesus is baptized by John and then is led by God's Spirit into the wilderness to prepare for what was ahead. Wildernesses are wild-nesses— pieces of our environment that can make us or break us. I've experienced a few in my years, and I usually find them without a map. But Jesus had an idea of what was coming and prepared himself by fasting.

As a spiritual practice, fasting is saying no to things like alcohol, social media, or Hulu, not because those things are inherently bad, but because saying no to them trains us to say no to other, more dangerous kinds of gratification.

Jesus was giving up food in order to have the spiritual stamina he would need when the tempter came, dangling shortcuts to glory in front of his face.

—BKS

What is something you've given up before in order to become stronger, faster, smarter, etc.?
What is something you'd be willing to fast from for a season to become more spiritually prepared for wisdom?

SATURDAY—3RD WEEK OF LENT

Then he went down with them and came to Nazareth, and was obedient to them. His mother treasured all these things in her heart. And Jesus increased in wisdom and in years, and in divine and human favor. —Luke 2:51-52

When my daughter was on the brink of womanhood I worried, even though she wasn't doing anything death-defying or dangerous. Unless by dangerous you mean working her mother's last nerve.

When they're toddlers, children expand their young egos with that annoying No! phase. My child postponed her No! phase for a decade while honing her skills in sarcasm.

So when pubescent Jesus misses the caravan home from Jerusalem, forcing his parents to return and track him down, my sympathies lie with his mother.

Don't you know that Jesus rolled his eyes dramatically before snarking "Why were you searching for me? Did you not know that I must be in my Father's house?"

Brink-of-manhood Jesus has been in the temple arguing Torah with the men, expanding his ego. Scripture does not say that Mary, panicked and tired from searching for her missing child, backhanded the smart-mouthed savior, but I can imagine her wanting to.

She and Joseph lead Jesus back home to Nazareth where Jesus was obedient to them.

As Jesus grew, Mary must have depended on the God-given practices she had instilled: dedicating him to God as required (2:39), observing Passover (2:41), and, of course, the big "Let it be" she gave the angel when it told her she was pregnant.

The beginning and end of this passage link obedience with growth in wisdom (2:39-40, 51-52). When parents, whether divine or human, provide structure and expect obedience, they instill internal discipline. When children rebel, they grow in courage and experience.

Obedience and rebellion, discipline and experience: these are the framework for wisdom.

God gave us the law to shape us for wisdom. We choose spiritual practices, such as obedience, to curb our adolescent "No!"s and strengthen our souls so that as we increase in years we, like Jesus, may also increase in divine and human favor.

—EOR

When adolescent urges toward rebellion control you, how might you use obedience to build self-discipline?

SUNDAY—3RD WEEK OF LENT

And when he comes home, he calls together his friends and neighbors, saying to them, "Rejoice with me, for I have found my sheep that was lost." —Luke 15:6

On the Discipline of Celebration

When my son, Nick, was four years old, we lost him at a theme park. We were in one of those big souvenir shops right by the park's exit gate. Of course, we panicked. The staff at the store knew exactly what to do—I figure this wasn't their first preschooler rodeo.

They asked everyone to stop what they were doing and look for my son. In a matter of a couple minutes, he was back in my arms. Sure, I was upset that he'd gotten away from us. But I was so relieved he was safe, all I wanted to do was buy everyone in the store a funnel cake.

We've all lost things. Small things like car keys. Big things like a preschooler. Sometimes finding them is simply a relief. But sometimes, it's a reason to party.

Here, a shepherd finds a lost sheep, one of a hundred sheep, and he gathers his friends to celebrate. Later, a woman loses a coin—one of only ten she has to her name. When she finds it, she tells her friends and they rejoice together. And after that, a father, whose son has left home, throws a huge party when his wayward kid returns to him.

Celebrating the good things that happen, even small things, is a spiritual practice. Some of us minimize our successes, which can make drawing attention to them more challenging than, say, fasting. It's often easier to toast the good things that happen for others than it is to invite them to rejoice with us. But when we acknowledge and share our achievements, we give our friends an opportunity to show us love— something they like to do, and something that helps us see ourselves the way they do.

Whether for ourselves or someone else, keeping an eye out for a reason to celebrate, and then drawing attention to it with an attaboy, a cake, or a text to a friend that says "I did it!" is a way that we can make joy and gratitude something we experience on the regular. And couldn't we all use more of both?

—BKS

What is something you can celebrate today? How about right now?

MONDAY—3RD WEEK OF LENT

Leave your gift there before the altar and go; first be reconciled to your brother or sister, and then come and offer your gift. —Matthew 5:24

On the Discipline of Reconciliation

Ever been on the receiving end of the silent treatment? You know, where someone isn't speaking to you, but you don't know why? I have. It can be funny to watch in a rom-com, but in real life, it's no fun.

Of course, what the injured party is (isn't) saying is you hurt my feelings, or you weren't listening the last twelve times I asked you not to do that. As the person who did the thing that hurt the other person, it is on me to go to them, take responsibility for what I did, and make things right.

We don't make altar sacrifices anymore, but what Jesus is saying here is: don't lay your lamb down at the altar if someone has something against you.

Sometimes I know what I did that wronged someone else. And sometimes it's a big deal. Making reconciliation in this context means owning what I did—or failed to do—and humbly asking forgiveness from the person I hurt. That is pretty impossible to do if I think I'm right, if I believe I'm owed something in return, or if I'm just downright stubborn. But until I lay down my pride, it will not only stand between me and the person I hurt, but also between me and God.

And that's the point. When my behavior has caused a rift with someone, and I don't do all I can to repair the relationship, then it causes a rift with God too. If I want to please God, then I have to be mindful of how I'm treating others.

—BKS

Do you have a relationship that needs repairing?
What steps can you take to practice reconciliation?

TUESDAY—3RD WEEK OF LENT

I say to you that everyone who looks at another with lust has already committed adultery in his heart. —Matthew 5:28

On the Discipline of Self-Control

God created us as sensual beings who touch, taste, smell, see, hear, and experience. God also created beauty, beautifully, and made us sensitive to it. It is both fleshly and divine to experience the pull that beauty can have on us. It draws us nearer to God's own nature, to what God must feel when observing God's own creation.

That's not lust.

Lust is seeing an object or person, being drawn to it, and wanting to possess it. When we lust, a person is transformed in our minds into an object to be used or won. We lose sight of their dignity and self-determination. It's a tragedy, as the loss of holiness and humanity always is.

When I see a human being I find compelling and have a bodily reaction, that alone is not a problem. That's just how we're all made: stimulus then response.

Lust happens when I take stimulus/response and let my imagination run wild.

Lust isn't about sex, or even really about attraction, but about the rush I get. It's about the power and ego boost that comes from asserting myself and getting what I want.

But when I do that, I don't in any way take into consideration the well-being of the other person. In a split second, my mind can turn that human being— someone with their own desires, strengths, and history— into a kind of toy, or a tool, to be used to my own ends.

So how do we conquer lust? By dealing with our craving for power, as well as our feelings of powerlessness. By turning our thoughts toward the wholeness of the other person, seeing them as a subject, not an object.

Practices to counter lust include looking at people we find compelling and thinking through the fact that they are human beings too, with families, histories, struggles, etc. Or, when we are wrestling with our own powerlessness, we can learn to counter lust by affirming our power—reminding ourselves that we can and do make choices, and that we are not being deprived of our desires.

—EOR

Where is lust (the compulsion to conquer or possess another person) a problem for you? How can you address it and deal with it?

WEDNESDAY—4TH WEEK OF LENT

He asked them, "How many loaves do you have?" They said, "Seven" … He took the seven loaves, and after giving thanks he broke them…and they distributed them to the crowd. —Mark 8:5-6

On the Discipline of Sacrifice

It had been a long day. The thousands who had gathered to hear Jesus teach were tired and hungry, and they still had to walk home. Jesus' disciples were hungry too. Between them, they had seven loaves of bread and a few small fish. When Jesus asked for their dinner, the disciples handed it over. There's no record of a scuffle, of words exchanged, or of any sore feelings. They just gave it to Jesus, not knowing what he was about to do with it.

Sacrifice is a concept we all understand. I've been on the receiving end of my parents' sacrifices, probably more than I realize. I've done without things so that my kids had what they wanted and needed. That's just a given. But I've never emptied my bank account to buy shoes for the homeless. I've never given one of my kidneys to a stranger who desperately needs one. I've never given my dinner to someone hungrier than me.

Sometimes God asks us to hand it over. And it's usually awkward, uncomfortable, even painful. We don't always know how our sacrifice will benefit someone else. We can't always trust its recipient. But because we trust God, we know that when we give it, God blesses it, and multiplies it.

Sacrifice as a spiritual practice can start small. Giving up lattes for a month and giving the money to a local homeless shelter to provide coffee for its guests might be a good starting point. Or delaying a weekend getaway and giving what you'd spend to support refugees who are starting a new life where you are.

—BKS

What is something valuable to you that are you willing to sacrifice to train your soul for good?

THURSDAY—4TH WEEK OF LENT

At daybreak he departed and went into a deserted place. And the crowds were looking for him; and when they reached him, they wanted to prevent him from leaving them.
—Luke 4:42

On the Discipline of Solitude

Jesus had been dodging religious legalists, healing the sick, rebuking demons, and teaching constantly. I'm exhausted just thinking about it. We go and go and go and then we're surprised when we run out of gas. Why is that?

Our reserves of power are pretty small. AAA batteries at best. God's power is enormous. Jesus of Nazareth knew the limits of his body and spirit—how big his battery was. So to do all the things he did, he charged up with God's power, sneaking away at daybreak to be alone with God the Almighty.

We don't know exactly what he did while he was alone, but it's a good bet that he prayed, meditated, regrouped, and recharged. Jesus didn't spend time by himself with God in order to rest from his work. He drank in God's energy, God's power before he had to do what he did.

If you're a parent, or a caregiver, or a pastor, or just a person who cares about people who aren't you, let me remind you how vital solitude is.

Those who tend to the needs of others face hazards—physical, emotional, and spiritual. We risk our souls sticking to the wrong things, such as unhealthy attention or adoration. We also risk having our spirits become blocked by cynicism, negativity, and just plain burnout.

Regularly setting aside time to drink from God's infinite power source is critical for refilling our spiritual batteries. Solitude is a discipline of gaining strength from God.

Time alone can be hard to get. We have to admit our need to anyone who depends on us and then ask for their support.

Maybe all you can manage is a bath or some deep breathing while a little one is napping.

Maybe you have more freedom and can negotiate an afternoon hike by yourself, take a long drive in the country, or even plan a solo weekend retreat.

But remember: For solitude to have its healing effect you must aim for minimal distractions and interactions, as well as plenty of space for quiet, prayer, reflection... and rest.

—BKS

How can you make solitude a regular part of your life?

FRIDAY—4TH WEEK OF LENT

But I say to you that listen, "Love your enemies, do good to those who hate you, bless those who curse you, pray for those who abuse you." —Luke 6:27-28

On the Discipline of Prayer

Throughout the Gospels, Jesus asks us to do some pretty crazy things. Among the craziest is expecting us to love our enemies. Of course, he knows it's more than we can do on our own because it's more than he could do on his own. But he showed us, all the way up to his last breath, that he could love those who hated him, and bless those who wanted him dead. And the crazy thing is, so can we.

We access God's power, courage, and well of love through prayer—consistent, expectant, soul-baring prayer. It gives us perspective when we're unsure, peace when we're anxious, and stamina when ours is gone. Turns out the result of this kind of prayer is often grace: the ability to do what we could not otherwise do.

Loving one's enemies is never easy. In fact, I'd argue it can't be done without God's help. When someone has hurt us deeply, wanting their good is truly hard. But in those cases, we can plead with God to do what we can't.

If prayer is difficult for you, you might begin by reading the prayers of others, as in *The Book Of Common Prayer* or any of the countless collections available. You might also try writing out your prayers in a journal, or picking a time each day to go to God.

Loving those who've hurt us or who wish us ill is among the hardest things we do. Let God do the heavy lifting.

—BKS

Who is your enemy?
How can you pray for them today?

SATURDAY—4TH WEEK OF LENT

They went to him and woke him up, shouting, "Master, Master, we are perishing!"
— Luke 8:24a

On the Discipline of Rest

Jesus was tired and looking for a respite from the crowds, so he got into a boat with his disciples and set out to cross the Sea of Galilee. After a bit, Jesus fell asleep and while he was sleeping, a storm came up suddenly. The boat began to fill with water and the disciples—who, by the way, were experienced fishermen and had no doubt encountered rough water before—woke Jesus in a panic, probably because he was sleeping through the tumult. He rebuked the wild wind and waves and everything was calm again.

Then Jesus asked them, "Where is your faith?" (8:25)

In the middle of the storm the disciples feared for their safety, didn't trust their own abilities to keep the boat from sinking, and didn't lean on the faith they professed. Conversely, Jesus could rest because he trusted everyone—including God—would be okay and that they could manage the world without him for a bit.

Rest requires trust. If I'm worried about paying my mortgage, saving my marriage, or keeping my career afloat, I won't rest. I'll keep doing everything I do to right the ship, so to speak. But if I trust that everything in my world is in capable hands and that all will be well, I can let go of the wheel and rest.

To practice rest I might delegate a responsibility and let go of the outcome, so that the video game I play to relax is actually restful. The point of rest is not just about taking a break, but also giving up control and trusting that everything will be fine while you do.

—BKS

What are some actions you can practice in order to deepen your trust in God and others so that you can experience rest?

SUNDAY—4TH WEEK OF LENT

Now as they went on their way, he entered a certain village, where a woman named Martha welcomed him into her home. —Luke 10:38

On the Discipline of Fellowship

Jesus brought all his disciples to Mary and Martha's house for dinner. Mary hung out with the disciples and listened to Jesus tell stories while Martha stressed out over getting their meal together. When Martha finally lost her cool, Jesus assured her that Mary had done nothing wrong, even implying that Martha could join them too.

The fact is these kinds of gatherings were the heartbeat of family life in Jesus' day. The kind of fellowship small groups in churches aspire to have. It was in community that children were raised, physical needs were met, and souls were filled. In John 21, resurrected Jesus cooked fish and invited his disciples. Of all the things Jesus could've chosen to do, fellowship was right at the top of his list.

When my grandmother died, friends from her tiny, tightly knit community brought countless casseroles, covered dishes, Jello salads, and sweets when they stopped by to offer their condolences to our family. The stories, laughter, and tears were a balm for my grandfather's broken heart. In times like those, where there is inexpressible pain and grief, love can be expressed and felt through fried chicken and fellowship.

Because of the pandemic, most of us have felt isolated to some degree. Depression, addiction, and anxiety are at troubling levels. What if the remedy for this isolation is reaching out with kindness, hope, and love, and allowing ourselves to receive the same?

It's true that sometimes what we want and need is time and space to process and mourn. And sometimes, fellowship is how God chooses to remind us that, in the midst of everything, we are not alone.

—BKS

How do you allow fellowship into your life?
How might you practice it with others?

MONDAY—4TH WEEK OF LENT

In the morning, while it was still very dark, he got up and went out to a deserted place, and there he prayed. —Mark 1:35

On the Disciplines of Solitude and Prayer

Once again, Jesus sneaks off by himself to pray. How else was he going to get a little peace and quiet? With his notoriety growing, people were always chasing him with their questions, their afflictions, and their accusations. Claiming solitary time with his Father was getting harder and harder to do.

For Jesus, prayer was preparation.

When Simon finds him, he has been praying about the corner he knows his ministry is about to turn. He is confident when he says, "Let's go do what I came out to do."

Connecting with God refilled his spirit, renewed his strength, and steadied his resolve.

Solitude makes room for uninterrupted, spirit-filling, soul-focusing prayer. That prayer gives us what we need to face what we see coming, and what we don't.

Like Jesus, we all lead crowded, noisy lives, with people who count on us. But when he knew he needed time with God, Jesus was fine with stepping away from everything and everyone to get alone and pray.

Am I fine with stepping away? My sense of duty, and my guilt over maybe letting someone down, has held me in place many, many times. I am learning that most things can wait. But when the thing I need is prayer, I will only recognize it if prayer is a practice.

—BKS

Where do you find solitude?
How can you make solitary prayer a spiritual practice?

TUESDAY—4TH WEEK OF LENT

God is spirit, and those who worship him must worship in spirit and truth. —John 4:24

On the Discipline of Worship

Leading people in the worship of God is something that I do. I can create a worshipful environment. I can orchestrate activities like music, prayer, and silence. I can give people words to say, sing, and even pray. But if those with me aren't actually worshiping, then they might as well be at a Benton Stokes concert.

When we worship God, we express the beauty, goodness, grace, and power of God. That's what liturgical activities like singing and prayer are for. They focus our attention on the awesome attributes of God, allowing us to see God more clearly, and gain the vital perspective that gives.

Jesus distinguishes worship as a practice from worship as an internal experience. The spiritual exercise of worship always involves words, phrases, and behaviors we value, even when we are worshiping alone. The experience of worship results in awe, peace, gratitude, joy, and more. We need both. And the ways we go about it are as diverse as we are.

Worship as a discipline is an act of will or habit.

Worship as an experience is an act of mind and body.

When we worship in spirit and truth, we join our spirits with the Holy Spirit, and we ascribe to God what we know to be true. Giving God praise and adoration, and doing so with mind, body, soul, spirit, and will, is the kind of worship God enjoys.

—BKS

When do you feel most engaged in worshiping God?
Why do you think worship is sometimes hard for you?

WEDNESDAY—5TH WEEK OF LENT

Now about eight days after these sayings Jesus took with him Peter and John and James and went up on the mountain to pray. —Luke 9:28

On the Discipline of Transparency

When I was first coming out, I didn't call up everyone in my contacts and say, "Hey, I'm gay." There are a few, hopefully obvious, reasons why. But mostly, I was only willing to come out to those I thought would love and accept me after the big conversation.

Turns out I was lucky. And so was Jesus.

He didn't share his coming out with everyone either. Peter, James, and John had proven themselves to be faithful disciples. Yes, there was a risk they'd sell their story to the tabloids. Or maybe run for the hills, never to be seen again. It was not a given that Jesus' reveal would go the way he hoped. But he wanted to share this thing about himself with his close friends, so he took the chance and chose to be transparent.

Allowing ourselves to be seen always comes with risks. Rejection hurts. But when we hide, we settle for a version of ourselves that is less brilliant than we were meant to be. We deprive the world of our glory.

For Jesus, his glory was his divine nature. Because we were all created in God's image, we each have some God-ness inside us, a spark that is fanned into glory as we nurture and share it.

As I've become more and more open about all kinds of things in recent years, I've allowed more of my own glory to show. And God uses that in ways I'll never even know.

—BKS

Who are you willing to show your glory to?
How can you share your glory with the world?

THURSDAY—5TH WEEK OF LENT

And Jesus said, "Neither do I condemn you. Go your way, and from now on do not sin again." —John 8:11b

On the Discipline of Forgiveness

The Pharisees had Jesus in a conundrum for sure. What they were about to do was completely within the realm of the law.

Adulterers were stoned. Yes, it was barbaric, but it was the understood punishment for the crime—and adultery was a crime. Was Jesus going to contradict the law of Moses in front of them, God, and everybody?

Jesus knelt and started writing in the dirt. It's unclear what he wrote, but his scribblings figured into the men's reactions as he offered a proposition: If any of you is sinless, go ahead and hit her with a stone (v. 7) They all dropped their rocks, one by one, and went home.

Forgiveness is releasing one's right to revenge or repayment. Because of the law of their society, it was within the rights of the Pharisees to stone the woman. They relinquished that right, and in doing so, forgave her. Jesus himself forgave her as well when he said to her, "I don't condemn you either. Go and sin no more."

Forgiveness is a big thing to ask and a big thing to give. I know what it means to lay down my stone, and it isn't easy. I've also been the offender who received forgiveness. Both brought me peace and freedom. Forgiveness is powerful like that.

—BKS

When have you chosen to forgive someone?
When have you received forgiveness you knew you didn't deserve?

FRIDAY—5TH WEEK OF LENT

Mary took a pound of costly perfume made of pure nard, anointed Jesus' feet, and wiped them with her hair. —John 12:7

On the Discipline of Accepting Care & Love

Suppose you are a person who gives. A lot. You give your time, your resources, your attention, your care. You give to your friends, of course, but also to strangers you don't even know. People in need seem to find you, and you help them. You're that person.

Now suppose someone who loves you empties their savings account to send you on a spa vacation to Bali. She does this because 1) she thinks you deserve it, 2) she wants to share her gratitude with you for what you've done for her, and 3) she knows you need care, but won't do it for yourself. She's been paying attention, like a good friend does.

Now, you have this frenemy who finds out about the gift and points out that if HIS friend was going to spend HER savings, she could help a lot of people. And he would be happy to oversee the dispersing of generosity.

You could respond to your frenemy from a place of guilt or shame saying, "You know, you're right. Others need care more than I do" and return the gift. Many of us would. But instead, you take to heart what your friend gave you, acknowledge the magnitude of the gift—and the love behind it—and get on that plane for Bali.

When we accept care from someone, especially when we actually need it, it isn't a selfish act. Instead it grows our compassion for others, especially for the giver.

—BKS

When have you accepted care from someone who loves you?
Who do you love who really needs your offer of care today...whether they accept it or not?

SATURDAY—5TH WEEK OF LENT

He went to Nazareth, where he had been brought up, and on the Sabbath day he went into the synagogue, as was his custom. He stood up to read... —Luke 4:16

On the Disciplines of Study & Sabbath-Keeping

Jesus, the rebel.

Jesus, the table-turner, the prophet, the countercultural feminist lover of outcasts.

Do you know that Jesus?

Me too. I like that Jesus. He's totally rock-n-roll.

But this passage makes me look at another Jesus, who probably never even owned a motorcycle jacket like the one in my closet.

The Jesus in Luke 4:16 is a study-er, a sabbath-keeper, a traditional traveling rabbi, a respecter of the law and of tradition. Even as an adult he does what he is supposed to do, which is what his parents did, which is what their parents did.

Imagine Jesus having to fill out one of those little biographical boxes on job applications. Or completing his social media profile. Prophet. Rabblerouser. Son of Man, and of Joseph, son of Jacob of the line of David.

Every time you think of Jesus breaking boundaries and naming hypocrisy, think also of the Jesus of Luke 4:16.

Jesus, still connected to his childhood home, goes to visit. And while he's there he heads over to the local adult education center—the synagogue—on the Sabbath, because that is what he is in the habit of doing.

Jesus is in the habit of study, in the habit of keeping the Sabbath, in the habit of honoring his ancestry.

The real Jesus was formed by a lifetime of spiritually strengthening habits—study, Sabbath, honoring family, and others—into a man who could also be a rebel, a prophet, a rescuer and healer.

That is the power of spiritual practice that becomes habit: it shapes our souls and our selves into wall-crushers, derision-riskers, humble servants of God and others.

My Jesus spent his life preparing to welcome rebellious sinners like me into his Father's house. Seems like he might have gotten that whole lifestyle thing right.

—EOR

What spiritual preparation(s) are you making a regular part of your life?

SUNDAY—5TH WEEK OF LENT

On the third day there was a wedding in Cana of Galilee, and the mother of Jesus was there. —John 2:1

On the Discipline of Celebration

Jesus loved a party. In the Gospels, there are many accounts of Jesus hanging out with friends, feasting, laughing, telling stories. It's not surprising that his first miracle happened at a wedding. Celebration is a big part of life with God.

I grew up with the notion that Jesus was a pretty serious guy. And that God was a cranky, old deity. Many of the depictions of Jesus show him looking wistful, pained, or melancholy. Sure, he had those moments, as we all do. I think Jesus had a lighter side too. People wouldn't have been so drawn to him if he were always a wet sweater.

As for us, there are plenty of times when we don't feel like celebrating. Life is full of disappointment, trips to the DMV and the dentist, and legit reasons to be downtrodden. But those times are made easier when I picture a joyful God, dancing to Motown, laughing at a funny story, and celebrating life's big and small milestones with us.

Jesus didn't have to turn water into wine. He wanted to, maybe because he loved a party. Just like his Father.

—BKS

What is one thing in your life (or in the larger world) that is worthy of celebrating? What are three small actions you can take to celebrate today?

MONDAY—5TH WEEK OF LENT

Now during those days he went out to the mountain to pray; and he spent the night in prayer to God. And when day came, he called his disciples and chose twelve of them, whom he also named apostles. —Luke 6:12-13

On the Disciplines of Solitude & Prayer

I don't always trust myself. When it comes to making decisions of any magnitude, I can end up paralyzed, afraid of making the wrong choice. Maybe you've been there. I've sometimes delayed and deferred until the choice just never gets made, at least not by me.

Jesus was at one of those important crossroads. He needed to choose the twelve men who would continue his work after he was gone. Because he'd made a habit of pulling away from the crowds and his friends to pray, he could hear and recognize his Father's voice when he needed discernment. After spending the night in prayer, Jesus was able to name his apostles.

Discernment is divine insight, perceptiveness that doesn't come from research, option-weighing, or gut instinct. When I get stuck on a decision, I ask God for discernment. But here's the thing: if I haven't made a habit of spending time alone with God in prayer, how am I going to recognize God's voice if discernment is offered to me?

Jesus knew God's voice, and so can we. But it requires consistently talking to and listening for God in quiet, solitary moments. It takes practice.

—BKS

What is a decision you're making that could benefit from discernment? How will you know God's voice if you hear it?

TUESDAY—5ᵀᴴ WEEK OF LENT

Then Jesus told his disciples, "If any want to become my followers, let them deny themselves and take up their cross and follow me. For those who want to save their life will lose it, and those who lose their life for my sake will find it. For what will it profit them if they gain the whole world but forfeit their life? Or what will they give in return for their life?" —Matthew 16:24-26

On the Discipline of Ego-Denial

Jesus had an ego. All humans do. The tempter knew this when he approached Jesus in the desert. The temptations Jesus faced—to feed everyone, to rule the world, to prove he was the Son of God—all fed his ego. Saying no to them took real fortitude. But because he had practiced denying himself by fasting, by not having to have the last word, by living in humility, he was able to withstand the temptations and say no to his own ego.

When we deny ourselves, we trade our ideas of what we deserve, or what we think should be, for what is in line with the Spirit.

Like a doctor who quits her successful practice to treat patients in a third-world country, because that's what she feels led to do. Or an ordinary guy who donates his tax refund to feed homeless folks instead of spending a weekend with his friends in Tahoe.

It's hard saying no to my ego because my self-image is wrapped up in what I've achieved, what I possess, and how I present myself to the world. But denying myself gets me unstuck from a specific idea of who I am, or what I deserve. It frees me up to serve God in ways I didn't even know were possible. And my spirit grows stronger as it is becomes more closely aligned with God's Spirit.

—BKS

What is something you could deny yourself in order to grow closer to God?

WEDNESDAY—6TH WEEK OF LENT

It will not be so among you; whoever wishes to be great among you must be your servant, and whoever wishes to be first among you must be your slave.
—Matthew 20:26-27

On the Disciplines of Ego-Denial & Service

I started out at Starbucks as a part-time barista.

Before long, I realized I really liked working there. I was promoted to store manager in about six months. I enjoyed making lattes, chatting up customers, doing dishes, and taking out trash alongside my baristas. I'd often take on the task nobody loved doing to remind myself what it means to serve.

Jesus was the consummate servant-leader. He found joy in taking care of the needs of others. He didn't expect the disciples to do anything he didn't do himself. He also didn't expect to be called King.

Great leaders don't name themselves leaders and then demand people to follow. They lead by example, serving everyone with respect, and putting themselves last.

Service requires self-denial. I can't serve others well if I'm telling myself I deserve better. I learn to say no to my ego by doing without, by not having to have the last word, and by choosing to be last in line.

—BKS

What are some qualities you've seen in servant-leaders you admire? What one step can you take to cultivate those qualities within yourself?

THURSDAY—6TH WEEK OF LENT

He was praying in a certain place, and after he had finished, one of his disciples said to him, "Lord, teach us to pray, as John taught his disciples." —Luke 11:1

On the Discipline of Prayer

Those of us who pray in public—pastors, teachers, rabbis, worship leaders— are prone to a number of annoying habits.

Any of these sound familiar?

Some pray-ers call God by special names that can be confusing and exclusionary.

Some use flowery language, or big vocabulary words that do more to draw attention to the pray-er than to God.

Some sound like auctioneers, while others sound like they're on C-SPAN.

Some end every clause with "Father" or "Lord" as if everyone (God included) needs to be reminded who's being addressed.

Not to criticize anyone's intentions, but the bottom line is this: we overcomplicate our prayers.

Whether praying in public or alone with God, it serves us well to remember the prayer that Jesus taught his disciples. When we pray the way Jesus did, we simply acknowledge that God is giving and forgiving, powerful and wise, and so much bigger than we are.

Jesus' prayer is offered humbly, giving God reverence and worship. It is not me-focused, but us-focused, expressing the bodily needs and soul needs of everyone. It is simple and sincere, without fancy or frivolous language.

It is surprising what we learn about ourselves and about God when we pray like Jesus did.

—BKS

A practice to try on:
Pray the Lord's Prayer, pausing after each phrase to reflect on its meaning to you in that moment.

FRIDAY—6TH WEEK OF LENT

He went to him and bandaged his wounds, having poured oil and wine on them. Then he put him on his own animal, brought him to an inn, and took care of him. —Luke 10:34

On the Discipline of Service

What does it mean to love my neighbor?

If I define love as willing the good of another person, then I guess I could start by not bringing them harm. COVID-19 has given me opportunities to love my neighbor every time I leave my home. And heck: wearing a mask is easy.

Beyond that, loving my neighbor can get messy. It starts with paying attention to the needs of others around me. Obviously, if someone is lying on the side of the road, injured and afraid, I'm probably going to notice. But then I have to choose whether, and how, to get involved.

Samaritans weren't very liked by Jews. They differed over many things, including the chosen place to worship God. So when Jesus makes a Samaritan the protagonist of his morality tale, those in audience where aghast.

Good men—priests, scholars, leaders—pass by their nearly-dead neighbor. The bad Samaritan tends to the traveler's wounds, puts him on his animal, takes him to an inn, and pays for his room, promising to return the next day to check on him. Turns out anyone can love well.

Love is often expressed in service. Giving a neighbor a ride to the doctor, buying a meal for someone who's hungry, or doing simple home repairs for an elderly person are all ways we love each other. Loving my neighbor simply starts with asking myself, "How can I help?"

—BKS

What is one action you can repeatedly take to train yourself to better notice the true needs of those around you?

SATURDAY—6TH WEEK OF LENT

This took place to fulfill what had been spoken through the prophet...The disciples went and did as Jesus had directed them. —Matthew 21:4, 6

On the Discipline of Submission

It feels good to be celebrated. Now, while we've established that Jesus was maybe the least egotistical guy that ever lived, he did, in fact, have an ego.

If I were Jesus, a ride through Jerusalem while people chanted "Hosanna! Blessed is he who comes in the name of the Lord!" would've felt at least a little gratifying. I mean, consider everything he'd denied himself up till now. Finally his work was being lifted up.

But honestly, I think Jesus would've been fine forgoing the parade if it would've made the dark days to follow any easier. Entering Jerusalem unannounced meant riding past the rebels the Romans were crucifying. Jesus had to know this might not go well for him. But he had chosen to do it, and saw it through, because of love.

Jesus was willing the good of everyone there—and all of us—as he accepted the hosannas and arrived at what was to come.

I'll be honest: I don't like to submit. I respect authority, but I like for it to be my idea. Submission, even to God, often feels like it bumps into my kingdom...because it does.

There are things over which I have a modicum of control that I prefer not to hand over. In this passage Jesus was handing over all the control he had, or felt like he had, to God's will.

I'm not convinced he knew exactly what was about to happen, he knew—as do we—that doing what God asks is the good and right thing to do.

Submission was about to become the central theme of Jesus' remaining days.

—BKS

How can you make submission a central theme for your life in the coming days?

SUNDAY—6TH WEEK OF LENT

At that same hour Jesus rejoiced in the Holy Spirit and said, "I thank you, Father, Lord of heaven and earth, because you have hidden these things from the wise and the intelligent and have revealed them to infants; yes, Father, for such was your gracious will." —Luke 10:21

On the Discipline of Celebration in the Midst of Mystery

God loves to use foolish things to confound the wise, to humble the intelligent, to exalt the simple, or just to remain impossible to figure out. Whyever that is, I'm confident that God's ways are both perfect and higher than mine.

I love that Jesus found such joy in the absurdity of his Father's mysterious ways. The Holy Spirit was rejoicing too—maybe the Trinity was just having a big cosmic laugh. At any rate, Jesus understood, better than anyone, that God doesn't work the way we do.

In God's upside-down kingdom, the weak are strong, the poor are rich, and the uneducated are wise. Babies are in on it too. The whole thing is bonkers!

Jesus took a moment to really revel in what was happening. In retrospect, I sometimes see what God has done in my life and I smile, or even laugh, at how the right pieces fell into place. But I rarely catch it in the moment. Jesus saw it, stopped what he was doing, and thanked God right then and there.

I want to enjoy what God is doing in my world. That begins with noticing God at work. I get there by shifting my focus from myself through practices like fasting, and giving my attention to God through solitude and prayer. Then as I pay attention, I celebrate what God is doing—also a spiritual practice.

—BKS

When was the last time you experienced joy by noticing what God was doing in your life?
Right now, take a moment to notice and to celebrate.

MONDAY—6TH WEEK OF LENT

He answered, "I tell you, if these were silent, the stones would shout out."
—Luke 19:40

On the Discipline of Worship

I've always been fascinated with studies of nature-versus-nurture. You know, where kids—often twins or adopted children—are studied during childhood and adolescence to see which of their traits can be attributed to genetics, and which are shaped by environment.

I'm a middle-aged guy, and I'm still noticing things that I do that are just like my mom or my dad. It's weird.

I love Jesus' comeback to the cranky Pharisees who want him to tell his people to stop their praising. He says, If they shut up, the stones will start shouting. That's because the worship of God exists in the DNA of everything.

We all come pre-loaded with the desire to worship God. It's in our nature.

As we grow, our environment influences whether we choose to worship God or to worship someone or something else. That's the nurture part. There are countless attention-grabbers competing for my adoration. I won't list them all, but heck, my own ego is in there swinging.

Because God gives me the freedom to decide who or what I worship, I don't always choose well. So worshiping God is a spiritual practice that focuses on engaging my whole self in the praise and adoration of my Creator, and nothing and no one else.

—BKS

What competes with God to be the object of your worship? Why do you think that is?

TUESDAY—6TH WEEK OF LENT

If we live by the Spirit, let us also be guided by the Spirit. —Galatians 5:25

There are six parts to each of us: mind, body, will, environment, spirit, and soul. Nobody has a livable, physical life if they're missing any one of them. Also— and this is important—none of our parts is inherently evil.

Mind, body, will, and environment are pretty easy concepts to grasp, but spirit and soul are a bit more ephemeral.

My spirit is my divine spark, created in God's image. It connects me to God, kinda like a cosmic USB cable of infinite length. Everyone's spirit is unique, sacred, and beautiful. When my spirit vibes with God's Spirit, I feel at peace. When it doesn't, I don't. That's when I'm more likely to mistrust myself, and doubt God's care for me.

So what can cause my spirit to get out-of-sync with God's? Lots of things, but most often, I look at what's going on with my soul.

Our souls stick to things. They aren't ever really satisfied by anything but God, but certainly will attach to other things if we let them. To keep my sticky soul from doing that, I have to be intentional about what I feed my mind, how I treat my body, and how I allow myself to be affected by my environment.

For example, if I choose to cyberstalk my ex, while eating a box of Little Debbie's snack cakes, with some firestarting relationship coach on the tv, then I'm giving my soul lots of unhealthiness to grab onto.

Over time, any one of those things could have repercussions for my soul. And none of those things would ever satisfy it, causing me to consume more and more, while feeling increasingly empty.

Getting to a place of soul-satisfaction and true spirit-peace requires us to choose things like kindness, patience, and self-control (*see* 5:22-23). Spiritual disciplines, like fasting and prayer, help us get in the practice of being more self-sacrificial and loving.

—BKS

What is something your soul likes to stick to?
How do you know when your spirit is out-of-sync with God's Spirit?

HOLY WEEK

WEDNESDAY OF HOLY WEEK

Then he poured water into a basin and began to wash the disciples' feet and to wipe them with the towel that was tied around him. —John 13:5

On the Discipline of Service

So Elton John—whom I admire a great deal as a musician, a songwriter, and a human—came to my house in San Jose and made me dinner. He also did my laundry, and cleaned up my bathroom, which was a mess. After he folded my socks and loaded the dishwasher, he signed my favorite Elton album, and was on his way.

Okay, that didn't happen. (Did I have you going??) But if it had, it would've been almost as weird as this:

Jesus and his disciples had just finished their Passover meal. Jesus stood up, took off his tunic, and tied a towel around his waist. He poured water into a basin, and then made it really awkward for the disciples—he went around the room, washing their dirty, sandal-funky feet.

There are a few remarkable things about this. In their culture, feet were washed only by the lowest servant in a household—it was like the dirtiest, most undignified job you can think of.

Also, a teacher could not demean one of his students by asking them to wash his feet, so the idea that a teacher would wash a student's feet was unthinkable. I mean, can you imagine someone you idolize kneeling down and washing your feet? Or doing your laundry? Or cleaning your house? I can't.

One more thing: the disciples often bickered about which of them was most deserving of Jesus' favor. None of them would have offered to wash everyone's feet. But by humbling himself this way, Jesus is again demonstrating the last-shall-be-first nature of his Father's kingdom.

No one is great just because they say they are. The last becomes first by choosing to be last.

Serving others is messy. It can be thankless and humiliating. It also helps us become more like our Servant-savior Jesus.

—BKS

When have you served someone else, really truly expecting nothing (including gratitude) in return? How can you make service a regular practice in your life?

MAUNDY THURSDAY

He said, "Abba, Father, for you all things are possible; remove this cup from me; yet, not what I want, but what you want." —Mark 14:36

On the Disciplines of Transparency, Prayer, & Submission

You've been to Gethsemane. Not the garden, but the point of crisis it is known for. You have faced a reality—a diagnosis, a relationship impasse, a reckoning of some sort. This new reality brought difficult choices, emotionally charged actions and reactions, and outcomes both surprising and predictable.

You probably prayed. You might've tried to bargain with God. I did both.

I can tell you that if I'd been Jesus, facing the cross, I'd have been looking around Gethsemane for an exit that didn't involve running into Judas and some burly Roman soldiers. Jesus didn't do that. But he also didn't start down that awful road without first asking God, "Could this be accomplished some other way?"

When I came to my Gethsemane, I wasn't staring down my own death, but the death of my marriage. It had followed years of self-discovery, excruciatingly honest conversations with my wife, and many painstaking steps toward self-acceptance. I'd begged with God repeatedly for another way, but I knew being honest about my sexuality meant breaking up my marriage. It was the only way we'd both find healing and peace.

Though I knew God would be with me, I really didn't know how it would turn out.

Even if Jesus knew what would happen after—I'm not convinced he did—he couldn't see all the awful that was coming, even if he had an inkling. Still he trusted God, and after he pleaded for a reprieve, he made a vow of surrender. Not what I want, but what you want.

—BKS

What's your Gethsemane? How did—or will—you face it?

GOOD FRIDAY

Then Jesus said, "Father, forgive them; for they do not know what they are doing."
—Luke 23:34

On the Discipline of Prayer

I have a hard time asking God to forgive some people.

Anti-maskers, anti-vaxxers, right-wing rioters, and voting-rights thieves: all hard. I want God to rain locusts down on rich people who say they pay too much in taxes, and to raise an unsightly rash on those who think people of color, queer folks, and immigrants have too much power already. (I don't pray for these things, but I want to, sometimes.)

Growing up in the South I heard older ladies cluck, "They don't know any better" when people behaved in small-minded ways. I don't believe ignorance is the culprit, but it does cause me to pause and pray: for myself, to love them, and for them, that God would change their hearts.

On the day Jesus died, no one knew exactly what they were doing when they betrayed, denied, and crucified him. Sure, the Romans knew they were squashing a likely uprising. And the Pharisees were surely ridding themselves of a challenge. His accusers, both the powerful and the rabble, had clear, compelling reasons.

But they didn't know they were murdering the One who would always love them.

As he was dying, Jesus prayed, "Father, forgive them, for they do not know what they are doing." He was praying for the Romans and the Pharisees, and Judas and Peter, and you and me. He knew that when we are hard-hearted, or frightened, or arrogant, we do awful things without realizing just how horrible they are.

Unlike me, Jesus had no trouble asking God to forgive. He had spent his whole life practicing prayer-filled love.

—BKS

Who can you pray God's forgiveness for, today?
What has kept you from praying for them before?

HOLY SATURDAY

On the sabbath they rested according to the commandment. —Luke 23:56b

On the Discipline of Waiting

Imagine that someone you love very much, to whom you have devoted your days and nights and heart and mind, dies and you are not allowed to be near them.

You aren't allowed to say goodbye because you would be infected by them, forcing you to isolate for days.

Because you would be unsafe, and you would bring danger to everyone around you.

Because it is against the law, and you believe in the rule of law.

It used to be tough to understand the situation the women disciples were in. Almost impossible to imagine not racing to the most important person in your life.

It's not so hard to imagine now, years into COVID, is it?

The execution of rebel leaders and crowd favorites could inspire riots in Jerusalem. Killing Jesus on a Friday afternoon assured the rulers of a certain level of managed pain: Friday evenings and Saturdays were the Sabbath, when those who loved God and did what God mandated stayed near home.

Jesus had loved God and had done what God had commanded. So had his followers. Everyone knew that when they crucified a rebel leader, his followers would be next to die. The rulers of Jerusalem could count on Jesus' followers scattering.

And, for the Jews, though washing and tending a dead loved one was a sacred act, it also infected you ritually, made you unable to attend temple or be around others.

At this point it's all not so hard to imagine, is it?

And so the women who loved Jesus waited for Sunday's dawn. They waited through the dark horror of the Sabbath evening, through Saturday's sorrowful celebrations, and through the next dangerous night. They waited for Sunday to finally say goodbye.

Waiting is so hard. Torturous even. Waiting is also a spiritual practice that trains us to live in the current moment while anticipating the next.

—EOR

How are you training for this moment? What are you choosing to not act on for the sake of what is to come?

EASTER

EASTER SUNDAY

Jesus said to her, "Mary!" She turned and said to him in Hebrew,"Rabbouni!" (which means Teacher). —John 20:16

If I had busted out of a tomb like El Chapo did from Puento Grande prison, I'd saunter into my favorite watering hole, order up a seltzer, and casually say to the shocked server, "Yeah, man, just got tired of death."

Not Jesus. Jesus trusted his truth with a tiny and peculiar group. He took three of his apprentices up a mountain to see his coming out as savior of Israel as long-gone Moses and Elijah showed up in a literal blaze of glory.

Then he told them to not tell anyone what they saw.

Later, on the third day after his death, Mary was at Jesus' tomb, terrified that his body had been taken. In her weeping she mistook him for the gardener when he walked up. But when he said her name, she recognized the sound and responded without hesitation, "Teacher!"

Mary could have told anyone she wanted that she'd seen him. But she wouldn't have been believed. So when Jesus appears, it's no stunt reveal, no subversive proclamation to a gossip. It's her friend showing up, revealing his own hidden truth, to reassure her and give her hope.

Unlike me and El Chapo, Jesus didn't want people to be impressed by his miraculous feat. He wanted to share the most important parts of himself one by one with people he could trust.

Jesus didn't aim to impress with wildly improbable events. It's just that that death couldn't keep him from showing up for a friend.

Jesus wants us to know him so intimately that we know the sound of his voice when he speaks our names. Even if people don't believe us when we say that he conquered death, or think we're nuts when we say we trust him, he'd rather show us his real self, his deeply loving self, than have us go gaga over some pyrotechnic show.

Jesus escaped from a physical tomb. Our tombs tend to be things like self-doubt, envy, anger, loss, and grief. Jesus would rather we escape from our own tombs than be overly impressed by what he did with his.

—BKS & EOR

When have you recognized Jesus' voice? What tombs have you yet to leave?

EASTER MONDAY

When he was at the table with them, he took bread, blessed and broke it, and gave it to them. Then their eyes were opened, and they recognized him; and he vanished from their sight. —Luke 24:30-31

Kids absorb the ideas adults repeat to them.

Getting dressed for my childhood church meant using bobby pins to secure a little lace handkerchief on my head because it's respectful. To this day I feel just a little naked going bareheaded during Worship.

I also knew that when taking Holy Communion you must never bite down on the host (the flat wafer used in some ancient-tradition churches) because you'll be biting Jesus.

The mental picture of me biting Jesus still haunts me. When I take Communion in a church that uses hosts I wait for that little dry bread to dissolve in my mouth, however long it takes, while everyone around me is chomping on Christ's body.

That ritual dining event we call Communion or Eucharist matters, and not only because the Apostle Paul spent a good chunk of 1 Corinthians talking about it. When you take Communion as a spiritual practice, Jesus shows up.

Two disciples are walking to Emmaus on Resurrection Day. Jesus starts walking with them. They don't recognize him, even though they walk together for hours while Jesus lectures them on the scriptural and historical relevance of his death and detombment.

They get where they're going and invite this chatty stranger in. Only at the table, when he breaks the bread, do they recognize him. It is in the breaking of the bread that they really see Jesus.

Jesus was with them the whole day, but when they remembered him with bread, he showed up in a wholly different way.

I suspect those two disciples, those spiritual kids, remembered everything about Communion after Jesus repeated it with them.

—EOR

How might you incorporate Holy Communion into your worship practices, even when your church doesn't? How can you make room for Jesus to show up?

TUESDAY—1ST WEEK OF EASTER

Jesus said to them, "Come and have breakfast." Now none of the disciples dared to ask him, "Who are you?" because they knew it was the Lord. —John 21:12

I love breakfast. I love when a friend shows up unexpectedly and says, Let's have breakfast. I've never had a friend come back from the dead and invite me to breakfast but that would be nice too, I suppose.

Jesus had to know his disciples were feeling lost without him. Like we feel when we can't hug those closest to us. Thanks to COVID-19, we know what that feels like, don't we?

Jesus always liked fellowship. He enjoyed time with his friends like we do. But imagine this: you have an all-expense-paid trip to Bali (or Heaven), and instead of hightailing it to the airport, you choose to wait and surprise your friends with a visit first. Maybe Jesus didn't handle goodbyes so well. Or maybe he just really enjoyed hanging out with his friends. Plus: breakfast.

Anyway, there was fish—Jesus told them to cast nets off the right side of the boat—and there was bread. There was a fire and a beach. And a bunch of awesome friends. A pretty perfect breakfast scenario, if you ask me.

Fellowship can be a life-giving thing. Sharing food, drinks, laughs—that stuff matters. I'm lucky: I live with people I enjoy spending time with. Still, I don't think fellowship with friends is something I'll take for granted the way I used to, before COVID.

—BKS

How has fellowship felt different for you since before the days of COVID?
How will you invite Jesus to breakfast?

WEDNESDAY—1ST WEEK OF EASTER

With great power the apostles gave their testimony to the resurrection of the Lord Jesus, and great grace was upon them all. —Acts 4:33

Stories are powerful. Think of the stories that were read to you as a kid. I loved *The Berenstein Bears* and anything by Dr. Seuss. We never forget stories that help shape the way we see ourselves, each other, and the world.

Jesus was a storyteller. Most of his best teaching is in the form of parables.

We love a true story. When someone shares a first-person account of something life-changing that really happened, we're riveted. Testimonies are one kind of true story.

In the years of the early church, the apostles shared their testimonies with all who would listen. People were drawn to the details of Jesus' death and resurrection. Sure, Jesus' story had a hero, some villains, a mysterious twist, and a happy (albeit bittersweet) ending. What's not to love about that?

But, of course, there was much more. This true story was causing people to believe in a risen Savior, raised to life by the One True God. Churches were forming and growing. Families were living in community, sharing all their belongings and their earnings. The Gospel was living among them, and the apostles kept sharing.

The power and grace in their words and actions brought a new kind of life to people everywhere they went. And you know, there is power in our testimonies too.

—BKS

What is the story you and God are writing together?
Who needs to hear it?

THURSDAY—1ST WEEK OF EASTER

We know love by this, that he laid down his life for us—and we ought to lay down our lives for one another. —1 John 3:16

Loving someone is willing their good, even if the thing that's good for them isn't the thing you'd choose.

I watched Forrest Gump recently. Forrest is a person who loves well. In Vietnam, he runs back into the jungle amid gunfire to save his best friend, Bubba, and pulls out three other soldiers as well.

Forrest's love for Jenny is pretty darn close to unconditional. He rescues her from abuse a number of times over many years, even though she doesn't return his love until her life is nearly through.

Thing is, really loving someone is hard. It requires much more than affection or attraction does. It might go against everything you feel, or think, or want. It might mean you don't swoop in and save the day, even though you could. Sometimes it means getting out of the way, not knowing what happens after that.

Love costs us something.

In the final days and moments of his life, Jesus perfectly modeled that kind of love for us. He laid down his pride, his desires, and ultimately his life, because of love.

—BKS

What is love asking of you today?
What are some ways you can love those in your life well?

FRIDAY—1ST WEEK OF EASTER

And this is love, that we walk according to his commandments —2 John 1:6

God's commandments to the Israelites—Torah, which was familiar to most early Christians—were all about living in community, as a set-apart people of God. That meant that living according to Torah would result in both honoring God and respecting neighbor.

For the Jews, loving others—willing their good, even if it hurts—would happen more organically if one was religiously following God's commandments than if one wasn't. In other words, you wouldn't steal from your neighbor, lie to your brother, or treat a stranger badly, because God's law didn't allow for it.

We modern Christians don't follow Torah, though most of what Jesus taught was founded on its principles. Remember Jesus was a student, and later a teacher, in the Temple. So we need look no further than his teachings to understand that loving each other is an imperative of God.

All this talk of Torah comes down to this: we are more likely to act in love toward others if we follow Jesus' teachings than if we don't. And we are more likely to follow Jesus' teachings if 1) we know what they are, and 2) we have spiritual practices that help us live (and love) like Jesus did.

—BKS

Thinking back on the spiritual practices we talked about during Lent, which ones might help shape you to love others as Jesus did?

SATURDAY—1ST WEEK OF EASTER

And he said to them, "Go into all the world and proclaim the good news to the whole creation." —Mark 16:15

I'll admit that I struggle with evangelism.

I've attended churches where evangelism was like cold-calling strangers, showing up on their doorsteps with the sinner's prayer locked and loaded.

I've also been on the receiving end of evangelism that looked like multi-level marketing—a friend of a friend invites you to coffee, then starts asking you about your walk with God, and tries to sell you on their brand of Jesus.

I find both approaches to be awkward, intrusive, and insulting.

When I was in college, I hung out at the Wesley Foundation, an on-campus Methodist-supported ministry. We had Movie Mondays, where we'd eat pizza and watch a thought-provoking movie, then discuss it with the campus pastor moderating. Those nights were really good for me because I made friends with kids whose faith backgrounds were nothing like mine. Our conversations were organic and honest, full of questions without easy answers. There was no endgame—just talking.

I learned a lot and shared a lot, and the fundamentalist fortress around my brain started to crumble.

To me, that's what evangelism should look like. There is beauty in conversation where beliefs are shared without expectation or condescension. I've had many such conversations that helped me see God, myself, and the world differently. I'm better because of them.

—BKS

What does proclaiming the good news look like to you? How does your belief in God make its way into your conversations with friends and strangers?

2ND SUNDAY OF EASTER

Surely goodness and mercy shall follow me all the days of my life, and I shall dwell in the house of the Lord my whole life long. —Psalm 23:6

Psalm 23 is the psalm that gets read a lot at funerals. With good reason.

It is comforting to remember that God is with us in our grief, restoring our souls with green pastures and still waters, and walking with us through dark, sorrowful places.

The verse in Psalm 23 that resonates most with me is the last verse, where David asserts that goodness and mercy will follow him as long as he lives.

I believe the goodness David is talking about is God's God-ness.

Suppose life is a cosmic little-league baseball game. God is the parent who cheers for you so loudly it's embarrassing, who puts a band-aid on your knee after you awkwardly slide into third place, and who takes you to Baskin-Robbins after your team loses. That's God's God-ness. It includes things like God's constant presence, companionship, and care.

Mercy here isn't the not getting what we deserve definition we're all familiar with. Instead, mercy is like a soft place to land when we fall. God is with us, ready to catch us and comfort us, not just when we're grieving, but always.

Then there's the idea that I am already dwelling in the house of the Lord and will do so my whole life long.

Because we are already in eternity, we don't have to wait until our mortal existence is through to sit and feast at God's table.

—BKS

What does goodness and mercy mean to you?
How could you use Psalm 23 in a difficult time?

MONDAY—2ND WEEK OF EASTER

But Peter said, "I have no silver or gold, but what I have I give you; in the name of Jesus Christ of Nazareth, stand up and walk." —Acts 3:6

Once when I was 17, I was driving my Karmann Ghia on a freeway with four passengers. (Four passengers is a lot for a Karmann Ghia.) One of them was my girlfriend-at-the-time, Shannon, who was Pentecostal.

When it was time to slow down before taking an offramp, I realized my brakes weren't working. I let everyone know they should hold on, and I used my hand brake to slow our considerable speed.

As we approached the traffic light at the end of the ramp— which happened to be red—we had no hope of coming to a stop. So Shannon exclaimed, "Turn green in the name of Jesus!" And it did.

We rounded the turn with a squeal, and I kept working the hand brake. Then before the next light, which was also red, she exclaimed even louder, "Turn green in the name of Jesus!" And it did.

This happened three times.

Now I don't know if it was Shannon's faith, or just lucky traffic-light timing, that allowed us to get home without ever having to come to a complete stop. (We eventually coasted to a stop in my backyard, and my beloved Karmann Ghia was fine, except for its lousy brakes.)

But the thing I continue to be so impressed by is that Shannon's knee-jerk response to a crisis situation was to invoke the name of Jesus. That is never my first response, whether the crisis is mine or someone else's. I do whatever is in my power to make things better. I might pray and call for help. But I don't jump in like Peter did, as if the power of Jesus' name is at my disposal to save the day.

What would happen if I did? What if we all did? How weird would that be?

—BKS

Have you ever invoked the name of Jesus? What happened?

TUESDAY—2ND WEEK OF EASTER

The Lord is my shepherd, I lack nothing. He lays me down in green pastures.
—Psalm 23:1-2a

In high school I was a Future Farmer of America, raising sheep and goats and working horses in exchange for stall space. The school farm brought in dozens of lambs every year for students to raise, show, and eventually slaughter. I lasted through just one sheep cycle because eventually they'd all have to be butchered and I didn't have the stomach for it.

I should say: almost all had to be butchered. There was a ram at the school farm who was a grumpy so-and-so. He'd haul back and butt everyone who came into his pen. It really hurt, causing almost-grown men to wipe their eyes along with their bruised thighs.

The ram liked me. I don't know why. For months he butted me until he didn't and he'd come when I called him in from the pasture. Maybe it was because I visited him every day, even over school breaks when no one else came around. Maybe the ram knew that if I was there he'd have everything he needed: food, petting, and safety from loud, clumsy boys.

When I was with him, the ram could rest.

When county fair time came around we took all the season's lambs to be shown and sold. We took the ram too. I washed his wool, trimmed his feet, fluffed him up. He didn't appreciate the admiring crowds and was constantly wary, restless, butting the fence to send them scattering.

In the evening, after long days of school and showing and butting, I'd clean his pen, feed him grain, and pluck stuck things from his huge woolly head. Finally he'd lie down in the fresh straw, able to rest. And I would lie with him, my head on his side, the two of us stretched out in the quieting barn.

Sheep don't lie down in their pastures or pens unless their stomachs are full and they feel safe. Neither do we. Those rare times we let down our guard and truly rest, it is because we feel safe and cared for by our Shepherd, whether we realize it or not.

—EOR

When do you truly rest? How might you take advantage of God's protection and provision more often?

WEDNESDAY—2ND WEEK OF EASTER

All who obey his commandments abide in him, and he abides in them. And by this we know that he abides in us, by the Spirit that he has given us. —1 John 3:24

At the Last Supper, Jesus leveled the room with some cryptic—and not-so-cryptic—foretellings. The disciples were understandably rattled, so he went on to offer them some reassurances. One of them was this: that they would never be without God's presence because he would ask God to send another Advocate who would never leave them (John 14:16-17).

That Advocate is the Holy Spirit. We also know Her as the Helper, the Comforter, or the Paraclete, if you prefer Greek.

The Holy Spirit baffles many Christians.

To some, She is God's fire, reminding us of God's might, power, and mystery.

To others, She is God's breath, reviving and renewing our tired spirits.

I've experienced Her as both, and as neither. She is enigmatic, but if you know God, then you know Her too.

The Holy Spirit reminds us that God abides in us.

There've been times in my life when I've been wracked with grief, or riddled with questions and fears. In those moments, I've felt the Holy Spirit sit with me, listen to me, and cry with me.

Sometimes when worshiping with others, I've felt Her moving through the room, provoking prayer and prompting testimony.

I believe that, while choosing to follow Jesus is an act of our will, it isn't without the involvement of the Holy Spirit, helping us see ourselves as people who need a loving God.

—BKS

How have you experienced the Holy Spirit?
How did you know it was Her?

THURSDAY—2ND WEEK OF EASTER

And all of you must clothe yourselves with humility in your dealings with one another, for "God opposes the proud, but gives grace to the humble." —1 Peter 5:5b

I used to know a guy who was arrogant. Like really arrogant. His ideas were the best ideas ever thought of. His plans were mind-blowing. He made no mistakes—at least none he ever owned up to. And he made no apologies.

Unsurprisingly, he wasn't nearly as awesome as he thought he was. In fact, a little humility would've gone a long way to earning him the respect he wanted so badly.

We've all known people who are a bit full of themselves. Most of the time, all their boastful talk is an attempt to hide their insecurities and distract from their failures.

But as someone who is typically a pretty humble guy, nothing gets me riled up like arrogance. And then you know what? I become prideful about my humility, which is the opposite of humble.

Everybody has a kingdom—the part of reality each of us can influence, affect, or control. If you cut me off in traffic, interrupt me when I'm talking, or flirt with my boyfriend, our kingdoms are clashing. This is the stuff that starts wars. If we don't approach those kinds of conflicts with humility, it can get ugly.

I think of it this way: if I'm full of myself, there's no room for things like love, joy, patience, kindness, and the like.

When I refuse to yield my kingdom to God's—and sometimes to yours too—I become the kind of person no one wants to be around. It's life-destroying for you, and for me too.

—BKS

What are ways you can practice being humble? How can you show love to someone who is arrogant (even if that someone is you)?

FRIDAY—2ND WEEK OF EASTER

Out of the depths I cry to you, O Lord. Lord, hear my voice! —Psalm 130:1-2a

I'm a terrible swimmer.

When I was a high school senior, I went with my marching band to Orlando. It was June, it was hot, and it was Florida, so of course, we went to a water park. This one had a wave pool.

First thing, my friend, Susan, headed there and coaxed me to join her. In our zeal to get into the water, neither of us spent the $5 to get a mat, which is essentially a life-saving device for a non-swimmer like me. But no big deal, the waves weren't on anyway, and I had no intention of getting in over my head.

A short time later, the warning horn sounded and the waves started. Sure, I thought about getting out, or spending a little snack money on a mat, but I didn't. I stayed with Susan, bobbing up and down in the moving water.

As the waves got higher, the undercurrent pulled us further out, and pretty soon, I couldn't feel the bottom. The water rolled over my head, wave after wave, and I started to panic. When I couldn't get a breath between waves anymore, all I could do was pray and hope that Susan, or someone, would see me drowning.

Susan got the attention of the hunky lifeguard in the red swim trunks, who blew a whistle, and jumped in. That warning horn sounded again, the waved stopped, he swam to me, pulled me out, helped me to a chaise, and sat with me while I coughed up what felt like ten gallons of chlorinated water.

I was mortified, having caused a scene barely an hour into our day. But I was alive. (Thanks, Susan.)

Maybe you've been drowning before. If not in water, maybe in debt, or doubts, or depression.

Maybe you couldn't get the words out to ask for help.

Maybe you were just counting on God, or someone, to see you, and help you. Maybe that's where you are now.

I'd like to say that's the last time I had a harrowing experience in water. It isn't. And it isn't the only time I screamed silently out of desperation, both in and out of water. But every time we call out, God hears us, sees our need, and pulls us to safety.

Sure, we may feel foolish for needing to be saved, but the truth is, we all need saving sometimes.

—BKS

When have you called out to God in your distress?
How did God respond?

SATURDAY—2ND WEEK OF EASTER

Jesus also said, "With what can we compare the kingdom of God, or what parable will we use for it?" —Mark 4:30

There's a picture of me that always reminds me of the Kingdom of God.

Some years ago, my friend and ministry partner Benton (whose contemplations you've been reading) played a concert on acreage behind my house. The event was large, and a bunch of people had worked hard to pull it off, including me. Stage and chairs, equipment and publicity meant weeks of hard work.

Weeks of work, and of prayer. I spent hours asking God for guidance and help, listening to God's responses and silences, and taking in the encouragement God sent me through friends.

That night, when I'd finished welcoming the crowd, I sat down on the ground where I could see both the stage and the audience. Benton was in good voice and spirits, and the crowd was relaxed and happy. Even the weather cooperated, which in Nashville is no small miracle.

During the concert someone snapped a photo of me. It's a terrible image, vanity-wise: I'm tired and sweaty and need a haircut. My bra strap is down my shoulder; my shirt and jeans don't really fit.

In that photo, my face is everything: it beams.

If you saw the picture, you'd have no idea where it was taken, or why, but you'd know what joy and peace and love feel like.

Jesus struggled to explain the experience of living in God's kingdom, so resorted to parables and similes: finding a treasure, recovering something precious you'd lost, the poor fed and prisoners released.

Words can't capture what it's like to live your daily life in constant companionship with God. When your mind is burdened with worry and your body is in pain, your soul has access to a deep well of peace and hope. Your spirit can recharge its batteries with God's power.

Jesus didn't have a camera. So with words he tried to explain the wholeness and peace that came from his connection with God.

Scripture says the crowds didn't really understand.

When I forget what the Kingdom is like, Jesus' words don't always help. But I have that picture, and it's close enough.

—EOR

What helps you remember joy in God's presence?

3RD SUNDAY OF EASTER

[The Kingdom of God] is like a mustard seed, which, when sown upon the ground, is the smallest of all the seeds on earth; yet when it is sown it grows up and becomes the greatest of all shrubs —Mark 4:31-32a

It doesn't take much to change someone's day, year, or life. Just a seed really.

I'm not well-versed in chaos theory, but I get the gist of the butterfly effect. You know, the idea that a butterfly moving its wings in Kansas, let's say, can seriously affect weather somewhere far away, like in Japan.

Applied more broadly, chaos theory suggests I can do something seemingly inconsequential that has unintended outcomes, for good or for ill, that I probably will never even know about.

It's like when somebody got the idea to pay for the stranger's latte who was in line behind them at Starbucks. And for hours, people were paying for each other's coffees. Until finally, somebody took the free drink. So in reality, that initial act of generosity materially benefited someone hours later, though sending the kindness down the line certainly brightened many people's day.

Fact is, we sow seeds all the time. A smile. A kind word. An inspirational Instagram post.

On the flip side, a selfish or careless act can ruin somebody's day—or life. None of us lives in a self-sustaining bubble, and our choices impact people we don't even know.

We see it in the viral nature of information and entertainment these days. Made-up facts and offensive antics make their rounds. And people get hurt.

So we can choose to drop seeds that end up growing into resentment, intolerance, self-importance, and the like. Or we can plant seeds that yield goodness, compassion, understanding, and love.

Kinda like the Kingdom of God.

—BKS

How have the actions of a stranger made your day, or life, better?
What is something you can do today to sow a seed of kindness?

MONDAY—3RD WEEK OF EASTER

Now the works of the flesh are obvious: fornication, impurity, licentiousness, idolatry, sorcery, enmities, strife, jealousy, anger, quarrels, dissensions, factions, envy, drunkenness, carousing, and things like these. —Galatians 5:19-21a

Paul's listing of the works of the flesh is quite extensive. I referenced the New Revised Standard Version of the Bible, as I usually do, and some of these words required definitions. (Disclaimer: I went to Webster's, not the original Greek. I also editorialized a little.)

Fornication is defined as consensual sexual relations between two people who aren't married. Licentiousness is lacking legal or moral restraints, especially disregarding sexual restraints.

Sidebar: Things like purity culture, conversion camps, and objections to sexual education in schools, as well as opposition to contraception, and on and on, have shown churches to be out-of-touch with where society (including many Christians) lands on issues of sexuality across the board. I do agree that sex of all kinds is inherently fleshly, since it involves our bodies.

Surprisingly, sorcery has nothing to do with Harry Potter. It is actually the use of power gained from the assistance or control of evil spirits.

Enmity is positive, active, and typically mutual, hatred or ill will.

Strife is bitter, sometimes violent, conflict or dissension.

Dissension is partisan and contentious quarreling.

And factions are parties or groups, especially within government, that are often contentious and self-seeking.

Carousing makes me think of those westerns I used to watch with my dad as a kid, with barmaids in petticoats, and gunfights in the dusty street. But it is actually less interesting: drinking liquor freely or excessively.

I don't mean to make light of Paul's list of fleshly works. I do mean to point out that it is important to consider what was going on culturally when we read Paul's letters.

Each of them was written to a group of new Christians that was learning how to follow Jesus. Each baby church Paul exhorted had its own challenges, struggles, and learning opportunities. We can't fully grasp what Paul was writing, or why he was writing it, without understanding the historical and cultural context of each letter.

Since I'm not going to do a deep-dive into First Century Galatia to unpack Paul's list, I'd like to offer my own version. This is not meant to replace or challenge Paul's list, but just to remind myself (and maybe you) of some modern life-destroyers common to our 21st-century, American culture. I encourage you to write your own list as well.

Life-destroying works of the flesh aren't always obvious, but here are some that are hard to deny:

> objectifying someone for sexual pleasure
>
> worshiping things or people that aren't God
>
> trusting spirits that aren't God's Spirit
>
> provoking unrest
>
> obsessing over what someone does or has
>
> seeking revenge
>
> bullying
>
> encouraging intolerance (in all its many forms)
>
> drinking irresponsibly
>
> partying to escape being responsible, and
>
> anything else that destroys life—yours or someone else's.

—BKS

**Now...what's your list of life-destroying works of the flesh?
Write it out.**

TUESDAY—3RD WEEK OF EASTER

For the Lamb at the center of the throne will be their shepherd, and he will guide them to springs of the water of life, and God will wipe away every tear from their eyes.
—Revelation 7:17

When we were visiting my grandmother for Christmas a few years ago, she had a massive stroke. My mother, my sister, and I sat in the floor of her bedroom and held her while we waited on the ambulance to arrive. We told her she would be all right. We prayed over her.

I don't know if she had any idea we were there or what was happening. In the days that followed until she passed, I don't know what, if anything, was going through her mind.

I hope she was catching glimpses of the heaven she'd spent her life preparing for. Streets of gold, gates of pearl, the whole nine yards. I hope she was at peace. I believe she is now.

I don't think a lot about heaven. When I was younger, I was scared of death, mostly because I could never be sure if I was headed up, or down, when it was my time to go. But these days, I don't live my life with heaven as my endgame. I mean, I believe I will be with God when this life ends for me, but I have no real concept of what that will be like.

There is one thing I am confident of: there will be no more pain, grief, sorrow, loneliness, depression, illness, or death. God will wipe the last of our tears, and whatever happens after that will be rainbows and roller coasters.

If death is something you worry about, I hope you'll reach out—to us, to a friend, to a therapist, to God. I hope knowing that God is with you <u>now</u> (and not just after your mortal body gives out) gives you courage, peace, and joy as you face this life, and whatever happens next.

—BKS

What about death causes you to worry or to be afraid?
What ideas about heaven give you peace?

WEDNESDAY—3ᴿᴰ WEEK OF EASTER

Do not rejoice over me, O my enemy; when I fall, I shall rise; when I sit in darkness, the Lord will be a light to me. —Micah 7:8

I deal with depression.

There've been times I couldn't make even simple decisions, like what to eat, or what to wear. When everything felt so big and consequential that I didn't want to get out of bed. It's like I was wandering in a fog, dragging a ball and chain. No clarity, no hope.

If you've spent any time with me at all, you know that I'm typically an upbeat, optimistic guy. I like to spread hope and share light. When I was at my lowest, the guilt of not being able to be that guy made everything so much worse. The voices in my head were loud and condemning. The shame I felt was debilitating.

There were times when I would literally sit in darkness. But somehow I knew God was with me even then. And over time, a combination of medication, therapy, affirmations, and time with God helped me find my hope again.

Maybe you have had, or are currently having, similar experiences. Maybe you, or someone you love, is living with depression, anxiety, or some other condition that causes a loss of focus, motivation, and hope. If this is you, please tell someone who loves you.

Being depressed doesn't mean your faith is weak, or that your relationship with God is broken.

It means you need to tend to your mental health just as you would your physical health.

Spiritual health, mental health, and physical health are all part of well-being, and they're all connected. Don't be afraid to take action toward your spiritual or mental health. You'd get a broken leg set, after all.

—BKS

If you have felt any of the ways I've described, how will you address the depression and/or anxiety in your life?

THURSDAY—3RD WEEK OF EASTER

Hear this, you that trample on the needy, and bring to ruin the poor of the land, saying, "When will the new moon be over so that we may sell grain; and the sabbath, so that we may offer wheat for sale?" The Lord has sworn by the pride of Jacob: "Surely I will never forget any of their deeds." —Amos 8:4-5a, 7

It is not the man who has too little, but the man who craves more, that is poor. —Seneca (Roman philosopher)

I understand wanting to be prosperous. I mean, nobody daydreams about sleeping under a bridge when they have a house in the suburbs. And to be clear, there is nothing wrong with money—having it, needing it, or working to earn more of it.

However, God does not owe us, nor promise us, financial prosperity.

I used to own a cafe. Even though I worked really hard and managed my business in a God- and people-honoring way, I didn't get rich making sandwiches and lattes. In fact, I accrued quite a lot of personal debt while trying to keep my cafe from sinking.

I prayed in frustration about my lack of income, and doubted I'd ever get back on my feet. God didn't answer my prayers by wiring thousands to my checking account. But God did help me find the courage and resourcefulness to make different choices, and to dig out of debt.

I think it's nearly impossible to be a person of faith in our prosperity-obsessed culture and not struggle with wanting more. But throughout the Bible, we are warned about the trappings of materialism and greed—that to find out where our treasure is, all we need to do is follow our money.

We are also taught that, instead of chasing wealth, we should seek contentment, and share what we have with those less fortunate. Jesus was clear that holding loosely to what we have, and caring for the poor and the needy, are part of living in God's upside-down kingdom.

Our reward will not likely be a mansion in the Caymans or a flush retirement account. But we will have the peace and joy that come from serving others, the way Jesus did.

—BKS

What is your relationship with money like? What would happen if you applied God's priorities to your spending habits?

FRIDAY—3RD WEEK OF EASTER

For I desire steadfast love and not sacrifice, the knowledge of God rather than burnt offerings. —Hosea 6:6

God likes you.

God smiles when you notice the beauty of the wildflowers that grow beside the road near your house. God chuckles when you tell a dad joke and everyone groans.

God sighs relief when your flight lands safely.

God likes it when you are content.

God sees how you prioritize the needs of your family over your own and would like you to take better care of yourself.

God knows you regret what you said in that argument with your partner, and that you don't know how to take it back.

God isn't surprised that you have anxiety over your finances, and that you wish you'd made different choices in your thirties.

God is on the dreaded phone call with your sister about your mom's memory loss.

God knows you haven't slept a solid eight hours since the 90s.

God wishes you'd quit that job you hate so much, and trust that the money will come from somewhere else.

God likes the things you think are too different, too weird, too scary, too _____ about yourself. God thinks you're special and spectacular.

God hangs on your every word when you pour out your heart.

God doesn't love you out of obligation and isn't looking for reasons to be mad at you. (God doesn't get mad at you.) God isn't waiting for you to make some grand gesture to prove your love and devotion. (God isn't impressed with grand gestures.)

God just wants your actual love and devotion.

These are all things God wants you to know. Oh, and this: you are God's treasured child.

—BKS

What are some ways you can remind yourself that God treasures you? Why do you think it is so easy to forget?

SATURDAY—3RD WEEK OF EASTER

See, the former things have come to pass, and new things I now declare; before they spring forth, I tell you of them. —Isaiah 42:9

My son, Nick, is smart, focused, and ambitious. He is also funny, levelheaded, and thoughtful. But this isn't really about Nick.

Coming back home to Tennessee for his college graduation—to celebrate my son and his accomplishments—reminded me again that life marches on. Nobody stays the same, and I'm certainly not the same person who left Tennessee here for California in the fall of 2019.

Sitting on my old plaid couch in my old studio apartment in the basement of my parents' house conjures up all kinds of feelings. There's the loneliness I lived with here while struggling in a long-distance relationship for years. There is the stress I had over money, career, and parenting. And the depression that set in when I felt like none of it would ever change for the better.

There's also the banana pudding Mom made for me yesterday, the music I'm still creating with Dennis all these years later, and my kids, who keep making me a proud, happy dad.

Tennessee is home. But moving away has made me appreciate it differently. Like so many country songs tell us, we sometimes see things clearer in the rearview mirror.

Jobs, relationships, roles, ideas—they sometimes become old things, and then they pass away. We grieve, we grow, and we continue. We start a new career. We vote differently. We learn to smile when we hear someone else's name.

God is always doing new things. Knowing that makes it easier for me to try new things too.

—BKS

**What old things are passing away for you?
What new thing can you celebrate?**

4TH SUNDAY OF EASTER

By this we know that we love the children of God, when we love God and obey his commandments. —1 John 5:2

I'm an imperfect parent. But I'd say that's true of every mom and dad I know. Even the most loving, attentive, super-involved parents are actual humans with actual problems.

My mom and dad were also imperfect. They were young when I was born—22 and 25 respectively. They had moved to Nashville only a couple years earlier to start their life together. (I still thank them for making that move from rural Alabama.) They were learning how to be grown-ups, and married, and parents, in the city, all at the same time.

I was a precocious kid. I was creative, overachieving, emotional, and unlike every other boy they'd ever been around. They were winging it, learning as they went, and mistakes were made. But I always knew I was loved. And we all survived.

Thankfully, God offers us all the room we need to discover, fail, recover, and thrive, like the best parents do. Being grown-up children of God means we keep making mistakes, but even though God is a perfect Parent, God does not expect perfection from us.

When we love God, and want to love God better, we do the work to become less self-centered and more others-centered.

We do the work through spiritual practice, and choosing to yield our kingdoms to God's kingdom.

—BKS

What does it mean to you to aspire to be spiritually mature while accepting being imperfect?

MONDAY—4TH WEEK OF EASTER

Fight the good fight of the faith; take hold of the eternal life, to which you were called. —1 Timothy 6:12a

I think we agree that Christians are supposed to be fighting the good fight of the faith. But what is it we should be fighting for—or against?

According to a recent survey by Pew Research, evangelical leaders overwhelmingly believe these are the things Christians should be most concerned with:

> Christianity is the one true faith that leads to eternal life (98%)
>
> The Bible is the Word of God (98%)
>
> Abortion is usually or always wrong (96%)
>
> Society should discourage homosexuality (84%)
>
> Men have a duty to serve as the religious leaders in the marriage and family (79%)

Sit with this list for a minute.

Where did fighting racism land on the list? What about ending gun violence? Where is taking care of the poor, sick, hungry, and homeless? How about caring for our planet-in-crisis?

Seems to me evangelical Christians are picking the wrong fights.

Some of the items on this list just tear people down. Jews, Muslims, and people with spiritual and religious expressions that aren't Christian, are told they practice a lesser faith.

The spiritual standing of women is discounted, and their lives are considered less important than those of their unborn children.

And queer folks are discouraged from...existing...?

We are called to be life-giving, not life-destroying. We can do mighty things if we choose to stand for the things, and people, Jesus stood for. Sadly, those things didn't make the top five in the leaders' list.

—BKS

If you're honest, what would your "top 5 things Christians should be most concerned with" be? What do you want to do about living them out?

TUESDAY—4TH WEEK OF EASTER

Know therefore that the Lord your God is God, the faithful God who maintains covenant loyalty with those who love him and keep his commandments, to a thousand generations. —Deuteronomy 7:9

Trust doesn't come easily to most of us.

There's the base-level trust I have in my Uber driver, my barber, and my barista.

Then there's the next-level trust I have in most of my friends, my family, and my therapist.

The deepest trust I have is in those closest to me—my best friend, my partner, my parents, and my kids.

Any of these people may test, or even lose, my trust. Could take as little as a bad haircut, or as much as a string of lies or betrayals.

Then there's God.

Trusting God can be difficult when we believe untrue things about God. It's hard to trust a God who we think is easily angered, capricious, hypercritical, and unapproachable.

God gets blamed sometimes for terrible things that happen, like cancer, miscarriages, fatal car crashes, and deadly tornadoes.

Who would trust a God who has hurt them by allowing—or even causing—the pain they suffer?

I wouldn't trust that God.

But God doesn't cause the bad things that happen as a result of our individual or collective choices, or because of we've altered, with our actions, the order God created to sustain us. God also doesn't usually break natural laws on our behalf to swoop in and save the day. But we know that God grieves with us when we suffer, and promises to remain faithful, no matter what we face.

It isn't in God's nature to be anything but good. God is for us, never against us, always faithful, and worthy of our trust. When we suffer, and everyone does, it's easy to forget that.

Here is the bottom-line imperative for us all:

Don't believe anything bad about God.

—BKS

When do you find it hard to trust God?
What are some of the bad things you have believed about God?

WEDNESDAY—4TH WEEK OF EASTER

You shall put these words of mine in your heart and soul, and you shall bind them as a sign on your hand, and fix them as an emblem on your forehead. —Deuteronomy 11:18

Starting new habits—or changing old ones—is hard. That's because our brains are misers, designed to create shortcuts, and make as many behaviors automatic as possible. This frees up our minds for more pressing matters. Habits are meant to be hard to break.

Changing a habit requires a truly compelling reason, and some serious rethinking. For example, if you say you want to stop watching so much Netflix, but you keep watching because, well, you like watching Netflix, then what you really want is to stop wanting to watch so much Netflix. Watching Netflix scratches an itch that, once you know what it is, could perhaps be scratched another way, if you decided you wanted it to be.

It isn't enough to just resolve to eat healthier, go to bed earlier, or read your Bible every day. Doing those things must satisfy something in you that needs satisfying—or ease a pain that needs easing.

When we start to realize the benefits of a new behavior, we are more willing and able to spend the mental energy to make it a habit.

We get life-giving habits into our bones with practice. Spiritual disciplines help us form new habits by repeating life-giving behaviors and changing life-destroying thought patterns.

But making spiritual disciplines a part of our daily lives starts with seeing a compelling reason to do it in the first place.

—BKS

What spiritual disciplines—prayer, solitude, fasting, for example—are part of your life?
What did it take to make them habits for you?

THURSDAY—4TH WEEK OF EASTER

Why do you stand looking up toward heaven? —Acts 1:11b

When the dog is hungry, he sits at my feet, gazing upward, pleading for food.

When the dog wants to go out, he sits at my feet, gazing upward, pleading for me to put on shoes.

Are you sensing a pattern?

Our dog knows most good things come from me so when he wants a good thing, he gazes upward, wordlessly speaking his desires. If he doesn't get fed, or walked, or invited into a lap, he's done all he can.

The dog doesn't have much choice, being thumbless in a world of can openers and leash latches. So he tries to tell me what he wants, then hopes that I'm listening, and undistracted, and inclined to follow through.

You are not a dog. Do you pray as if you were?

Do you gaze up toward heaven, pleading for what you want, hoping God's listening, and undistracted, and inclined to follow through?

After he burst from his tomb, Jesus promised his disciples that they'd get all the power they needed. Then he left them by rising into the heavens.

Instead of doing any of the things they were capable of doing, they just stood there, staring upward.

They'd spent so many years gazing and waiting for him to speak or heal or cook fish that instead of claiming the power he had given them and doing all the good things he'd taught them to do, they just stared up and watched his feet vanish. Jesus isn't your master like I am for the dog.

Jesus is your master teacher: the one who knows how to do what you want to do, and wants you to know how too.

And God didn't create you to be a dog. God already had dogs. God made you to be glorious, to take the power you've been given and do the great things Jesus is teaching you to do.

Prayer isn't just powerless pleading. Prayer is a conversation with God about the things we are doing together.

—EOR

What glorious things could you do with God's power if you did more than gaze and plead?

FRIDAY—4TH WEEK OF EASTER

He placed his right hand on me, saying, "Do not be afraid; I am the first and the last, and the living one. I was dead, and see, I am alive forever and ever"
—Revelation 1:17b-18a

John was on Patmos, a small Greek island in the Aegean Sea, when he had the trippy visions we know from the book of Revelation. In this verse at the beginning of his strange journey, John is greeted by a version of the glorified Jesus—with hair like white wool, eyes like fire, feet like bronze, and a voice like an ocean. Don't be afraid, Jesus says, reassuring John that he is alive and holding the keys to death.

Fear is a part of living. Some fears are real and rational—like the one that causes you to head for the basement when the tornado siren sounds. Other fears are based on what-ifs, and worst-case longshots that aren't actually real.

But here's the thing about fear: whether or not the thing I fear is really real, the fear is absolutely real.

And acting—or not acting—out of fear can cause real damage.

In those moments of fear, have you ever heard Jesus say to your spirit, "Don't be afraid"? I have. Many times.

There was the time I lost my last music industry job and I thought my life in music was done. Then again when I signed my divorce papers and I was so afraid that my kids were going to hate me. Also when I walked away from the business I'd built, with a ton of debt, not knowing how I'd pay my bills.

I heard Jesus speaking fear-freeness when I moved to California, grieved a breakup, lived amid a pandemic. And I've heard it every day since.

Don't be afraid.

—BKS

What would you do if you weren't afraid?

SATURDAY—4TH WEEK OF EASTER

Then Moses, the servant of the Lord, died there in the land of Moab, at the Lord's command. —Deuteronomy 34:5

What of you should live beyond you?

There are two major stages of life: building ego and living wisdom.

Stage 1: Construct an "I" for yourself and the world through quests and failures, blacks and whites. Your self-image—success, failure, acclaim, embarrassment—defines you.

Stage 2: Your "I" limits you so you release it, giving your deepest self room to breathe. Resiliency and relationship develop wisdom, patience, kindness, and compassion.

Most people never get to Stage 2. They stop at its edge, clutch their carefully constructed self-image, and retreat.

We think of Stage 1 as The Whole Enchilada. We value success instead of love, wisdom, trust, and peace. Hence war, bad politics, midlife crises, and pitying Moses.

At age 25, Moses finds his role. For 95 years he leads the Israelites through famine and abundance, faith and idolatry, toward a promised land. Moses becomes "MOSES! The Deliverer Of His People!"

Finally, at age 120, he arrives. God tells Moses, "There it is. Everything you've worked for. But you won't get to enjoy it. It's for everyone else." Moses sees all he's worked for, dies, and is buried on its edge.

All those years, all that suffering and frustration, and Moses doesn't get any of the win.

Tragic, right?

Uh, no.

After he took credit for God's work (and God told him off) he realized how much his "I" was getting in the way. He trained a successor and passed his leadership on and kept walking toward his people's good.

There at the edge, he saw his people's future and God's faithfulness. What of him would live beyond him was enough.

You can keep defining yourself in terms of your quests and failures. You can resent all the things you couldn't have, all the Promised Lands you missed out on, and hate yourself (and others) for the mistakes you've made along the way.

Or you can focus on what of you is truly valuable to others, over the long haul, and keep walking toward that.

—EOR

What *do* you value? Are you sure? How can you tell?

5TH SUNDAY OF EASTER

Happy are those who do not follow the advice of the wicked, or take the path that sinners tread, or sit in the seat of scoffers; but their delight is in the law of the Lord, and on his law they meditate day and night. —Psalm 1:1

Am I choosing life?

I can choose to smile at a passerby on the sidewalk, or I can look at my feet as they pass. Did I do a bad thing by not making eye contact? No. Could I have made a positive difference in someone's day if I'd smiled instead? Maybe.

When we are intentional about making choices that make the world better, little by little, we become more like Jesus, and closer to God. Our souls long to be close to God, so making life-giving choices brings us peace and joy. Seems simple enough.

Here's the flipside: We don't intentionally make life-destroying decisions most of the time. It's the little self-centered choices we make that get us in trouble after a while. And because we don't always know how our choices impact other people, we sometimes do more damage to our bodies, marriages, kids, friendships, and spirits than we realize.

When we make choices that are life-destroying, we create distance between us and God. Then our souls start sticking to other things or people, while in search of that soul-satisfaction we're missing. Eventually, we can find ourselves far away from God, utterly dissatisfied with everything.

When I choose to smile at a stranger, I add light to the world, simply by making that choice.

The more we make life-giving choices—big and small—the more it becomes second-nature to us. Before long, we're all habitually smiling at strangers on the sidewalk. How cool would that be?

—BKS

What is one small life-giving choice you can make today?

MONDAY—5TH WEEK OF EASTER

I am confident of this, that the one who began a good work among you will bring it to completion by the day of Jesus Christ. —Philippians 1:6

I don't tend to leave things unfinished.

Unless you count the many song lyrics I've started over the years that were never completed or set to music. Or the stage musical I started writing a few years back. Or the tv shows I got bored with. Or the books...

Okay, maybe I sometimes start things I don't finish. But it's rare that I flake out on a commitment I've made to someone who isn't me. I rarely back out of a co-writing session, a video chat, or dinner plans. I pride myself on being a reliable friend, a dependable co-worker, and a good son and dad. I never like feeling as though I'm letting someone down.

Thankfully, whether I follow through or not, God always does.

Paul reminds the early Christians in Philippi that God has started a good work in them. Exciting things are happening, and there's momentum for even greater things. Then he assures them that the work God is doing will be completed before Jesus returns. Because God isn't one to ever leave a project undone.

Like with the Philippians, God works with us, in us, and among us, to accomplish great things. But it is our participation—our willingness to be the hands of feet of Jesus—that gets things done. We are required to show up, and to follow through.

We choose to work with, and against, God all the time. But when we yield our kingdoms to God's, we can count on the inspiration, strength, courage— whatever is required—do the thing God is asking us to.

—BKS

What work is God doing among you and your people right now?

TUESDAY—5TH WEEK OF EASTER

Our God is in the heavens; he does whatever he pleases. Their idols are silver and gold, the work of human hands. —Psalm 115:3-4

I'm not much of an idolizer. I mean, there are people I've known—in person and from a distance—that I've placed on pedestals. Most of them were musical influences, like Michael W. Smith, Bruce Hornsby, and David Foster. A few were pastor-types and writers, like Scotty Smith and Donald Miller. I also have friends that I look up to for their courage, faith, intellect, and creativity.

It's okay—important even—to have people you aspire to be like, and to learn from. That said, I understand that even the brightest of us is flawed. I can admire Steven Spielberg, Taylor Swift, and Barack Obama, for perfectly understandable reasons. But as brilliant, creative, and influential as they are, they are not worship-worthy.

Because we humans are worshipers by nature, we have sticky souls, always adoring someone or something. Maybe you aren't wowed by a shiny statue, like the Israelites occasionally were. But a golden calf is often disguised as a perfect persona or some other ideal—just as meticulously crafted, but way more breakable.

And what about those who haven't earned our acclaim at all? Celebrities and influencers with little to no discernible talent. Political figures without convictions, who just say what their adoring followers want to hear.

Christian personalities, who peddle Jesus for personal gain. They all get worshiped. And when they disappoint us, we're...surprised...?

Only God is worthy of our reverence, adoration, and worship. No one—no matter how famous, attractive, smart, funny, sexy, or influential—will ever satisfy the longings of your soul, or mine.

—BKS

Who do you idolize?

WEDNESDAY—5TH WEEK OF EASTER

So you have pain now; but I will see you again, and your hearts will rejoice, and no one will take your joy from you. —John 16:22

I have always felt conflicted over Jesus 2.0.

When I was a youngster at Fundy Fun Summer Camp, we were shown *A Distant Thunder*, a low-budget eschatological horror flick that scared the bejeezus out of me. The story took place in a post-rapture apocalypse, made up entirely of 1970s horror tropes, and draped in prophetic cliches. (Completely appropriate viewing for 12-year-olds in the woods without their parents, by the way.)

The intent was to scare us all into giving our lives to Jesus. All it really did for me was make me terrified of the End Times. All throughout my teens, I was afraid of losing my salvation, missing out on the Rapture, and being left to aimlessly wander a Godless hellscape. All while being chased by cloak-and-dagger baddies, eager to brand me with a 666.

The joy Jesus promised was completely papered over with a propaganda poster that shouted, Fear the Tribulation!

Here are a couple more concerns I have with millennialism.

I know Jesus returning as the Triumphant King is something many Christians long to see. But Warrior Jesus feels out-of-character to me. Kinda like Ninja Gandhi. I just can't seem to wrap my mind around it.

And then there's the blood-washed Bride of Christ (aka us) summoned to meet Jesus in the air, while people we know and love are left behind to survive in the aforementioned hellscape. I have a really hard time believing God would really do that.

Jesus never actually said any of these things would happen. But he did promise the disciples they would see him again, and that their hearts would be filled with joy that no one would ever take away.

I believe we will also be with Jesus in the next part of eternity. And I'm confident our hearts, too, will rejoice, free of fear and eschatological fiction.

—BKS

What are your ideas about the Second Coming?

THURSDAY—5TH WEEK OF EASTER

Happy is the nation whose God is the Lord, the people whom he has chosen as his heritage. —Psalm 33:12

I was a band geek. Marching band was my nation.

When you are in a marching band, you spend countless hours, standing on asphalt in hundred-degree heat. You learn the music and the drill, and you mentally rehearse the show in your sleep. You take it all very seriously, and you give it more than you thought you could.

You are in it with your closest friends, creating something together that will bring an audience to its feet. You wear your band jacket in the halls of your school with pride—doesn't matter if the jocks look at you like you're nerdy and weird.

You honor those who marched before you, and those who will march in your footsteps when you're gone, by giving your best all the time. And you open your arms to clarinets and trombones alike.

When band is your nation, you always have a home.

What bound me to my band-geek friends was the music, the camaraderie, and the common endgame. The music could've been something else. The goal could've been something else too.

My nation was marching band. Maybe yours was the softball team, or the debate team, or Girl Scouts.

I hope you've had a nation.

We long for that feeling of belonging, of working together toward something big. Not just as kids, but for our whole lives.

We all need more than acceptance. We need belonging.

—BKS

Are you part of a nation?
If so, what is it, and what does belonging feel like? If not, why not?

FRIDAY—5TH WEEK OF EASTER

The heavens are the Lord's heavens, but the earth he has given to human beings.
—Psalm 115:6

Do you know that old hymn *This Is My Father's World*?

> This is my Father's world
> And to my listening ears
> All nature sings and 'round me rings
> The music of the spheres

Now picture this: You have a sink full of dishes, garbage spilling out of your trash can, crumbs in your carpet, and a bathroom in need of super-scrubbing bubbles. Annoyed, you call your landLord and say, "Hey, can you come over and, like, clean up my place? I mean, technically, it's yours, and it's kinda your fault for renting it to a slob."

Yeah. Ever heard of eviction?

> This is my Father's world
> I rest me in the thought
> Of rocks and trees, of skies and seas
> His hand the wonders wrought

It isn't God's job to clean up after us. God created natural laws that govern things like climate, weather, and seasons.

We know that we can affect those things with our actions. We can harm, or help, our planet.

> This is my Father's world
> He shines in all that's fair
> In the rustling grass, I hear him pass
> He speaks to me everywhere

As people of faith, it seems to me we should lead the charge to care for the earth God gave us. Why do you think it is that we don't?

—BKS

This Is My Father's World was written by Maltbie Davenport Babcock.

So seriously: why don't we care for God's gifted world?

SATURDAY—5ᵀᴴ WEEK OF EASTER

God's eye is on those who respect him, whose hope for deliverance is in his love.
—Psalm 33:18

I give up.

How many times have you said that, out loud or in your mind?

When has your soul been trapped in a tiny room of worry, shame, or exhaustion?

What has brought you low, pinning you in a fetal position until the weeping ended?

Nothing, ever? Maybe your pain isn't that dramatic, or the challenges you face are mere raindrops on an otherwise sunny window.

"I give up" are the words we scream when we're staring at the empty page where an answer is supposed to be.

"I give up" are the words written on the wall of WTF?!!, the last ones we see when we crash headlong into the inevitable.

When that happens—when our current way of living or thinking is no longer sustainable and we run smack into a reality we don't want to face—we have exactly three choices:

1. To stay there, living in misery and hopelessness or dying by our own hand,

2. To go backwards, pretending that everything is really fine and it will all work out somehow, or

3. To change "I give up" into "I surrender," face the pain, deal with reality, and with God's help, move forward.

Surrender sounds like losing, and loss is our deepest fear. But surrender is really about accepting a situation, acknowledging that if you could fix it on your own you would have, and opening yourself up to the way forward that only God can empower.

When you surrender the idea that you are right, or surrender the idea that you have to figure it out alone, or surrender whatever falsehood got you into that place of despair...

When your hope stops being grounded in your own ability to power through, and starts being centered on the unbreaking, never-ending, mighty love of the one God who never leaves you on your own...

That's when a tiny ray of light pierces the wall of darkness, pulls you up off the floor, opens your mind, and makes new things possible.

Surrender is the prerequisite for resurrection.

—EOR

Is there some reality facing you today that calls for surrender, and with it, God's loving, helping hand?

6TH SUNDAY OF EASTER

The Lord God formed the human from the dust of the ground, and breathed into their nostrils the breath of life; and the human became a living being. —Genesis 2:7

99.5% of your body consists of 11 elements:

O+C+H+N+Ca+P+S+Mg, along with Na+Cl+K

Soil is also mostly 11: O+C+H+N+Ca+P+S+Mg, plus Si+Al+Fe

Physically, you are separated from soil by only tiny amounts of a few elements.

Mentally, spiritually, emotionally: you and the ground are worlds apart.

Dirt is never more than a physical hodgepodge of elements in varying amounts.

Even on those days when you feel like dirt, you are filled with what even the most fecund field lacks: the breath of the living God.

What is physical is measurable, made up of discernable bits, growing or decaying at a determinable rate. That's the dust of you.

The nonphysical you is spirit and soul, directly connected to the essence of the One living God.

You are a spiritual being living a material existence, subject to the pleasures and tragedies of the physical world but inextricably linked to the majestical, creative, all-encompassing, persistent love that is God.

When you are beaten down and worn out, tired and hurting from hauling around the weight of the world with all its suffering and histories and battles and injustices, remember this:

You are a wonder greater than the stars themselves, for every nonphysical crevice of you is overflowing with God's spirit.

—EOR

A practice to try on:
Breathe.

MONDAY—6TH WEEK OF EASTER

Now there are varieties of gifts, but the same Spirit. —1 Corinthians 12:4

If you attend a church, chances are you've taken a spiritual gift assessment. These assessments are kind of like a personality test you might take on Facebook, but written in Christian-ese. They give leaders insight into where you, the member, could be of use to the church.

I'm not knocking these assessments. Anything that helps us better understand ourselves, especially our strengths, is a good thing. But I will say that nailing down what our spiritual gifts are is kind of like nailing down the Holy Spirit. (Good luck with that.)

That's because when we are open to being led by the Spirit, She will often use us in surprising ways.

Sure, if you are a cheerful, outgoing person, welcoming visitors and handing out bulletins is probably a great place for you to serve. If you are good with money, and trustworthy, then maybe you should be the church treasurer.

Serving in your sweet spot is a win for you and for your church.

That said, following Jesus takes us out of our sweet spot on the regular. When we submit to the leading of the Spirit, we learn there is more to us than we thought. We can do things that are only possible with Her help and intervention.

Our willingness and availability become our greatest gifts.

The key to discovering and using your spiritual gifts is allowing yourself to be useful to God. That begins when you practice spiritual disciplines, pray to be a part of what the Spirit is doing in your world, and then go where She leads.

—BKS

Be still and think for a minute before answering:
When has the Holy Spirit been able to change a situation for the better—to bring comfort to someone who needs it, or to give someone the aha! moment they've been praying for—because you were there, willing, and available?

TUESDAY—6TH WEEK OF EASTER

Now you are the body of Christ and individually members of it. —1 Corinthians 12:27

For about nine months before moving to California in 2019, I visited various churches around Nashville to see sense of what other churches do. I'd been on staff as a worship leader for ten years, so it had been a long while since I'd just sat in a pew.

The place I enjoyed visiting most was Christ Church Cathedral, an Episcopal congregation downtown.

The building is old, built of stone, complete with gorgeous stained glass and a stunning chancel area. Feeling of sacredness in the space? Check.

The music at Christ Church is stunningly good. Because their worship is centered around classical music, I wasn't compelled to question their song choices, or rearrange their parts in my head. Their singers are mostly paid professionals and their organist is world-class, so no pitchy altos or bad notes. I was able to rest in their musicianship and just worship.

All of their pastors are smart, thoughtful, appropriately funny, and eloquent. The sermons are poignant, succinct, and thought-provoking. No hourlong ramblings or incoherent illustrations.

And of course, because they are Episcopalian, I was worshiping alongside other LGBTQ+ folks, which made me feel welcome.

While all of those are perfectly good reasons to choose a church, I was surprised by what really attracted me to Christ Church. Being there made me realize that church wasn't about my tending to my personal relationship with Jesus. Instead, I came to be a part of something bigger than me. I came to share liturgy and Scripture and Eucharist with people doing the same thing in churches all over the world.

Being one of many reminded me of something that's easy to forget: worship isn't about me. Or about you. It is about joining our hearts, minds, and voices in the worship of our living God. Experiencing that at Christ Church gave me the perspective I needed to be a more intentional, impassioned follower of Jesus.

—BKS

Why do you keep choosing your church? If you're not part of a church, how much of that is about you and not the church?

WEDNESDAY—6TH WEEK OF EASTER

And you shall know that I am the Lord, when I open your graves...I will put my spirit within you, and you shall live. —Ezekiel 37:13-14

I watched the first couple seasons of *The Walking Dead* a few years ago. I'm not a fan of horror, but I find zombies to be fairly comical creatures. Just reanimated flesh and bones, incapable of reason, or emotions, driven only by survival.

I've felt like a zombie before.

It was a while after my divorce. I was dealing with running my own business, and the financial stresses that go along with that. I was trying to keep a long-distance relationship together, which left me feeling jealous, lonely, and resentful. I was also co-parenting teenagers ('nuff said), and figuring out how I felt about God, myself, and everything else.

I was depressed. Fear, shame, and guilt were deep in my bones. I was stumbling around, doing the daily minimum, but feeling pretty dead inside.

Even in my zombie-like state, with little to give, God gave much to me. Friends kept showing up, reminding me that I was loved, and worthy of love. I rediscovered passions from my youth, like drum corps and roller coasters, that started giving me joy again. I slowly—very slowly—started to trust myself to make life-giving choices.

Prayer, meds, friends and time helped me get through the fog of depression, and to find hope.

God opened my grave. Not in a single, dramatic moment, but over time, in subtle and not-so-subtle ways. The Holy Spirit was close by through that entire season, and through every season since.

If you find yourself in a grave, please talk to someone—a trusted friend, your pastor, a therapist. God s Spirit offers life to you, and to all of us.

—BKS

Have you ever felt like a zombie?
What brought you to that place and how did you find life again?

THURSDAY—6TH WEEK OF EASTER

Cease to do evil, learn to do good; seek justice, rescue the oppressed, defend the orphan, plead for the widow. —Isaiah 1:16b-17

Have you ever gotten lost? I have a pretty good sense of direction from behind a steering wheel. But put me on a trail and I can get turned around easily. One of my biggest fears is getting lost in a forest at night. (Heck, the idea of just being in a forest at night gives me the willies.)

It's one of the problems with depending upon GPS, right? We pay attention to the voice and not to the place, which means that we get wherever we're going without knowing how it happened, or how to get home.

Getting lost is especially easy to do when you're not paying attention.

In Isaiah 1, God lays out a case against the people of Judah. They were being rebellious and arrogant. But then, God offers an invitation to them to change, a prescription for finding their way back home.

The six actions that God put before Judah are the same things Jesus taught in the Gospels. They are directions for us to find our way when we've strayed from our True North.

We start by examining our actions and attitudes to see where we veered off-course. We fix what we can, make amends, ask for forgiveness, start again, do better.

We stop defending ourselves and start standing up for the defenseless. That means seeking opportunities to help and serve those disadvantaged, ostracized, bullied, and ignored.

Then we make it a point to pay attention to what's going on with our own souls. What are drawn to that isn't God and why?

There's always a way back home. But first, we have to recognize how lost we are.

—BKS

When have you been lost?
How did you find your way back?

FRIDAY—6TH WEEK OF EASTER

To set the mind on the flesh is death, but to set the mind on the Spirit is life and peace. —Romans 8:6

Ever wake up with a thought in your head that pretty much wrecks your whole day? Like a memory of something your ex said to you? Or a thing you read in the news? Or a frustration from work?

I wake up like that and it takes a lot of effort to shake that kind of thought. It comes charged with feelings and a list of what if's a mile long. I usually feel powerless to change the thing I'm thinking about.

But I can change my thoughts.

Now I'm not saying it's easy. But the big problem is that our thoughts become ideas, and then over time they turn up as beliefs.

Once ideas become beliefs, which are just ideas we're willing to act on, they are much harder to change.

Negative beliefs lead us toward depression and anxiety, sometimes even violence and self-harm.

Positive beliefs build our self-confidence, deepen our trust, and allow us to see the best in others and ourselves.

It all starts with what we think about.

To set our minds on the Spirit, there are a few tried-and-true spiritual practices that help: repeating positive affirmations, practicing gratitude, monitoring what we feed our minds, shifting our attention to the needs of others, and of course, asking God for help.

—BKS

What are you thinking about today?

SATURDAY—6TH WEEK OF EASTER

If the world hates you, know it hated me before it hated you. —John 15:18

Go Ducks!

Gryffindor? Me too!

Red Vines forever, Twizzlers never!

Whether you share an interest or a blood line, being part of a community gives companionship and safety. Anywhere your tribe is, you belong. You're home.

Maybe you're a Green Bay Packers football fan. Driving through the land of the Dallas Cowboys you feel out of place and disoriented. You pull into the parking lot of your favorite chain restaurant and are relieved by the familiar signage. Suddenly you spy a Packers bumper sticker and relief turns to joy. Your tribe is here!

Belonging makes us feel like the world's okay. Even when the world isn't okay and we know it.

Jesus' first apprentices had belonged to a large community. They knew the rules, were invited to the parties. Some of them weren't liked very much (we're looking at you, Tax Collector), but they were part of Israel. They belonged. It was home.

When they decided to follow Jesus, Peter, John, Mary, and the rest thought they were still Jews, connected by blood and history. But, as he told them "if the world hates me, it's going to hate you too." As Jesus got hated, his followers lost their community and its companionship and safety. They didn't belong anymore.

When you follow the Way of Jesus, you're going to go against the dominant culture, no matter what your dominant culture is. Following his Way isn't normal, not even in churches, because you wind up putting that allegiance first: above church, above country, above family, above tribe.

Following Jesus changes everything, including where you find home, where you belong.

The day before I was accepted into seminary I was living as a Christian in mostly queer culture. Not the day after.

I had thought I was adding to my current life. My tribe thought I had become untrustworthy, bizarre, even dangerous.

That's one of the many reasons so many people identify as Christians, but so few follow Jesus wherever he leads. He happened to lead me to seminary and away from the life I knew. It wasn't fun.

At all.

And that's why if you do follow him, try to live his way, no matter where you feel like you belong you'd better find your home in the present Kingdom of God.

—EOR

Where do you find belonging?
What's your real home?

7TH SUNDAY OF EASTER

So you are no longer a slave but a child, and if a child then also an heir, through God.
—Galatians 4:7

I have a good friend who used to say he experienced God as his boss. As long as he was doing things for God—and doing them well—then he was in God's good graces. His relationship with God was very much based on what he was willing to do.

So he started and led a ministry for teens at our church. He sang on the worship team every Sunday. He committed to being mentored by our pastor, and even preached a few times. He probably did lots of other things I never knew about.

But after a while, all the doing became exhausting. So he stopped. And without all the doing, he had no longer had a job. Or a boss.

I used to experience God as a cosmic scorekeeper.

Like everything I did, or didn't do, was being tracked. My salvation was always touch-and-go. Only God and my scorecard really knew if my soul was eternally secure at any given moment.

Some of us experience God as aloof, faraway, and uninvested. As if we—and our planet— have been abandoned to our own devices.

Others experience the opposite: God as micromanager, with a divine hand in every little thing. Like nothing happens without God's nod of approval.

None of these perceptions of God—or of ourselves—is true.

We are not slaves, working to appease an easily disappointed God. We are not pawns or puppets. We are not unseen, unheard, or unloved. And we are not victims of God's whims or tantrums. It is inconsistent with God's nature to be cruel, capricious, or unjust.

Instead, we are children of a loving Parent. We are cherished, treasured, and deeply loved by God, who desires good things for all of us, and loves us with an unbreakable, everlasting love.

—BKS

How do you experience God?

MONDAY—7TH WEEK OF EASTER

The Lord bless you and keep you; the Lord make his face to shine upon you, and be gracious to you; the Lord lift up his countenance upon you, and give you peace.
—Numbers 6:24-26

June is Pride Month, a celebration of all things queer. For LGBTQ+ people, it's a time to feel empowered. Rainbow flags are flown in public places. There are parties, parades, and high-fives from allies. If you're queer, like me, it's nice to feel seen and celebrated.

Pride also draws bigotry and homophobia out into the open. Some queer folks feel unloved and unsafe. Many are tired of the tensions, tired of hiding who they are to keep peace, and tired of repeating the same conversations.

Sadly, there is a predictable uptick in violence against LGBTQ+ people during Pride. And much of it is perpetrated under the guise of defending traditional Christian values—which must grieve God a great deal.

So pride can deal us soaring highs and crushing lows at the same time.

God gave Moses a blessing to give to the Israelites. It's used often as a benediction in Christian worship services.

I'd like to offer my own take on this blessing for all of us misfits—queer or not—as we enter any month of Pride:

May God bless and keep you, wherever you find yourself right now.

May you know that God sees you, hears you, knows you, and loves you.

May you feel accepted and embraced by our loving God, as you are.

And no matter what is going on around you, may the peace of God dwell within you always.

—BKS

What blessing would you offer oppressed people celebrating their identity and belonging?

TUESDAY—7TH WEEK OF EASTER

Let love be genuine; hate what is evil, hold fast to what is good. —Romans 12:9

Some things that are good, in my opinion: a summer day at Cedar Point, laughing hysterically with a friend, Mom's banana pudding, watching my favorite drum corps perform from the top of the stands on the 50yard-line, a well-crafted Manhattan, sharing a new song I just wrote for the first time, spaghetti with meat sauce, leading worship from behind a piano, sleeping in, HGTV at the end of a mentally exhausting day, and hanging out with my kids—anytime, anywhere.

Likewise, here are some things I believe are evil: movies inspired by eschatology, conversion camps, bubble gum on hot asphalt, putting children in cages, voter suppression, most reality tv, Uber's surge rates, white supremacy, slimy food, addiction, mass shootings, traffic, and Christian nationalism.

You may ask: "How do you know what is good and what is evil?"

"Well," I would answer, "it's a carefully-applied algorithm, based on personal experience, research and observation, societal norms, and my gut."

These days, there isn't much that we can all agree is objectively good or objectively evil. Christians can't really claim any authority in that department anymore (if we ever really could) since we can't even agree amongst ourselves.

In Romans 12:9 Paul's telling everyone to be genuine. But then there's the question of what is genuine. If I know someone really well, I might be able to tell if they are being genuine when they say or do something. But really, all I can do is choose to be genuine in my own actions and interactions, and trust that others are choosing the same.

So what does it mean then to let our love be genuine? I think it means we are to love everyone without motive, expecting nothing in return.

And how do you hate what is evil? By staying away from things that make you think badly about yourself, God, or others.

And what about holding fast to what is good?

I think that means that you search for, and find joy, hope, and peace—wherever they happen to be—and then you hold onto them with everything you have. Because they are what make life sweet, unexpected, and marvelous.

—BKS

How do you know when love—yours or someone else's—is genuine?

Bonus question: Name ten things you believe are good.

WEDNESDAY—7TH WEEK OF EASTER

I praise you, for I am fearfully and wonderfully made. Wonderful are your works; that I know very well. My frame was not hidden from you, when I was being made in secret, intricately woven in the depths of the earth. Your eyes beheld my unformed substance. In your book were written all the days that were formed for me, when none of them as yet existed. — Psalm 139:14-16

When I was a kid, I was skinny. Really skinny. I had copper hair, freckles, and ears that stuck out a little. I was shorter than most of the kids at school my age. And I was clumsy, ill-equipped for athletics.

I had (and still have) a tic that appeared when I was feeling stressed or anxious. My kindergarten teachers thought I had a learning disability because I couldn't tie my shoes.

But I was smart. I got the nickname "The Walking Dictionary" when I was in second grade. (I've always liked words.) I was also easygoing, optimistic, and eager-to-please (still true).

I was a late bloomer. I passed for pre-teen, even after I was driving. I was skinny till I turned 30. Now in my 50s, I'm a little overweight and mostly gray.

Why am I telling you all of this?

Each of us is perfectly imperfect. We see our flaws in the mirror. We tell ourselves we aren't _____ enough. But the truth is, we are exactly as God designed us.

I used to want to be anything but different. But my years have taught me that different is beautiful.

Our differences give us reason to shine, and shining is a good thing.

We were wonderfully made and deeply cherished by God even before our first breath. Freckles, tics, and sticking-out ears included.

—BKS

What is a difference about you that you can celebrate today?

THURSDAY—7TH WEEK OF EASTER (ASCENSION DAY)

So when they had come together, they asked him, "Lord, is this the time when you will restore the kingdom to Israel?" He replied, "It is not for you to know the times or periods that the Father has set by his own authority. But you will receive power when the Holy Spirit has come upon you; and you will be my witnesses in Jerusalem, in all Judea and Samaria, and to the ends of the earth." When he had said this, as they were watching, he was lifted up, and a cloud took him out of their sight. —Acts 1:6-9

"Are we there yet?"

That's the cliché, right? The family is in the car for a long road trip. Less than 15 minutes away from home, little Billy pipes up excitedly with "Are we there yet?" Then, 3.73 days of boredom-inspired questioning later, Dad (who drives the car) snaps at Billy, "Does it look like we're there yet?"

Experience informs me that adults ask "are we there yet?" far more often than children.

Is this the last mask mandate?

Will my boss finally give me that promotion?

Is this the year Black folk stop getting killed by police?

Will my kid stop cutting this time?

Is this the time when you will restore the kingdom to Israel?

At the beginning of the book of Acts, Jesus has been driving the rabbinical car for three years. He's been killed, and resurrected, and appeared all over Galilee to demonstrate God's power.

You'd think that by now his followers would have the sense to trust him and his Father. Maybe even start to get a glimpse of the fact that the restoration of Israel as an earthly power wasn't the point.

But they're anxious for the result they long for. They're tired of trying to do the right thing. They're painfully aware of everything they've done wrong up until now, and they're looking to Dad to set everything right so they can just stop and really, really rest.

Aren't we all? At least sometimes?

Jesus gives his unsatisfactory answer: "Does it look like we're there yet?" which in first-century Galilee sounds like, "It is not for you to know."

But Jesus isn't snapping at them like Billy's dad. He's reminding them that while they may be focusing on the wrong things and may not know when their desires will be satisfied (if at all), they do not have to simply wait for someone to do something. They have power to act and will have even more when the Spirit comes alongside them.

—EOR

Are you underestimating your own ability to effect change or focusing on the wrong kind of change needed? What do you want to do about that?

FRIDAY—7TH WEEK OF EASTER

O Lord, how manifold are your works! In wisdom you have made them all… When you send forth your spirit, they are created; and you renew the face of the ground.
—Psalm 104:24a, 30

Want to know the biggest difference between God and you?

God is never finished creating, and God's creations are never finished being created. Or re-created.

If you put together flour, water, salt, and yeast to make bread, when are you finished creating your loaf?

When is that song you've been working on for 10 years finished?

If you see streaks in the paint you put on the wall yesterday, do you feel like you have to paint the wall again?

It doesn't matter how you answer: you understand what it means to be finished with something. You know what it feels like to think you're finished and then to discover there's more to do.

You live in linear time with material objects that come into and go out of existence. Of course you have markers for "done."

God doesn't seem to have those same markers. You ever notice how at the end of one of the creation stories in Genesis, God comes to the seventh day and rests? God doesn't wash God's hands, put away all the tools, and head to another project. God just rests.

Then God creates some more.

When God sends forth God's spirit (or God's breath, depending upon your translation), things are created and the face of the ground (aka "adamah"—the same word as for humanity) is renewed.

God breaths and we are renewed, re-created.

God sends God's Spirit and we are born again, and again.

—EOR

When you experience renewal—of your strength, focus, determination, hope—what can you do to notice the presence of God's Spirit in the mix?

SATURDAY—7TH WEEK OF EASTER

Elijah said to Elisha, "Stay here; for the Lord has sent me as far as Bethel." […for the Lord has sent me as far as Jericho…for the Lord has sent me to Jericho…for the Lord has sent me to the Jordan…] But Elisha said, "As the Lord lives, and as you yourself live, I will not leave you." So they went down to Bethel… —2 Kings 2:2, 4, 6 (adapted)

The best piece of advice I've received in my long life was this: choose your teachers, not your classes.

Sally didn't intend it profoundly: I was a kid and she was talking about college. She was a visual artist— charcoal and watercolor, mainly—and the wife of my mother's ex-father-in-law. I'm not sure I had seen her before then, and I'm not sure I ever saw her after. But for some reason her words stuck with me.

Choose your teachers because human beings teach us more than the subject matter of their expertise.

At the end of the Elijah (teacher) & Elisha (apprentice) passage, Elisha asks Elijah for a double share of his spirit. It's a bold request, a student asking his teacher to make him even better than the teacher himself. Elijah grants it and Elisha continues leading and teaching as Elijah had (but, one presumes, better than Elijah had).

I don't believe Elijah could have refused, because the transfer and amplification of his spirit was based on Elisha's having stuck close over the long, tiresome journey. Elisha literally followed in Elijah's footsteps for years, watching his teacher, listening to his teacher, eating when his teacher did, sleeping when he did.

Because Elisha was a good student, sticking close, taking wisdom when he found it and discarding foolishness when that's what was offered, over time he absorbed Elijah's spirit as well as access to the Spirit that made Elijah great.

Had Elijah been a scoundrel, or unwise, sticking so close to him would have spelled disaster for Elisha. Haven't we all seen disciples of a fool become twice as foolish themselves? But Elisha chose well, so Elijah and experience and God blessed him.

I've added a codicil to Sally's advice over the years: Choose your teachers but make sure they are learners too. Good teachers aren't perfect people, but they admit their mistakes and learn from them.

I'm grateful for the good teachers in my life, the ones in the classroom as well as the ones who live with me. They've made me better than I could have been without them, and pointed the way to the Spirit by being the people they are.

—EOR

Who has taught you well?
Have you stuck close enough to inherit their spirit?

PENTECOST

PENTECOST SUNDAY

Likewise the Spirit helps us in our weakness; for we do not know how to pray as we ought, but that very Spirit intercedes with sighs too deep for words. —Romans 8:26

Fifty days after the first Easter, the Holy Spirit made her presence known. It was the Feast of Weeks, and the Apostles and other Jews from as far away as Mesopotamia, Rome, and Libya, had gathered in Jerusalem for the event, to celebrate the harvest.

Because of the diversity of the group, many languages were being spoken at once. That is, until a gust of wind moved through the place where they were meeting, and something strange happened.

Everyone heard everyone else speaking in their own native language. Words were no longer a barrier between them.

Everyone was understood.

Have you ever felt like no one understands you? Like your intentions are misread all the time? Like you might as well be from Mars, or Berkeley, or Alabama?

Maybe you don't say what you really mean, because you don't think it will make any difference.

Maybe you say exactly what you mean, but your words are always getting twisted.

Maybe you just say nothing, because there aren't words for what you feel, and no one is paying attention anyway.

Even if you are constantly feeling misunderstood, you—your words, your intentions, your actions, your heart—matter.

Just like on Pentecost, the Holy Spirit is still breaking down our barriers to understanding. She opens ears, minds, and hearts to the things we need to hear, and the things we need to say. She even interprets our silences to God when we don't know how to pray.

—BKS

When has the Holy Spirit helped you understand someone else, or to be understood yourself?

For the rest of the season of Pentecost, use Common Time days, beginning where you left off.

On the last day of the season of Pentecost, contemplate the entry called "The Last Saturday Before Advent."

See the Chart of Days on pages 5-6 for help.

COMMON TIME

COMMON 1

Put away from you all bitterness and wrath and anger and wrangling and slander, together with all malice, and be kind to one another, tenderhearted, forgiving one another, as God in Christ has forgiven you. Therefore be imitators of God, as beloved children —Ephesians 4:31-5:1

Ever seen a small child step his tiny feet into his mother's high heels, carefully put on her favorite necklace, and wobble down the stairs? I have, and the only thing I could think was "please don't tumble down all those steep wooden steps on *my* watch!"

That's what young children do. We try on being our parents. Or our aunties. Or the local pastor or songwriter or whomever captures our imagination.

Children learn to become the people they will be by imitating the people they admire.

My child doesn't have my hair or my nose, but (God love her) she's absorbed my conscious use of words, because when she was little and phrased sentences illogically I would raise an eyebrow and ask, "do you mean *[fill in the formal meaning rather than the colloquial one]* or something else?"

I'd like to say I don't do that anymore but I would be using "anymore" incorrectly.

When the writer of the letter to the Ephesians tells them to imitate God, it sounds crazy hard. "You want me to create all that exists or ever has, Paul? How 'bout I just turn water into wine, huh?"

But that's what safe and cared-for kids do, right? Try to be like the parent who loves them?

Achieving a great imitation of God isn't the point. Recognizing that God is the kind of parent you might want to imitate—that's the point.

God is the sort of parent who has put away anger and bitterness because God cherishes you, God's own beloved child. God is the sort of parent who is kind, tenderhearted, and forgiving.

When you consistently work to remember that, although your demon voices may tell you otherwise, God treasures you, it's a little easier to be decent to others. Even the others you don't like very much.

So go ahead and put on God's high heels and necklace. Wobble down the steep wooden stairs, in full confidence that the parent who waits at the bottom is honored, and smiling with joy.

—EOR

Don't be shy: name one (or more) ways you resemble your Parent God.

COMMON 2

> May all kings fall down before him, all nations give him service. For he delivers the needy when they call, the poor and those who have no helper. He has pity on the weak and the needy, and saves the lives of the needy. From oppression and violence he redeems their life; and precious is their blood in his sight. —Psalm 72:11-14

You're painting a portrait of an emperor—a king who has gathered so many nations under his control that there are lesser kings below him. A king over many kings.

How would you depict him?

Would he be standing atop a mountain, his raised fist clenching a sword? Or sitting on a throne, his crowned minions groveling before him? Or standing behind a plexiglass lectern, his teleprompter flowing words of arrogant defiance? I'd go for a toga and a semi-automatic weapon, just for effect.

The Psalmist paints a different picture of a ruler worthy of other kings' fealty. He's not violent or proud. He wields kindness and compassion instead of a sword, rescuing his people from oppression and bloodshed instead of cheering it on.

What a weird king.

This is the Hebrew Scriptures we're talking about, the part of the Bible that many Christians think portrays a vengeful, bloodthirsty god.

Yet here we are, extolling a supreme ruler who is honored for his deliverance and mercy.

You don't have to wait for Jesus to think maybe God is a good guy after all.

It's humans we have to watch out for. Particularly ourselves, because we may honor a tender heart when it's written into literature but we do love our kings.

We bow down to celebrity and ruthlessness (when it's on our side).

We admire kings of industry who could solve a good amount of the world's poverty, much of it caused by themselves, by opening their coin purses.

We tend to prop up exactly the kinds of idols we'd find troubling in a portrait.

To topple tyrants, we have to shine light on our own ideas about strength and worth.

To get different kings, we have to have different hearts.

—EOR

Ask yourself: "Whom do I cheer for in movies? Do I envy the privately owned rocket ship, enjoy the "secret" information, repeat the snide remark, shake my head at "ignorance"?
And then: "How can I speak back to my own desire for kingship, or at least my will to be right?"

COMMON 3

> Now when all the people were baptized, and when Jesus also had been baptized and was praying, the heaven was opened, and the Holy Spirit descended upon him in bodily form like a dove. And a voice came from heaven, "You are my Son, the Beloved; with you I am well pleased." —Luke 3:21-22

I've been a teacher, a supervisor, and a parent for a long time, which means I've had lots of opportunity to tell people what a great job they've done.

Some folks like getting rewards of money, trophies, or certificates. Others want a public shout-out: a sign on a bulletin board or a presentation from a dais. Still others enjoy acquiring points or wins, measuring their increasing value by the growing pile.

And then there are those who want their parent or teacher, or boss or spouse or child to look them straight in the eye and say: I am so proud of you.

Three of the books of the Christian Scriptures—Matthew, Mark, and Luke—describe the scene at Jesus' baptism. All three have the crowds, and John the Baptizer, and something about repentance. The book known as John refers to the Spirit descending on Jesus but skips the event itself.

All four books suggest that John thought Jesus' wanting to be baptized was strange.

Overly self-effacing, maybe. But Jesus insists, so John obliges.

In Matthew, the voice from the heavens introduces Jesus to the crowd, saying, "This is my beloved son..." It's like God invites Jesus up onto the stage, puts His arm around Jesus' shoulder, and shouts, "this is my kid. Isn't he great, folks?"

But in Mark and Luke, God's pleasure is communicated straight to Jesus. "You are my Son, the Beloved; with you I am well pleased."

It's not clear whether the crowd hears the heavenly parent claiming their kid; God's praise and pride weren't directed toward them. If God needed the crowds and John to know Jesus was special, they'd have realized it when they saw Jesus receive his prize in the form of a dovelike Holy Spirit.

The One Jesus called "Father" looked him straight in the eye and said: I'm so proud of you.

Jesus got approval from the one person who really mattered, claimed his beloved identity, and went on to be the decent, humble kid he knew his dad wanted him to be.

—EOR

How do you like to receive praise? When do you really take it in and make it part of who you are?

COMMON 4

> Therefore take up the whole armor of God, so that you may be able to withstand on that evil day, and having done everything, to stand firm. Stand therefore, and fasten the belt of truth around your waist, and put on the breastplate of righteousness. As shoes for your feet put on whatever will make you ready to proclaim the gospel of peace. With all of these, take the shield of faith, with which you will be able to quench all the flaming arrows of the evil one. Take the helmet of salvation, and the sword of the Spirit, which is the word of God. —Ephesians 6:13-17

Most days I get dressed without thinking much about it. My closet is full of black pants and shirts because I can grab them before the sun's up and still be confident of a close match. I work from home, so unless I am meeting with a client my hair can be mussed and my face bare and barely washed.

Some clothing choices require more thought. If I'm going someplace special I might put on heels or my wedding pearls, because I rarely wear them so they feel special too.

If depression or anxiety are making the day harder, or I have to see people I find draining, my clothes have to not only cover me but serve as fortress walls.

What I wear can help me feel safe in a world that isn't always easy or kind.

When people conceal a knife or a pistol in their pocket with no intention of using it, they're doing the same thing, I imagine, though my leather jacket is a lot less likely to accidentally kill somebody.

On those hard days, when a specific pair of socks feels like armor, my goal isn't to start a fight, or be on the offense, or even to impress. Armor isn't designed for attack; its purpose is to defend from an unpredictable enemy (which in my case is body chemistry and ancient shame).

In the biblical letter to the Ephesians, Paul warns of difficult times. Early Jesus-followers were persecuted, arrested, and murdered, so Paul's giving a heads-up. His advice isn't to take up arms and slaughter the infidels, nor is it to take an AR-15 into a crowd. Paul tells them to suit up in truth, and righteousness, and faith, and salvation and whatever will get them ready to proclaim the good news of peace.

The only offensive weapon Jesus-followers are to use is Spirit-inspired words. Lest we think that means we should bludgeon people with the Bible, Paul explains that he means prayer, and petition, and declaring the good news of God With Us—the gospel of peace.

Each day, before I get dressed in pre-coffee black or a blazer and belt, maybe I should spend a few minutes with God, the only security my soul really needs.

—EOR

How do you prepare your mind and soul for hard days?

COMMON 5

Little children, keep yourselves from idols. —1 John 5:21

By now you know that God isn't terribly worried that you're going to pick up a statue of Thor and prostrate yourself before it, no matter how cute the guy who plays him in the movies is.

God knows you understand that rain is a function of atmosphere, not a gift from Tlaloc, so if you want to have a pen-and-ink of that Aztec god you just go right ahead.

Those aren't your problem idols, are they? They aren't the ones that are going to distract you from God.

My child is currently worshiping her rationality and independence. When she wants something, particularly if her parents don't approve, she turns to Logic and Belligerence in the hopes that They will bestow her desires upon her. Since she cannot see that God is perfectly fine with rationality and independence she's holding tightly onto God's nonexistence.

My own idol tends to be Self-Sufficiency. When I'm running on my own power I feel invulnerable, so I'll just give a little wave to God as I race by. Even when I start running out of steam, or smack into a wall of reality, my first impulse is to give myself a "You Got This" speech rather than reaching out to the One who never left my side.

Our idols are the images we cling to even when they don't serve us. Our idols can be self-images or ideas about others or the world.

Conspiracy theorists cling to the idols of Persecution and Inside Information. White supremacists have a whole pantheon, including Victimization. Liberal Christians can place Deconstruction (among other things) between themselves and God, just as Evangelicals tend to bow to Certainty and Paternalism.

Saying no to idols means retraining our thinking, accepting our vulnerability, and like little children, being curious rather than condemning. Having regular spiritual practices that right-size both God and others help, as do honest friends and good therapists.

But to keep yourself from idols you have to start with the question below.

—EOR

What do you cling to instead of the God of love and peace?

COMMON 6

And your life will be brighter than the noonday; its darkness will be like the morning.
—Job 11:17

You know the story of Job: He lost his wife and kids. Lost his flocks and his wealth. His friends turned on him. He got very, very sick.

He went from being a pillar of his community to being pitied. He had every right to feel as though he'd been exiled to darkness. I mean, wouldn't you?

Even in the midst of his suffering and grief, he held as tightly as he could to God's reassurance.

"Your darkness will be like the morning."

For me, darkness has been depression, a daunting mountain of debt, and a lack of self-confidence that left me afraid of almost everything. I was not as certain as Job that God would meet me on the other side of my troubles. But eventually, with help, I was able to see what my life looks like in the morning. And of course, God was there.

If you find yourself in darkness, God wants you to know that you are not weak or faithless for feeling unsafe, unsure, or afraid. Neither have you wandered off so far that God has given up on finding you, and reaching you.

Overcoming your darkness does not require superhuman faith. Instead, it starts with refusing to believe God is to blame for where you are or what you face. It also relies on you believing that God deeply loves and treasures you.

When you can begin to see yourself as loved and lovable—and God as your Protector and Champion—then light will begin its way through the cracks.

—BKS

When have you found yourself in darkness?
When did you realize your darkness was becoming morning?
If you still feel overcome by darkness, what is one thing you can do—or ask for help with—that could move you closer to morning?

COMMON 7

Now when Simon saw that the Spirit was given through the laying on of the apostles' hands, he offered them money, saying, "Give me also this power so that anyone on whom I lay my hands may receive the Holy Spirit." —Acts 8:18-19

Spoiler alert: Simon's offering money to Jesus' disciples Peter and John in exchange for spiritual powers doesn't end well.

And while in his tiny tirade Peter curses the money he's been offered, I don't think the money was the problem. Jesus' disciples were dependent upon offerings in order to continue traveling, teaching, and healing. Money *per se* had no moral encumbrances.

Money is neither good nor bad. In fact, money is exchange-worthy only because we agree it is. If tomorrow the world decides that cat hairballs are better for transactions than paper, coin, or electronic packets, hairballs will become valuable.

In first-century Palestine, most people didn't have much money so having some was actually pretty cool, just like it is now.

Where Simon went wrong was in thinking that a) Peter and John could convey spiritual power, b) the Holy Spirit was manipulable, and c) the spectacle of receiving the Holy Spirit was the point.

Simon wanted power to control others by utilizing the Spirit, as if She were no more than a special effect, like a smoke machine at a magic show.

God's power belongs to God, not the human being through whom it flows. The disciple Peter made a lot of mistakes, but thinking that God's power was really *his* power wasn't one of them. He must have been appalled at the idea that he, Peter, had anything of God's he could just hand over.

God chooses to work through us only when our egos aren't in the way. Anything the Spirit did through Peter and John She did because they knew they weren't the ones doing it.

If you see a politician or doctor or evangelist or musician acting as though they and the Spirit are in cahoots you can assume that, really, all the credit belongs to them.

Or if your pastor's sermons bring down the house but his daily doings are less than savory, he's doing it all on his own. No God involved.

Or, if some daily miracle happens and you start to think that maybe you brought it on, through prayer or candle-lighting or tithing, you might want to just stop to say thank you to the Spirit who is wiser than you are, and is never, ever, for sale.

—EOR

When have you been inclined to be impressed with spiritual special effects, rather than the steady goodness of a life lived with God?

COMMON 8

For surely I know the plans I have for you, says the Lord, plans for your welfare and not for harm, to give you a future with hope. —Jeremiah 29:11

I've turned to Jeremiah 29:11 many times to steady myself when life has felt uncertain.

You see, I'm an Enneagram Six, which means I like to know what's coming. I don't enjoy surprises. I have contingencies for my contingencies should things go sideways.

To me, the Unknown doesn't feel like an adventure—it feels like an abyss.

I've been offered things before that sounded too good to be true—and they were. I've been promised prosperity and success that never came to be. I've trusted the wrong people and wound up in debt, brokenhearted, and scared.

As a result, I've learned to not trust people too quickly.

Over time, I've developed a lack of trust in myself too, especially when the stakes seem high, or when others could be hurt by my decisions.

But when I read Jeremiah 29:11, I remember that God's hands are bigger than mine, and I am safe in them. I remember that God wants (and intends) good things for me.

In other words, I remember that God can be trusted.

God doesn't promise us lives without pain, grief, or conflict. Neither does God assure us of material wealth or success.

What God does desire for us is that we flourish, and grow into people who are kind, loving, joy-filled, and at peace. God wants us to live in light, and to be light.

Disappointment, fear, and grief will always be difficult to face. But I'm learning that our trustworthy, faithful God will be beside me again and again, always desiring my best.

—BKS

How would you live if you truly hoped?

COMMON 9

Be strong and courageous; do not be frightened or dismayed, for the Lord your God is with you wherever you go. —Joshua 1:9

Moses was dead. The Israelites were about to cross the Jordan River and enter the land that God had promised them, which meant they would have a battle on their hands. Joshua, their new leader, had many reasons to feel dismayed.

Have you ever felt dismayed?

Dismay is defined as a "sudden or complete loss of courage; utter disheartenment; sudden disillusionment; (and/or) agitation of mind" (Thanks, Dictionary.com)

You might be dismayed when your spouse tells you they want a divorce. Or when your boss tells you your job has been eliminated. Or when you're facing your own battle—with addiction, disease, anxiety, you name it.

It's hard to be strong and courageous all the time. And if all we have to go on is what we can see and feel, what lies ahead of us can seem insurmountable.

God reassured Joshua, saying (something like), "You've got this. Do all the things you've been practicing. Follow My lead. I'm with you."

God reassures us too, in much the same way. Doesn't mean the next, best step is an easy one. Doesn't mean that it won't take time to regroup, recover, and heal.

But it does mean that, because God is with us, we can draw strength and courage from God. We can act with confidence based on a history of how faithful God has been when we've faced difficult odds before.

—BKS

When have you felt dismayed? How did you summon the strength and courage to move ahead? What does that tell you about God and yourself?

COMMON 10

By the tender mercy of our God, the dawn from on high will break upon us, to give light to those who sit in darkness and in the shadow of death, to guide our feet into the way of peace. —Luke 1:78-80

Sometimes I want to sit in darkness. I want to put on my headphones and soak in *Pretty Hate Machine* (Nine Inch Nails) or *Folklore* (Taylor Swift)—whichever resonates.

I want to sit with my righteous anger, self-pity, and indignation. I want to answer insult with insult, and be as mean and hurtful to those who oppose me as they've been to me and those I care about.

But since tweeting my ire isn't Jesus-like, I close my curtains, throw covers over my head, and feel everything. I don't want peace. I want justice.

I know. Dramatic.

But after a while, daylight inevitably finds the cracks in my blinds. I reluctantly begin to admit to myself that I might not be altogether right, or fair, or kind. I remember that justice isn't something I dole out, just something I pray for.

Then head down, tongue held, I inch my way back to pursuing the way of peace.

Sure, we say we want peace. The problem is we also want to be right. And chasing peace means laying down our right to be right. It means putting others first too, which is also hard.

So how do we choose dawn over darkness?

Living like Jesus requires us to open our minds, our hearts, and our hands. So that when we speak up, it's for the least of these, the defenseless, and the wronged. And we do so with love, not hate.

—BKS

When have you sat in darkness with your back to the Light? How did you find your way back to the way of peace?

COMMON 11

Then the Lord God said, "It is not good for man to be alone" —Genesis 2:18

I'm lucky. I live with good friends. We laugh, watch Netflix together, enjoy cocktails on the patio, dance in the kitchen, go for walks, and marvel at sunsets.

It is good to have friends around. Family too. (Sometimes they're the same people.)

When God made Eve as a companion for Adam, God knew that we would be prone to loneliness. We need laughter, deep (and not-deep) conversation, physical touch, and other shows of affection, empathy, and love. It's how we were made.

COVID-19 challenged us in many ways. The isolation it forced upon many of us was devastating. Church moved online. Our jobs moved home. Schools went virtual. Vacations, weddings, and graduations all got canceled.

For some, loneliness, fatigue, and depression weighed heavily. There was a pervasive sense of uncertainty and dis-ease. Some of us became sick, or knew others who did. Some suffered deep loss. And the isolation lingered.

Its effects—the grief and trauma—will be with us for a very long time.

Because of the pandemic, I've discovered a greater appreciation for singing with other people, watching a movie in a theater, enjoying a live concert, even eating at a restaurant.

I won't ever again take for granted the time I get to spend with people who make me think, laugh, and become better.

Fact is, we need each other. Sometimes that means we reach out, anyway we can. And sometimes it means we take an outreached hand.

—BKS

What did you learn about yourself—what you needed, what you missed—during the lockdowns of COVID-19? How has it changed the way you relate to other people and to God?

COMMON 12

Finally, brothers and sisters, whatever is true, whatever is noble, whatever is right, whatever is pure, whatever is lovely, whatever is admirable—if anything is excellent or praiseworthy—think about such things. —Philippians 4:8

We are what we think.

Most self-help books tell us that, to change our lives, we have to change what we tell ourselves, what we let into our minds, and what we do with what we know.

I recognize that I more easily and clearly focus on God when I feed my mind with excellent, praiseworthy things that aren't, by nature, polarizing.

I mean, does anybody sling hateful rhetoric at redwoods, or daisies, or red pandas?

All that thinking on good things leads to one thing—truth.

I'm not a philosopher, but the concept of truth, to me, has always seemed straightforward. Truth is what is true—that is, what agrees with fact or objective reality.

I guess the big problem with nailing down what is true these days is that we often can't seem to agree on what the facts are, or whether reality can even be objective.

Spend 15 minutes on Twitter or Facebook away from your "friends" and it'll become clear that we don't all agree on what's true. Or much of anything else.

Dr. Martin Luther King, Jr. accepted the Nobel Peace Prize in 1964 and in his remarks, he said, "I believe that unarmed truth and unconditional love will have the final word."

There is something pure, lovely, and admirable about the idea of unarmed truth. It has nothing to prove and needs no defender. It simply (and powerfully) is.

Maybe it's naive, under the specter of fake news and alternative facts, to think that we could all embrace one truth. But what if embracing that one truth, instead of twisting facts and creating realities that serve us, could save us from injustice, poverty, and more?

—BKS

What makes something true? What would it take for us to pursue God's honest truth, without self-serving arguments, motives, and politics?

COMMON 13

For his anger is but for a moment; his favor is for a lifetime. Weeping may linger for the night, but joy comes with the morning. —Psalm 30:5

Sometimes the night lasts for days, weeks, years.

Ask the woman who finally gets an all-clear after two years of hoping, praying, and chemo. Ask the man who's still struggling to keep a roof over his family's heads ten months after losing his job.

Consider the seasons of your own life when you seriously questioned, "Will things ever get better?"

During my longest night, I faced divorce, debt, and depression. There was some weeping, but mostly there was jaw-clinching, smile-forcing, and prayer-pleading.

In the beginning, I suspected that God might be mad at me. I knew I was mad at myself, and guilt and shame had me by the shoulders. But soon I realized it was God's favor that was sustaining me. It was God's encouragement that helped me hang on till morning.

Nehemiah 8:10 says "The joy of the Lord is your strength." I don't think I understood that until I believed I'd run out of strength, stamina, and options. When I finally (really) believed that God was in my corner, I began to see the sun peek over the horizon.

If you're in the middle of one of those will-this-ever-end nights, know that God is not mad at you. In fact, God treasures you like a Parent treasures their child. It is God's desire that we all live rich, full lives, where joy is the rule, not the exception.

—BKS

Where are you finding joy today?

COMMON 14

O give thanks to the Lord, for he is good; for his steadfast love endures forever. Let the redeemed of the Lord say so, those he redeemed from trouble and gathered in from the lands, from the east and from the west, from the north and from the south.
—Psalm 107:1-3

Psalm 107 tells of a reality where wanderers find welcome. Where the hungry are fed. Where those in darkness find light. Where the poor in spirit are raised up and the powerful are brought down.

Where springs of water appear in the desert.

I drove across the New Mexico desert when I moved to California a couple years ago. I was fascinated by how life persists in an environment that, on the surface, appears to be so antagonistic to it.

I kinda feel like most of us live in a desert most of the time. Where there are forces that make welcoming wanderers and helping the Light-deprived harder than it should be.

Justice, or even fairness, for the downtrodden is often out of the question. And the powerful? Their wealth and influence grow at the expense of those with less already.

But the question occurs to me: In the desert where I live, what if I'm meant to be the spring?

What if we're all meant to be springs? Watering desert places by standing up to bullies, opening doors for outsiders, and caring for the impoverished, all while drawing from the Source of all life?

We can help usher in a Psalm 107 reality now. By learning to live as Jesus did through spiritual practices such as prayer, hospitality, and self-denial. We can choose to give life rather than destroy it.

And when we pray "Your will be done on earth as it is in heaven," we can be the answer to that prayer ourselves.

—BKS

What is one way (or maybe three) that you can be a spring in the desert where you live?

COMMON 15

I cry to God Most High, to God who fulfills his purpose for me. —Psalm 57:2

I grew up in a church that stressed the importance of walking in God's will. So much so that I was sure if I stepped outside of God's will, I would most certainly be doomed to hell.

This was made even more frightening because I believed God had a *specific* plan for my life that I was expected to follow to the letter. A purpose that I had to discover. Like a cryptograph in an escape room or a Dan Brown novel.

I made the assumption, as a 16-year-old boy feeling *called* to do *something* by God, that I ought to study and become a pastor. (Felt like a safe bet.) So I enrolled at the nearby college my denomination supported, and majored in pre-seminary religion.

It did not take me long to figure out that I wasn't cut out to be a religion major. I came to understand that a calling need not be pastoral or even vocational. Turns out God's will isn't a blueprint I am expected to figure out and follow.

What God cares about is how I live my life. Do I make choices that are life-giving? Am I concerned about the things God is concerned about? Do I practice living like Jesus did?

By the way, I'm not meant to do any of that without the Holy Spirit's guidance and help. That's why I can cry to God, and expect a response, when I feel like I'm struggling to fulfill—or even find—my purpose.

—BKS

Have you cried out to God for help living out your purpose? What happened?

COMMON 16

Therefore, since we are surrounded by so great a cloud of witnesses, let us also lay aside every weight and the sin that clings so closely, and let us run with perseverance the race that is set before us —Hebrews 12:1

In the video for one of my favorite Taylor Swift songs, *Shake It Off*, Taylor is a terrible dancer surrounded by world-class performers. She bumbles through ballet, streamer dancing, hip-hop moves, and modern dance. It's pretty hilarious.

In spite of her awkwardness, she is unflustered as she repeatedly sings "shake it off." By the time she reaches the last chorus, she is flailing about with other nerds like herself in a joyous free-for-all.

Perseverance is kind of like that.

To persevere is to press on, no matter what difficult thing lies ahead. Even with God by our side, we may feel outnumbered or outclassed. We may look ungraceful and awkward. We will certainly get tired, often discouraged.

Persevering often means changing our old (ineffective, unhealthy) way of doing something to try a new (uncomfortable, even painful) approach. It might also mean humbling ourselves, asking for help, or closing a chapter so we can write a new one.

In the midst of all this pressing on, it helps to have people who love us, believe in us, and pray for us—people who have faced down their own struggles and made it to the other side. Like own cloud of witnesses.

One more thing to remember: We live alongside others who are going through their own hard stuff. They are doing their best to hold it together. Like us.

—BKS

When have you had to persevere? What were the challenges in front of you and how did you overcome them?

COMMON 17

I have learned to be content with whatever I have. I know what it is to have little, and I know what it is to have plenty. —Philippians 4:11b-12

A few years ago, I owned a business. Sometimes when the business was floundering, I would use my personal credit cards to pay for things it needed. I also charged my own necessities when the business couldn't pay me.

In other words, I leaned on my credit cards. A lot. My debts mounted quickly. So did my stress.

Meanwhile, standing on a street corner near my business, Shawn sold newspapers. He'd been homeless and had served prison time in a previous life. Shawn had a big, contagious laugh, and never met a stranger. He was saving up to buy a car and to start a t-shirt business.

Considering where he had risen from, Shawn would say he had plenty—enough money to pay for his one-room transitional apartment and food and bus fare. What more did he need?

Sometimes, like Shawn, I recognize what I have with gratitude.

Other times, I fixate on what I don't have, and I get resentful and envious.

Like when I was living in my parents' basement, working all the time, and not seeing an end to my financial struggles. Even though I always had everything I needed (and much more), I sometimes got grumbly about my three jobs, my out-of-control finances, and my living arrangement. Until someone like Shawn came along to remind me how good I had it.

Contentment is intentional. We naturally want more. Choosing to be satisfied takes retraining in the form of spiritual practice. But choosing to not spend, covet, and consume leads to contentment. And, from where I sit now, content is a pretty great thing to be.

—BKS

If you aren't content, what's holding you back? (Hint: it's not outside you.)

COMMON 18

And the people of Nineveh believed God; they proclaimed a fast, and everyone, great and small, put on sackcloth. —Jonah 3:5

Nineveh was a city with lots of people who were prone to wickedness. Jonah was a disobedient prophet who had just been discharged from a whale's belly. Seems like the makings of a Netflix comedy—stinky, skinny prophet shows up on Madison Avenue with a megaphone. (Cue the antics.)

But what happened in Nineveh is quite amazing.

First, Jonah actually went to Nineveh. Granted, it took a whale of a storm and a whale of a … *whale* … to convince him. But he went. And he didn't go alone. I mean, who pays any attention to a sidewalk prophet?

Second, the Ninevites believed Jonah's warnings that God would destroy them in 40 days if they didn't stop being so wicked. So clearly, there were other, bigger forces at work. The ears and hearts of Nineveh were already open to Jonah's message, before he even showed up.

So the Ninevites repented in sackcloth, and fasted. And God had mercy on their city.

I had a pastor once who often said something like, "Nobody turns to Jesus without the Holy Spirit first getting their attention." I believe that is true.

The Holy Spirit has a way of preparing us to hear what we're about to hear. I've also heard, "The Holy Spirit doesn't go where (s)he isn't welcome," which implies that we can opt not to be open to what God wants to say to us.

I think the lesson in this for me is this: Don't be afraid to be Jonah—God doesn't send us anywhere without going ahead of us first. And always be open to what God might be wanting to tell me, like, in this case, the folks in Nineveh.

—BKS

When has the Spirit used you to deliver a message? When have you been the recipient of a word from the Spirit that someone unexpected gave to you?

COMMON 19

They were astounded at his teaching, for he taught them as one having authority, and not as the scribes. —Mark 1:22

I've had classes with teachers who were born to teach. They love their subject and know it well. When light bulbs start popping up over their students' heads, they get super-excited.

I've also had teachers who phone it in. They talk like they're experts on a subject, but then leave it up to a textbook to teach it. Instead of inspiring A's, they threaten F's.

I learn a lot more from teachers who love to teach.

I get the sense that Jesus loved to teach. We know that he was hanging out in the temple as a kid, astounding the old guys with his knowledge. Even more impressive than what he knew was the confidence—the authority—with which he shared his knowledge.

Jesus *knew* what he was talking about because he *knew* his Father. It's the difference between knowing *about* someone and actually *knowing* someone.

I mean, from whom would you rather learn about Barack Obama—me or Michelle Obama? Michelle, hands down. She *knows* him and can talk about him in ways I can't begin to.

Jesus knew God in a way the scribes and Pharisees didn't. He was truly an authority on the Subject.

And like all great teachers, Jesus gives us—his students—what we need to be experts on the Subject too. By putting into practice the spiritual disciplines Jesus modeled for us, we can become more like him and have a relationship with God that looks a lot like his.

—BKS

Think back on great teachers you've had. How did they inspire you as well as teach you? Who is teaching and inspiring you today?

226

COMMON 20

In the same way, let your light shine before others, so that they may see your good works and give glory to your Father in heaven. —Matthew 5:16

I don't enjoy being the center of attention. I tend to be more of a nerdy wallflower in the world, watching the class clowns, student body presidents, and homecoming queens fight for the stage.

I often deflect the spotlight. But there is such a thing as too much humility.

In the verse that precedes this one, Jesus says, "No one after lighting a lamp puts it under the bushel basket, but on the lampstand, and it gives light to all in the house."

All of us have things we excel in, whether we recognize, embrace, and share them, or not. Some people love the lamp stand, while others (like me) are tempted to head for the basket. But who gains the benefit of our awesomeness if we keep it hidden?

Inspirational author Marianne Williamson in her book, *A Return To Love*, says it well: "We are all meant to shine, as children do. We were born to make manifest the glory of God that is within us. It's not just in some of us; it's in everyone. And as we let our own light shine, we unconsciously give other people permission to do the same. As we are liberated from our own fear, our presence automatically liberates others."

When you allow your light to shine, you inspire and motivate me to shine too. When you excel, I'm reminded that excellence is possible. When you thrive, I want to thrive.

God doesn't give any of us gifts to keep for ourselves. We are meant to share them, for the good of all of us.

—BKS

How will you share your light today?

COMMON 21

We know that all things work together for good for those who love God, who are called according to his purpose. —Romans 8:28

When I was a baby, I quickly learned there was a difference between "good" and "good for me." Pudding is good. Peas are good for me. I like things that are good. I tolerate things that are good for me.

That hasn't changed all that much.

I enjoy comfort. I'm into warm San Jose winters, broken-in jeans, and brunch. I'm less into exercise, kale, and dental checkups.

Sure, I understand that good-for-me things are important. They lower my cholesterol, build my character, blah, blah, blah. Doesn't mean I enjoy them when they're happening.

Romans 8:28 doesn't promise pudding. It does assure us that things work for our good when we make God's priorities our priorities. In other words, deferring our desires to God's.

Spiritual practices like fasting train us to want differently. They teach us to hold more loosely to material things and to think before indulging short-lived satisfaction that might prove problematic in the long run.

Spiritual practices help us think and act more like Jesus.

So while there are things I enjoy that aren't inherently bad (Milano cookies are the new pudding), I've learned that my life is richer because of the good-for-me things I partake in.

—BKS

What is a "good" thing that you could trade for a "good-for-me" thing for the good of your spiritual health?

COMMON 22

Be angry but do not sin; do not let the sun go down on your anger. —Ephesians 4:26

Sure, I get angry. But as a nice Christian, I feel conflicted about it and unsure how to express it.

When Christians talk about anger, they often point to Jesus upending the vendors' tables in the temple. Jesus was upset that this house of prayer had been turned into a flea market. He didn't hold back, calling the vendors "robbers" (Matthew 21:12-13). Surely if gentle Jesus can express anger, Christians can—and sometimes should—too.

But other Christians point to the Beatitudes, those verses in Matthew where Jesus talks about who is blessed. He mentions "the meek", "the peacemakers", and "the merciful."

He also says "Blessed are you when people revile you and persecute you and utter all kinds of evil against you falsely on my account" (Matthew 5:11). He goes on to say we should rejoice when that happens, because we will be rewarded in heaven.

The Apostle Paul puts it simply: Get angry, then get over it.

Anger is a natural, even primal, response to fear. It is sometimes reasonable and justified. But if we sit with anger long enough, it can become a more insidious creature like hate or revenge, or lead to lasting feelings of sadness or depression.

That's why dealing with it in the moment is so important.

We will get angry again. But next time, instead of telling ourselves to get over it or feeling guilty for feeling angry, I want to challenge us to ask the question below.

—BKS

Ask yourself when needed: "Why am I feeling this way? What is the real reason for my anger, also known as fear? How can I deal meaningfully with <u>that</u>?"

COMMON 23

Therefore I tell you, do not worry about your life, what you will eat or what you will drink, or about your body, what you will wear. Is not life more than food, and the body more than clothing? —Matthew 6:25

Why's it so hard to be fully present ... in the present?

My thoughts tend to jump ahead to what's around the corner or replay what happened yesterday, or last summer, or when I was 10. Sometimes they just take off to some other place, like wherever my kids are, or Hawaii.

Sitting still in a moment—paying attention to the chair I'm sitting in, the smell of soup cooking in the kitchen, the sound of kids laughing outside, my own breathing—takes real effort.

I blame worry for much of my distraction.

It's usually low-grade worry, not the hand-wringing kind. But it can be worry over serious things like money (do I have enough?), dating (when will I be ready for another relationship?), family (what do my kids really think of me?), and other life questions like "when will the pandemic finally be over?" and "would I rather have flight or mind control as my superpower?"

All those existential worries aren't going to go away, but I can be intentional about putting them aside while I write this post to enjoy how sitting by the fireplace in this comfy chair feels.

With practice, worrisome thoughts can become a smaller and smaller part of what occupies my mind.

It helps to remember that God's much-bigger hands are holding my future, my kids, and everything else I care about. After all, my needs are met. Most of my desires are too. So really, what do I have to worry about anyway?

—BKS

What are some worries you have? How might you practice trusting God (and others) to take care of those things?

COMMON 24

If a prophet, or one who foretells by dreams, appears among you and announces to you a sign or wonder, and if the sign or wonder spoken of takes place, and the prophet says, "Let us follow other gods" (gods you have not known) "and let us worship them," you must not listen to the words of that prophet or dreamer... It is the Lord your God you must follow, and him you must revere. Keep his commands and obey him; serve him and hold fast to him. —Deuteronomy 13:1-3a, 4

A real prophet is someone who sees the big picture, who notices things most other people don't. Prophets are truth-tellers and sometimes that means they bring warnings. They can see that if a troubling situation or trend continues, its outcome could be damaging, even devastating.

For example, Greta Thunberg, the Swedish climate activist, works to educate the public on climate change. She points out what will happen if we don't change our climate-threatening behaviors. She is a prophet because she draws attention to what many of us don't want to see, and points to what the consequences of our ignorance or denial will be.

Prophets can be powerful. False prophets can be dangerous.

Many committed Christians have been led astray because a false prophet convinced them a lie was truth. Most of us know professing Jesus-followers who, because of false prophecies (conspiracy theories, made-up news, twisted half-truths, and other fear tactics) are behaving in ways that are anything but Jesus-like.

It is surprisingly easy to be misled by someone who knows what to say to get the action or reaction they want. We've seen politicians, public figures, and pastors who were masterful at getting their followers to believe something and then to act on it. Even when that something was absurd or evil.

So how do we guard ourselves against false prophets?

By learning to recognize the voice of God.

How do we do that?

By spending time with God in solitude and prayer, like Jesus did.

When we know what God sounds like—what God would (and would never) say—then we will less likely fall for the lies of a false prophet.

—BKS

A practice to try:

If you avoid silent retreats, thinking you'll be anxious, bored, or fighting your "demon voices" consider this: you may need more time alone with God to get over it, rather than less. Try a half day away, somewhere quiet, without distraction of a book or phone or dog. If anxiety rises, notice it with curiosity, then offer it to God's care. When it happens again, do it again. Cry if you want. Yell. Run. Do be safe, but don't let the feelings scare you. Over time, exposing your soul to quiet and God will give you healing.

COMMON 25

The fear of the Lord is the beginning of wisdom; all those who practice it have a good understanding. —Psalm 111:10a

Solomon was a very wise man. Even before God granted him wisdom, the king did a wise thing by asking God to make him wise. He could've asked for the death of his foes or a long, prosperous life, but he didn't (which made God very happy, by the way).

In asking for wisdom, Solomon acknowledged that God was God and he was not. That's when wisdom begins for us too.

The nemesis of wisdom isn't ignorance or stupidity—it's arrogance.

God gives wisdom to the humble, the mistake-makers, and the overcomers—not the know-it-alls, the braggarts, and the bullies. I mean, if I have my sh*t together, why do I need wisdom?

Arrogance makes us think more of ourselves than we ought. Conversely, it causes us to see others—even God—as smaller than we ought. That's why calling yourself wise is a sure sign you're not.

Wisdom comes from falling down and getting back up. It comes from persevering.

The wisest people I know have years of life-learning under their belts, and they have scars to show for it.

I hope to be wise one day. And if I ever am, I hope I'm wise enough to never realize it.

—BKS

Who do you know that's wise? How do you think they got that way?

COMMON 26

Rejoice always. —1 Thessalonians 5:16

In modern English, to rejoice is to feel and show great joy or delight.

Rejoicing sometimes comes easily to me. Like when life is going exactly the way I want—when I feel over-the-moon happy, overwhelmingly positive, and maximally encouraged.

Like maybe 2% of the time (if I'm being optimistic).

The kind of rejoicing Paul is talking about here has nothing to do with how things are going or how we are feeling.

To truly rejoice is to treasure the joy we have found as children of our loving God, even when our circumstances may be decidedly joyless. Like when you don't get the job, but you know that, because you're cherished by God, you will be fine with whatever God provides in its place.

That kind of rejoicing requires spiritual practice. We must retrain our minds, souls, and spirits to reach beyond our go-to emotional responses when things aren't awesome.

One practice to try is beginning and ending every prayer by celebrating what you see God doing in your life, in your world, and among your people. Another is looking for beauty in not-obviously-beautiful places.

Anything that draws joy out into the open is a very good thing and gives us new reasons to rejoice.

—BKS

A practice to try:
In your journal or in the space below, write 10 reasons to rejoice today.

COMMON 27

Pray without ceasing. —1 Thessalonians 5:17

Where my grandfather lives, there is a church that is attended by most everyone in his tiny community. It is where weddings and funerals happen, and baby showers, and 4th of July barbecues.

It is also where the prayer chain begins and ends. Neighbors call neighbors and needs are shared. Those on the chain commit to praying for every request, earnestly and often.

It is imperfect: asking for prayer on behalf of someone else can sound a lot like gossip. But it can also start to look like praying without ceasing. Multiple voices and hearts lifting up the same needs throughout the day and night.

I know prayer is important and I think I pray a lot. When I'm driving. When I'm talking a bath. When I'm falling asleep. Even so, I don't come close to praying without ceasing.

But I don't think constant talking to God is what Paul is suggesting.

You know what it's like when you're working a crossword puzzle on the couch while someone you love is reading a book in the armchair? You can share the quiet space and oxygen and also break the silence anytime with an observation, a chuckle, or a sigh. The interruption is always welcome.

I think the kind of prayer Paul is talking about is more like that. We share a space with God where we can talk anytime about anything. God is always available and eager to listen.

Prayer is an always-open opportunity to trust God with what's on our minds and hearts. It's much more about us than it is about God. So prayer becomes more of a never-ceasing approach to living.

—BKS

Why do you pray?
Write down the reason.

COMMON 28

Give thanks in all circumstances. —1 Thessalonians 5:18

Can you come up with five things you are thankful for right now? (Don't overthink it!)

Here are my five this morning:

The big, comfortable shirt I'm wearing that my middle son, Nick, gave me for Christmas

My laptop, which provides me with a means to work and be creative, a way to stay connected with the world, and a near-bottomless well of streaming entertainment

Coffee, which is helping part the sleepy fog I woke up in

The conversation with my Mom yesterday, which reminded me who I am and what's important

San Jose winters, which aren't like Tennessee winters.

Finding things to be thankful for isn't hard. And yet, practicing gratitude can be. Especially when I'm not feeling grateful.

When winter comes, I have to work a little harder at gratitude. The short days and long nights wear on me. I'm inclined to isolate, bury myself in blankets, and hole up till April. It's easy to forget how good I have it.

Jotting down five things I'm thankful for *today* gives me perspective, lifts my mood, and points me toward hope. Being grateful is sometimes the one thing that can get me out of my bed and out of my head.

—BKS

When is gratitude tough for you?

COMMON 29

You are the light of the world. A city built on a hill cannot be hid. —Matthew 5:14

We all have some shine in us. And shining is something we were made to do. But to be the "light of the world" takes a little something more.

I'm not the light of the world when I write a new song, or when I record it, or when I share it on Spotify.

I'm not the light of the world when I give someone who's hungry a five-dollar bill, or when I wish the checkout person at Whole Foods a good day.

I'm not even the light of the world when I lead a congregation in worship or tell a friend that God cherishes them.

Even though we were all made to shine, being the "light of the world" takes more shine than any of us has in our back pockets. What we can do is learn to follow in the steps of Jesus, the capital-L light of the world.

In John 8:12, Jesus says, "I am the light of the world. Whoever follows me will not walk in darkness, but will have the light of life."

We are light when we put others first, when we're patient and kind, and when we give more than we take.

We are light when we devote ourselves to prayer and live lives that are joy-filled and peaceable.

We are light when we allow God to shine through us.

—BKS

What is one small, practical way you can be light in your world today?

COMMON 30

For where your treasure is, there your heart will be also. —Matthew 6:21

It's true, you can tell what someone values by looking at how they spend their money. But that isn't the only way.

We spend time too.

We work a heckuva lot. Because of the pandemic, more of us than ever work from home, making life/work balance tough. I also work a lot. Four part-time jobs to be exact.

We're on our phones and devices a lot too. I'm on my phone more than I care to admit, scrolling Instagram, doing crosswords, watching YouTube, and checking email. I also text my friends and my kids and I occasionally call my Mom. That's a lot of phone time.

I meet up with friends occasionally, have dinner with my housemates, watch a little *Ted Lasso*, HGTV, or *Northern Exposure*. I take baths.

And I sleep.

That's mostly it. When I seriously examine how I'm spending my time, it doesn't feel particularly overindulgent. But it doesn't feel especially virtuous either.

I wonder what you'd think of how I spend my time.

—BKS

Be curious and observe: What do you fill your days with? What do you think it says about what you value?

COMMON 31

Whoever pursues righteousness and kindness will find life and honor.
—Proverbs 21:21

When I decided to follow Jesus as a kid, I didn't really know what that meant. Heck, plenty of adults don't really know what that means.

The church I grew up in would say that I'd be deciding to follow Jesus over and over my whole life. It was not a once-and-for-all kind of thing.

I disagree with that church on most things, but that's not one of them.

Pursuing righteousness is learning how to fall down and get back up. It's learning to say I'm sorry, then deciding to make a change and making it. It's being in the world, and yet separate from it. It's being kind to the person who just treated you unkindly.

Following Jesus is a choice I make over and over.

Pursuing righteousness means, with every do-over, we become more and more like the Jesus we chose to follow—the process my old church would call sanctification.

We find "life and honor," joy and meaning, when we walk in the ways of Jesus, choosing life over death, light over darkness, again and again.

—BKS

What does following Jesus mean to you? Why do you do it?

COMMON 32

The Lord is the everlasting God, the Creator of the ends of the earth. He does not faint or grow weary; his understanding is unsearchable. —Isaiah 40:28

Have you ever been (as we say in the South) dog tired? I understood from an early age when my dad said he was dog tired, it meant he'd had a hard day, a physically draining day, and he was just done.

I had one of those days recently. I was sore and exhausted from an unusually trying day at my barista job. I was emotionally spent too, languishing in a dark headspace, triggered by an emotional dream the night before, and a lack of solid sleep.

I was feeling beaten-down. Dog tired.

God has a bazillion reasons to be dog tired. But thankfully, God doesn't nod off like a sleep-deprived parent while we toddlers stick our fingers in wall sockets.

God's understanding is unsearchable—that is, God doesn't miss a thing. Not the external factors that we fight against, nor the internal demons we wrestle with. Because God misses nothing, we can trust our never-sleeping Parent to keep us safe.

This passage in Isaiah goes on to say, "those who wait for the Lord shall renew their strength."

Waiting for the Lord means trusting that God will revive our weary spirits and provide everything we need, as God sees fit.

—BKS

What makes you dog tired? What can you do to trust God to help or handle things when you've reached the end of your strength?

COMMON 33

For the gate is narrow and the road is hard that leads to life, and there are few who find it. —Matthew 7:14

Two roads diverged in a wood, and I—I took the one less traveled by,
And that has made all the difference.
—Robert Frost, The Road Not Taken

Any queer, closeted Christian understands the implications of the less-traveled path. Choosing it has the potential for devastating losses—friends, family, church.

For me, it was about losing a marriage, the love and respect of my kids, my career in Christian music, and my church—the things I got when I chose the well-traveled path.

The things I thought God considered more important. But I was wrong.

What God cared more about was my spirit—the part of me that connects to the Divine. It was threadbare and lifeless. God cared that I was suffering. God wanted me to have peace and joy that wasn't swallowed up by fear and anxiety.

Once I started to realize *that* I found the courage to choose the less-traveled path. It was hard and painful in some ways, and I did lose some things, including my marriage.

But I found another church, and a side gig there as a worship leader. I went from writing songs for the Christian market—the theology of which I was finding shallow and unsatisfying—to writing songs that are more true to my experience, and singing them myself.

My relationship with my kids got better, since I wasn't hiding all the time. And my faith, though it took some time, became stronger than ever.

I don't know what the narrow gate looks like for you. I don't know what choosing it will cost you. But I can say for me, choosing it has made all the difference.

—BKS

Have you chosen the less-traveled path? If so, what has that meant for you? If not, what's stopping you?

COMMON 34

Now the works of the flesh are obvious: fornication, impurity, licentiousness, idolatry, sorcery, enmities, strife, jealousy, anger, quarrels, dissensions, factions, envy, drunkenness, carousing, and things like these. I am warning you, as I warned you before: those who do such things will not inherit the kingdom of God.
—Galatians 5:19-21

We are fleshly creatures. We live in a physical world with physical bodies. Our flesh, in and of itself, is neither good nor bad. But in his letters to the various New Testament churches, the Apostle Paul points to "the flesh" when calling out anything that isn't of "the Spirit."

To live in the Spirit is to pursue God and to bear the fruits of the Spirit. When we don't pursue God, we are prone to living self-centered—and sometimes self-destructive—lives.

The list of character flaws and grievous deeds Paul lays out is long, but not exhaustive. I don't personally default to sorcery or carousing when I'm not living in the Spirit, but I do tend toward laziness and overindulgence. Maybe strife doesn't make *your* list but vanity is somewhere near the top.

The point is, I know when I'm not living in close connection to God. I know what my less-than-holy tendencies are.

Naming them, recognizing them when they show up, and getting to the bottom of why they're a problem are key to overcoming them.

And the more "fleshly" behaviors I conquer, the more I default to living in the Spirit.

—BKS

What are some of your fleshly tendencies? How do you feel when you're in control of them? How about when they are controlling you?

COMMON 35

By contrast, the fruit of the Spirit is love, joy, peace, patience, kindness, generosity, faithfulness, gentleness, and self-control." —Galatians 5:22-23

Just as we are fleshly creatures with bodies, we are also spiritual beings with spirits that connect us with the Divine Spirit.

Sometimes our physical cravings and our spiritual needs conflict. While satisfying our bodily desires is not necessarily (or inherently) bad, it will take precedence over tending to our spirits if we aren't mindful.

When I "live by the Spirit" (Gal. 5:25), I pay attention to what my spirit needs in order to be close to God, the Source of its peace and power. Choosing spirit over flesh requires retraining my mind and body through spiritual disciplines like fasting and patience-building. It isn't something I can do with my will alone—at least not sustainably.

When I live by the Spirit, my life bears fruit—just look at Paul's list.

Loving others—or willing their good—becomes more effortless. Understanding my worth in God's eyes makes it easier for me to receive love, and to have love for myself.

Joy and peace are the results of trusting God and being certain that God is with me, no matter what.

The other qualities—being patient, kind, generous, faithful, and gentle—benefit everyone I encounter, especially those closest to me. And living by the Spirit helps me keep my physical cravings in check.

—BKS

Think of a time when you felt very close to God. What were you doing to keep your physical and spiritual needs in balance? What practices helped you "live by the Spirit?"

COMMON 36

Finally, beloved, whatever is true, whatever is honorable, whatever is just, whatever is pure, whatever is pleasing, whatever is commendable, if there is any excellence and if there is anything worthy of praise, think about these things. —Philippians 4:8

My mood is easily influenced by music. When I listen to Dua Lipa's *Future Nostalgia*, I feel upbeat and empowered. When I listen to Taylor Swift's *Folklore*, I sink into melancholy. When I put on classical music, I feel smart and cultured.

Changing what I'm feeding my mind can change my entire outlook.

In a former life, I listened to conservative talk radio. Of course, it impacted how I voted, but it also changed where I shopped (more Walmart, less Target), what I drove (a pickup), how I presented myself (less hair product, more flannel), and the people I hung around (white, suburban, evangelical).

Our thoughts become our beliefs when we act on them.

Over time, I started noticing how anxious, untrusting, and frustrated I was all the time. I realized how a steady diet of negativity had turned me into someone I didn't want to be. And worse, I saw how unlike Jesus I'd become.

I turned off Rush Limbaugh, traded the pickup, regained my sense of style, and opened my mind to new ideas. It took time, but I found peace and hope when I changed my thinking.

—BKS

Do you feel irritable, anxious, dissatisfied, unworthy, put-upon, or just plain unhappy? What kinds of news and entertainment are you consuming?
(If you don't know, try keeping a "consumption" journal for a week.)

COMMON 37

Anxiety weighs down the human heart, but a good word cheers it up. —Proverbs 12:25

Years ago, I owned a cafe in an office building. One of my regular customers, a woman who worked upstairs, was chronically unpleasant. I not-so-affectionately referred to her as Olga, a nod to her abrupt, stereotypically German personality. I mean, she threw an orange at the swinging door to my backroom to get my attention once.

Anyway, I learned from one of her co-workers that she had been battling cancer for some time. She was often in pain and her treatment was taking an emotional toll as well.

I learned her actual name and made an effort to chat with her whenever she came in. I kept her favorite pastry on hand. I shared little bits about myself. Pretty soon, she softened and I learned all about her daughter, who lived in Seattle with her wife, her husband and their dog, and of course, her fight with cancer.

We all encounter people who need kindness, whether they would ever ask for it or not. Sometimes the most prickly folks we run into are the ones who are hurting the most.

We can meet other people's anxiety and pain with negativity or we can choose to smile, listen, and encourage. Remember that sometimes, we're the ones who need a good word.

—BKS

When has someone met your physical or emotional pain with kindness?

COMMON 38

Just as I have loved you, you also should love one another. —John 13:34

We aren't born loving anyone but ourselves. As babies, all we care about is having our needs met and our discomforts eased. It's all we are capable of.

As we grow, we learn how to receive and show affection. We begin to feel the pull of attraction toward family, friends, people like us, and later, lovers. But affection and attraction aren't love.

When my son, Zach, was born, I knew instantly that I would step in front of a bus to save him. I'd forgo sleep, hand over all my discretionary income (okay, not all, but most), drive a minivan, and give up the tv if that meant he was happy and healthy. I'd still do all those things, and most anything else, for the good of my kids.

Love, the way Jesus is describing it here, is more like that. But it extends beyond my kids to everyone—even those I don't know and don't like.

Loving someone means willing their good, no matter what that requires of us. It also doesn't mean we get love—or anything else we want—in return.

In other words, love asks a lot of us.

Loving my kids is easy. Loving someone who criticizes, belittles, even hates me is hard.

That's why love is a choice, not a feeling. We are called to love each other even when we don't want to, even when our feelings would cause us to act without love.

—BKS

Throughout your life, who has taught you the most about what it means to love?

COMMON 39

Jesus took with him Peter and James and John, and led them up a high mountain apart, by themselves. And he was transfigured before them. —Mark 9:3

Jesus didn't share his (whole) story with everyone. It's not like most people would've believed it anyway. But when he knew the time was right, he took three of his closest friends—Peter, James, and John—up to a mountain and, well, came out.

I'd like to think Jesus was a bit nervous. I'm not convinced he knew how coming out as the Son of God would go.

When Moses and Elijah appeared—and who knows what the three of them were talking about—that had to be weird for everyone. And then God showed up and declared, "This is my Son, the Beloved. Listen to Him!" Doubly weird and probably more than a bit scary.

But Peter wanted to linger in the moment, asking if they could just build houses for Jesus, Moses, and Elijah and stay on the mountain. I'm sure Peter felt even closer to Jesus, being part of the inner-inner circle. And Jesus probably felt closer to his friends too.

It feels good to be known.

Anyone who has come out—as gay, Christian, Democrat, whatever—and felt accepted and loved understands that well. It also feels good to be trusted. Most of us have been Peter at least once in our lives.

Sometimes coming out is daunting and consequential. I get that. But we all benefit from one another's stories. Maybe it's time to share more of your story with someone you love and trust.

—BKS

When have you trusted someone with a part of your story that was hard for you to tell? How did it go?

COMMON 40

The light has come into the world, and people loved darkness rather than light because their deeds were evil. —John 3:19

There is strange comfort in darkness.

Like when you go through a breakup and all you want to do is cry in your pajamas while listening to sad songs on repeat. Eventually, most of us put away the ice cream, open the blinds, and take a shower. For some of us though, it's a bit more complicated.

It's true that some people love living in darkness. They don't want anyone to know what they're doing and they have no intention of changing their unhealthy, even nefarious, behaviors.

Some aren't in the darkness because they want to be, but because leaving it feels too hard, or even impossible. Ask someone who's in an abusive relationship with nowhere else to go.

For most of us though, darkness is a place we visit, where nothing is expected of us and no one can see what we're up to. Often, it's shame that leads us there.

But we were never meant for the darkness. We are called to live in the light, which takes effort, intention, and some self-denial.

Choosing light means also choosing self-respect, kindness, forgiveness, and love. And the Spirit empowers us to keep choosing light, which makes the Light even brighter.

—BKS

When was the last time you felt like lingering in the darkness? How did you find your way back to the light?

COMMON 41

I thank you that you have answered me and have become my salvation. The stone that the builders rejected has become the chief cornerstone. —Psalm 118:21-22

When I was 11 years old, at a summer camp in rural Tennessee, I gave my heart to Jesus.

At least that's what I thought I was doing.

The church where I grew up taught me that my soul's salvation depended on me making a choice to follow Jesus and no one else. It also taught me that the moment I disobeyed God, I'd be doomed for hell. My salvation was conditional. And complicated.

Thus began the ping pong match for my soul. Devil, Jesus, devil, Jesus.

Enter adolescence and hormones. Every time I noticed a boy, or a girl, and felt a tingle, I thought I'd failed God, and sent myself to hell again. That's a lot of pressure for a teenager, or anyone for that matter.

When I read the words of David—the divinely ordained, tender-hearted King of Israel who loved God, but sinned a little—I see someone who turned to God over and over again, not to avoid hell, but to reclaim who he was.

God never stopped being David's salvation.

I understand now that it's important that I keep choosing God. Not because I'm preoccupied with my afterlife, but because God gives me freedom from fear, self-doubt, and a host of other life-destroyers.

Turning to God reminds me who God is, and who I am.

—BKS

What does salvation mean to you? When have you needed to be reminded of who you are?

COMMON 42

To these four young men God gave knowledge and skill in every aspect of literature and wisdom; Daniel also had insight into all visions and dreams. —Daniel 1:17

It wasn't the vegetables that gave Daniel the ability to explain Nebuchadnezzar's dreams.

Or was it?

Daniel, on behalf of himself and his friends, Hananiah, Mishael, and Azariah (aka Shadrach, Meshach, and Abednego) asked if they could be served vegetables and water, instead of the food and wine served in Nebuchadnezzar's palace. King Neb's menu was outside what the boys' Jewish faith would allow them to eat.

This was a bold move because Daniel and his friends were at the mercy of a king who was hostile to Israelites.

God showed favor to Daniel and the king granted his request. As a result of their dietary differences, the young men became stronger and healthier than the others.

Nebuchadnezzar noticed them and gave them positions of honor in his palace, where God allowed them to flourish. That's when Daniel received his dream-decoding superpower.

It's true that sometimes just asking for what you want can get you punished, even killed.

Our best hope is that standing on convictions will change hearts and minds. Our last hope is that all will be well in the end because we did what God asked us to.

I'm not a disruptor by nature. But I know that sometimes, we have to push against the system in the name of what's right, fair, and just. And trust God for the outcome.

—BKS

When have you stood on your convictions? How did God come through for you?

COMMON 43

He reveals deep and hidden things; he knows what is in the darkness, and light dwells with him. —Daniel 2:22

I led worship at a progressive, affirming, inner-city church that was pastored by a gay, African-American man. During our Easter worship service in 2021, broadcast via Zoom, some strangers entered our virtual space and unleashed a prolonged racist, homophobic, anti-Semitic rage-rant.

Sadly, this kind of hate shows up in diverse faith communities a lot. Darkness creeps into sacred spaces, attempting to smother the light.

But the sad truth is, darkness doesn't need a terrorist to show it to its seat. We bring it in ourselves when we are intolerant, self-righteous, and unkind. We encourage it when we don't choose to be light.

Daniel reminds us that God reveals deep and hidden things. The Source of all light knows what's in the darkness. That includes the suffering that led to a violation of my church's sacred space.

God also understands the pain in everyone's heart, and what we are all capable of apart from the light.

Our hope is this: Those who dwell with God dwell in the light. Wisdom and power belong to God, and God gives knowledge to those who have understanding (v. 20-21).

Daniel received mercy from a disturbed tyrant, thanks to knowledge only God could've given him. And God empowers us too when we refuse to let our light be snuffed out.

—BKS

When have you faced the darkness? When have you chosen to be light?

COMMON 44

I do not judge anyone who hears my words and does not keep them, for I came not to judge the world, but to save the world. —John 12:47

For years we were in a church that was pro-gay but evangelifundy in sermon and Sunday school. So when my just-teenager asked, "Why would you run to a God who threatens to destroy you?" I bit my tongue and waited.

"Being Christian is about loving, but Everyone says God is going to send everyone else to hell unless they do what They tell them to do" she continued. "Why would you love that God?"

When she took a breath I didn't launch into my usual debunk-Christian-crap rant about humans liking to divide each other and learning about God from abusive parents and pastors. She knows all that.

I just waited.

"Wasn't that the whole point of Jesus?"

I'd like to report that I gave a pithy response that rescued her from existential despair. I'd like to give you a line that you can use anytime you run up against religious haters.

But you know better than that. You know that what people say can rob you of your sense of God's true love. You also know that trust in God doesn't come from what people say, but from how we behave.

Whether liberal or conservative, friends or family, queens or Queens; whether it's in our church or over dinner with our witty friends: if we run with a judgmental group, we're liable to wind up judgmental ourselves.

What we believe determines how we behave.

Jesus didn't just say that he wouldn't judge. Jesus actually didn't, not even those who wouldn't heed his words. Instead he opened his arms, again and again.

On that one day, rather than ranting I paused and got it right: I opened my arms, and for a split-second my hug-averse, God-doubting girl let herself be held.

—EOR

When you find yourself getting all judge-y, what can you do to re-open your mental arms?

COMMON 45

If we say that we have no sin, we deceive ourselves, and the truth is not in us.
—1 John 1:8

I'm not sure what a "high horse" actually is, but I know I've been on one a time or two. You know, when you get all arrogant and start preaching about someone else's behavior, often to direct attention away from your own?

We Christians get up on high horses a lot. We look down on others who don't share our views, or who just do things in a way we don't like. We act all holier-than-them, and enjoy the superiority. Happens among Episcopalians and Pentecostals alike, just not at the same dinner parties.

Thing is, most of us don't spend nearly as much time introspecting as we do critiquing and condescending. It's like what Jesus says about seeing the speck in someone's eye while missing the log in our own eye. We only see what we want to see. And our own sin is something we'd rather not examine too closely.

When we do admit to being less-than-holy, we might claim a mostly socially acceptable sin, without confessing anything too incriminating. Like coveting my best friend's vacation house, but never his husband. Or being a workaholic, but not an emotionally absent parent.

It's harder to judge others from a place of real humility.

When we say, or allow others to believe, that we are sinless, we are deceiving everyone, including ourselves, and the truth isn't in us. It would serve us Jesus-followers well to preach a lot less, and to be way more mindful of our actions. Remember: we are being watched too, and what we do can undermine someone's trust in a loving God.

—BKS

When is the last time you prayed for God to show you the life-destroying stuff in your own life?

COMMON 46

But whoever hates another believer is in the darkness, walks in the darkness, and does not know the way to go. —1 John 2:11

Before I moved to California, I spent a lot of time on Indeed and Google looking at worship jobs posted by churches here. Coming from conservative Tennessee, I just thought most West Coast congregations would be accepting of queer folks.

I was wrong.

I mean, I saw many postings from churches that advertised "all are welcome." But none of the families pictured on their websites had kids with two dads or two moms. Once I started digging, I discovered almost none of those churches were actually LGTBQ-affirming. I felt duped.

I have a good friend who has run into the same issue with churches that have theologically ambiguous names like The Quest, OmniSpirit, or Gravity Church. (One of those is actually affirming, but I bet you can't guess which one.) Why would a church be intentionally obscure about who they really are?

It seems some Christians consider the Great Commission a mandate to win all the souls they can, by whatever means available. As if hiding their true feelings about people who look, talk, or think differently than they do is okay, as long as it gets them in the doors. But what happens if these poor, misled seekers actually show up?

As Jesus-followers, doing and believing all the "right" things, whatever THAT means, isn't enough. If we don't love each other, none of the rest matters. We're just wandering around lost in the darkness.

—BKS

How can you welcome others who aren't like you into your life? How can you promote real acceptance among your people, and at your church?

COMMON 47

Do not love the world or the things in the world. The love of the Father is not in those who love the world. —1 John 2:15

There are things in the world that I love. Outrageous, I know, but it's true.

I love road trips to (almost) anywhere. I love cocktails at trendy bars. I love laughing at cat videos. I love talking politics with my grown-up kids. I love really good pizza. I love riding roller coasters. I love watching drum corps shows. I love writing songs.

Of course, when I say I love these awesome things, what I really mean is I enjoy them—that is, I find joy in the experience of them. I also find God in the things, people, and places that bring me joy. So finding joy in the world is not a bad thing.

However, when we *love* the world, we give it the devotion and adoration that God desires from us. We worship it. It's impossible to worship two things at once.

Some Christians put a pastor, a personality, or a President on such a pedestal that he or she becomes an object of worship. When our admiration for someone who isn't God causes us to do, or believe, things that are in opposition to what Jesus taught, or what the Bible teaches, it's a problem. Jesus-followers follow Jesus, not somebody else.

Same goes for ideas and philosophies, and more tangible things like career and family. While we can embrace these things, and find joy and fulfillment in them, it's important that our gratitude and worship belong to God, the Giver of all good things.

—BKS

How do you keep your love of this world in check? What does worship look like to you?

COMMON 48

Some Sadducees tried to corner Jesus with a convoluted question about death, marriage, and the afterlife. It's not too unlike some of the questions Christians pose today. Now it isn't that I oppose a spirited debate over what the Bible says about this or that. And of course, there are questions worth asking.

But here's the thing: it's rarely about the question. It's more about *why* we ask than *what* we ask.

I grew up in a church that had a lot of don't's. Don't dance, don't play cards, don't go to movies—the list is very long. As a kid, I used to think God was really just a cosmic score keeper, and that at the end of my life, a low score would send me to hell.

So I looked for loopholes, to make being a Christian feel a bit less oppressive. I asked questions like: "Is it dancing if my feet never leave the floor?" and "What if it's just Uno?"

Some get hung up on the minutiae of religiosity. What *must* I do, what *should* I do, and what *can* I get away with, and still go to heaven? It's all about the endgame. But what Jesus is saying here is, God is about the living, not the dead.

Yes, how we live our lives matters. But not because our afterlives are hanging in the balance. God is concerned about the quality of our lives now. Whether our actions and attitudes are life-giving, or life-destroying. It's less about the don't's and more about the do's.

—BKS

We experience heaven (life with God) and hell (life apart from God) in this life. What if you made choices based on the idea that you are already living in eternity? What would you do differently?

COMMON 49

Open the gates, so that the righteous nation that keeps faith may enter in.
—Isaiah 26:2

What would it look like if Christians were a "righteous nation"?

Throughout the Old Testament, God speaks to the Hebrews as a nation. While Jewish law required individuals to behave in certain ways, it was for the benefit of the entire community, in order to make them a different, set-apart, people.

Christians have never been a nation. Since the beginning, the capital-C Church has splintered repeatedly over opposing views on all kinds of things. There's are lots of historical reasons why we aren't all Catholics, or Baptists, or Lutherans.

Present-day Christians are more divided than ever. We all define and differentiate ourselves based on what we think about God, each other, how our culture should look and behave, and other things that aren't actually as critical as we think they are.

On occasion, groups of American Christians will come together in reaction to something like abortion or guns, but rarely do disparate Christians unite in meaningful ways to be *proactive* on something Jesus cared about.

For example, imagine if American Christians decided it was important to care for the poor. We could end poverty in this country without Congress having to agree on anything. With our resources, we could feed the hungry, house the houseless, employ the jobless.

But it would mean changing our priorities and setting aside our differences for the good of everyone.

—BKS

What are some ways you can encourage unity among the Christians in your life?

COMMON 50

Ah, Lord, great and awesome God...we have sinned and done wrong, acted wickedly and rebelled, turning aside from your commandments and ordinances. —Daniel 3:4-5

I was an evangelical for a long time. My spiritual life consisted of my personal relationship with God, and little else.

Liturgy, as I understood it, felt ancient and irrelevant. Church was there to give me a boost for my week with spirit-lifting music and friendly conversations—and a brief reprieve from guilt and shame. In short, all of it was all about me.

But God doesn't want it to be all about me.

God cares about *us*. All of us. I'm a part of us, and you're a part of us. When we go to God together, we begin to understand that we are a part of a much bigger us—the capital-C Church, the Bride of Christ, the people of God.

One of the powerful things we can experience as an us is confession. Corporate prayers of confession point out the ways we've missed the mark as a church, and they refocus us on what truly matters. Going to God together and confessing our life-destroying actions and attitudes gives life-giving perspective.

I still have a deep, personal relationship with God that—when tended to—satisfies my soul, fills my spirit, and gives me peace. But much of the hope I have comes from seeing my place at a huge table, where we all seek and find abundant life together.

—BKS

Do you see yourself as part of the capital-C Church? If not, what are some ways you might consider opening your life and your spirit to something bigger?

COMMON 51

Test me, Lord, and try me, examine my heart and my mind. —Psalm 26:2

I don't like being tested.

I know some people like the opportunity to show what they know. They find worth in beating expectations, ace-ing exams, and scoring high marks. I used to be one of those people.

But as I've gotten older, I put less stock in evaluations. I don't like having to prove myself. And most of the time, I'm not required to. At least not to other people.

You don't pray for God to test you unless you're ready for the answer.

You see, God isn't the boss who's watching your every move. Or the professor who enjoys seeing her students sweat through finals week. Or the parent who is hypercritical of his kid's grades, behavior, friends, and the rest.

Yes, it's important to make life-giving choices and to put more good into the world than we take. But it's not because God is waiting for us to fail, keeping track of our wins and losses, or giving us gold stars when we excel.

When I pray David's prayer, I'm asking God to hold up a mirror so I can see what's really going on with me—my thoughts, my doubts, my motivations, my compulsions. Why do I do the things I do? What or who am I worshipping? What is getting the best of my time, energy, and attention?

If I ask God to test me, it means I'm growing. And it means I'm willing to look closely at myself, and make changes, in order to be more like Jesus.

—BKS

When was the last time you prayed for God to examine your heart and mind? What did you learn? Is it time to pray David's prayer again?

COMMON 52

Truly I tell you, whoever does not receive the kingdom of God as a little child will never enter it. —Mark 10:15

When I was a kid, I created worlds for fun.

Sometimes they were idyllic small towns I'd crisscross with my Matchbox cars on the living room carpet. Sometimes they were bustling cities with shiny skyscrapers I'd conjure up as I rode my bike around our neighborhood. Sometimes they were far-flung galaxies complete with superheroes and perilous battles for the soul of the universe, inspired by comic books and Star Wars.

I can still imagine a Mayberry, a Metropolis, or a menace from outer space. But my ability to dream them into existence isn't what it used to be.

Kids have the capacity to believe incredible things. As we grow up, we start getting jerked around by adult realities and responsibilities. Experiencing that kind of wonder takes a lot more effort.

But it isn't impossible.

Approaching God with the wide-eyed wonder of a child means letting go of some things. Like needing to be right, or correct, all the time. Or leaping to defend the Bible, your church, or yourself when someone else's ideas about God are different from yours.

It means leaving room for possibilities. Imagining everything that could be. Trusting God the way a child trusts their Parent.

—BKS

What are some ways you could practice being childlike in the presence of God? And in the world?

COMMON 53

Humble yourselves before the Lord, and he will lift you up. —James 4:10

Merriam-Webster defines humility as "freedom from pride or arrogance."

C.S. Lewis once said, "Humility is not thinking less of yourself; it is thinking of yourself less."

Americans, as a culture, have a humility problem.

We see it clearly demonstrated in the absence of civility among our leaders, which encourages the populace to dismiss, insult, and belittle each other for all kinds of reasons. Some of the least humble voices are those of American evangelical Christians, whose actions (or inactions) are even louder than their words.

It's almost like we think humility is the opposite of strength and confidence. When that couldn't be farther from the truth.

Why do you think it is so hard for us to be humble?

Like other virtues that Jesus modeled for us, humility can be practiced.

By cleaning the office bathroom when you own the company.

By admitting you made a mistake.

By letting someone else talk and actively listening without interrupting.

By making sure others get acknowledged for the good they do.

By trusting that God will take care of you while you take care of someone else.

Humility is a state of being that we cultivate when we practice empathy, compassion, service, and trust. Humble is something every Jesus-follower should strive to be.

—BKS

What is one thing you can do to practice humility today? And tomorrow? And the next?

COMMON 54

Return to your rest, my soul, for the Lord has been good to you. —Psalm 116:7

I prayed for peace today. Not for the world, though it certainly needs it. I prayed for interior peace. For rest. For myself.

Lately, I've been feeling anxious, irritable, unsatisfied, and melancholy. Like I'm stuck in an emo pop song, or an itchy sweater. I can't seem to control my thoughts as they drag me to my past, linger on my what if's, and get riled at my how come's.

I could blame depression, grief, unresolved endings, the state of the world, even interference from the dark side, and they may all play a part. But knowing the cause doesn't necessarily point the way to peace.

So I've been reminding my restless soul that God has been—and still is—good to me. This helps center me, until my feelings (eventually) catch up.

I also have a best friend (and ministry partner) who gives amazing spiritual direction, as well as a terrific therapist. Both help.

I don't have a tidy ending for you with sunny advice and renewed perspective.

I will say this: If you're feeling the way I feel today, you're not a bad person, partner, parent, or Christian.

Try and be kind to yourself, looking at your emotions and thoughts with curiosity—not criticism or condemnation. Talk to someone you trust. Pray for rest.

—BKS

A practice to try:
Write down five small ways God has been good to you today.
Share them with someone and ask them to share too.

COMMON 55

If a kingdom is divided against itself, that kingdom cannot stand. —Mark 3:24

Have you ever felt conflicted?

I am an Enneagram 6, which means I don't trust easily. The person I struggle most to trust is myself. So inner conflict is a regular thing.

When I'm faced with a big decision—or even a not-so-big decision—I can become paralyzed, not wanting to make the wrong choice, and doubting my ability to make the right one. The fear of moving in the wrong direction will keep me at a standstill for months, even years.

When we are conflicted, it's like we're a kingdom divided. Overcoming conflict, even within ourselves, is always an exercise in trust.

Before I decided to come to California, I had every internal argument against it you can imagine. But I trusted Elane, my ministry partner and best friend, and I knew she would help me adjust and succeed.

I also trusted God's providence and provision, and that my family would be okay without me being physically present for a while.

Even though I wasn't sure I could trust myself, I knew God and Elane were trustworthy.

Over two years later, I know that I'm building God's kingdom here in ways I wasn't equipped to back in Nashville. My ministry and creativity are thriving here.

With every successful decision I make, I learn to trust that I can make good choices. Which helps me quiet those inner conflicts, and not feel afraid of making a misstep.

—BKS

Maybe you're conflicted over a job, a relationship, or a move to a new town. Where— or to whom—will you turn to find the confidence to make a decision?

COMMON 56

If you, Lord, kept a record of sins, Lord, who could stand? But with you there is forgiveness, so that we can, with reverence, serve you. —Psalm 130:3-4

I used to think God watched me constantly in order to catch me doing things I shouldn't be doing. Even committing my life to being a Christian wasn't enough to let me off the hook. God was always recording my sins in a giant ledger of iniquities that I'd have to answer for at the Pearly Gates.

So, of course, I felt defeated all the time. I could never be perfect enough to please a nit-picky God who could read my thoughts and surveil my every move.

Many Christians believe they are scum, reliant only on God's mercy to save them from certain damnation. Speaking from experience, this is not a foundation for life-giving faith, but the basis for an existence full of life-destroying fear.

The truth is, God isn't that petty and gets no pleasure from punishing us. God doesn't see us as a screw-ups and isn't waiting for us to fail.

The Creator made us in God's own image, which means we didn't start out defiled and unworthy. We aren't earning our way back from a sin deficit that we didn't create. We are beautiful, sacred, and worthy in the eyes of God.

If I spend my days bound up in shame and guilt over misguided ideas about God and myself, I will miss every opportunity I'm given to add light and hope to the world, which is God's actual desire for me.

—BKS

What ideas about God do you have that cause you to feel guilty, shameful, or afraid?

COMMON 57

Yours is the day, yours also the night; you established the luminaries and the sun. You have fixed all the bounds of the earth; you made summer and winter. —Psalm 74:16-17

I love roller coasters. They are freedom and fearlessness, anticipation and adrenaline. Arms up, pure joy. I love the build of the lift hill, the thrill of the drop, the speed, the airtime ... all of it.

For me, roller coasters are summer. So are drum corps shows, backyard barbecues, weekends in the Smokies, margaritas on the patio, sunsets at the beach, and twinkling fireflies. Most of my favorite things are summertime things.

But alas, summer can't last all year round. Even here in California.

Life is made of back and forth, give and take, yin and yang, ebb and flow. We need night as much as morning. much as June. That's the way God created the universe, and us.

Take circadian rhythms. You know how you feel when you travel across time zones, or only get five hours of sleep when you're used to getting eight? Our bodies crave a groove, and when that groove is disrupted, we feel it.

Our spirits need a rhythm too. Seasons of lament, anticipation, and celebration are all equally important to our spiritual health and well-being. That's why Lent precedes Easter. Without death, we don't experience resurrection. And if Christmas were every day, we'd lose the wonder of Jesus' birth.

Side note: Reading the Bible via the Daily Lectionary is a really helpful practice for moving through the calendar year in a way that acknowledges the rhythms of the Spirit.

As much as I love summer, I understand it wouldn't be nearly as fun without the other seasons. And if I'm being honest, there are things about winter I don't hate. Like Christmas.

—BKS

What do you notice about yourself when seasons change?

COMMON 58

Whoever is not with me is against me, and whoever does not gather with me scatters.
—Luke 11:23

One time, years ago, I was invited to lunch by the friend of a work acquaintance. When this guy extended the invitation, he made it seem like we had an urgent matter to discuss. It was weird, and I was afraid it was Amway. But for some reason, I agreed to the lunch, and when we met, he had his Bible in hand.

Now I'd been a Christian for close to 20 years that day. Even so, it became clear this guy intended to win me over for Jesus. His version of Jesus.

Our conversation was pleasant enough. Bible verses were quoted. I nodded. I shared my salvation experience when it felt like we might be revving up for the Sinner's Prayer. He downshifted. We finished our burgers, and I don't think I ever saw the guy again.

I think he thought he was doing the Lord's work, setting his sights on souls to win. He must've thought I was a good target. But I think God has better aim.

Makes me wonder if sometimes I think I'm doing good work for God's Kingdom, when really, what I'm doing is inconsequential, or worse.

What if I'm actually working against God?

There was a time in my life where I thought I had most of the answers to the big questions about creation, salvation, eternity, and such. Unsurprisingly, I thought I was also called to be a pastor. I was wrong on both counts.

I think the way to be relatively sure I'm working with (not against) God is to get out of the way. The thing that trips me up most is me—my ego, my self-righteousness, and my desire to look smart, pious, or darn close to perfect.

Instead, I'm pretty sure God uses me most when I am vulnerable, transparent about my failings, and at peace with not having all the answers.

It is my prayer for all of us Jesus-followers that we know when to speak up, and when to shut up. Sometimes God needs room to work.

—BKS

How do you know if you're working for God or against God?

COMMON 59

The righteous flourish like the palm tree, and grow like a cedar in Lebanon. They are planted in the house of the Lord; they flourish in the courts of our God.
—Psalm 92:12-13

Redwoods are kind of amazing. I've visited Muir Woods, an old-growth redwood forest and national monument, twice in the last month. I am in awe of these beautiful trees and their incredible resilience.

Here are a few facts:

Aside from logging, the most common killer of redwoods is windfall. That's because their root systems only grow 10 to 13 feet below the ground. But because redwood roots spread outward 60 to 80 feet, and interlace with those of other nearby redwoods, they are strong enough to hold each other up, even in the face of powerful winds.

Redwoods flourish in community.

The bark of redwoods contains tannins that make them resistant to most insects, fungi, and disease. And because redwood bark has very little resin, it is mostly fire resistant too.

Redwoods wear armor.

Because of their large size, long lifespan—2,200 years or longer—and rot-resistant wood, redwood trees can pull and hold at least three times more carbon from the air than the average tree. They combat climate change by keeping temperatures from rising, and cleaning the air we breathe.

Redwoods contribute to the common good.

Trees represent life throughout the Bible. The Psalmist compares the righteous to palm trees and cedars that flourish in the courts of God. When my life is done, I hope I can be compared to a redwood—someone who loved well, stood strong, and made the world a better place.

—BKS

In what ways are you like a redwood?

COMMON 60

And without faith it is impossible to please God, for whoever would approach him must believe that he exists and that he rewards those who seek him. —Hebrews 11:6

There's no certainty in a life of faith. Just belief and doubt. And we need both.

Without belief, there's no hope, only unanswerable questions, and inconsolable fears.

Without doubt, there's no room to learn, grow, and trust. Just rigid ideas and an unteachable spirit.

Christians are good with belief. So good that we treat our beliefs like they're facts. We defend them as if they're provable. Then when someone else's beliefs contradict ours, theirs are wrong. But because beliefs aren't actually facts, arguing about whose are right is pointless, and often just hurtful.

We like black-and-white binary truths that leave no room for what-if's and how-come's. That's because it's easier to be a good Christian if all you have to do is stay within the lines. That doesn't make for a very rich experience with God though. And it doesn't take into account that we all have different lines.

Sure, there are some things most of us can agree are capital-T Truth. But on most other things, you and I can read the same Scriptures, and attend the same church, and still have starkly different beliefs. Because, again, beliefs aren't facts. They are shaped by all kinds of things, including personal experience—past and present, race, gender, age, sexual identity, and on and on.

So when we read that we can't please God without faith, what does that mean exactly?

I believe it means, to please God, I must spend my life pursuing a deep, purposeful relationship with God by trusting, doubting, believing, practicing, asking, growing, forgiving, grieving, rejoicing, and becoming. It also means I'll never have all the right answers. And that's okay.

—BKS

What do you believe it means to have a faith that pleases God?

COMMON 61

Saul said, "When I saw I was losing my army from under me, and that you hadn't come when you said you would … I took things into my own hands …" —1 Samuel 13:11-12

In high school and college I swam competitively. My events were butterfly (because I had upper body strength) and long distance (because no one else would do it).

Butterfly was fun: dive in, work hard, done in a couple minutes, then personal triumph or defeat.

Long-distance was an obligation: dive in, keep swimming and swimming and endlessly swimming, bored out of my mind, anxious to be done. When I finished, the team gained points. Yippee.

I am not by nature a long-distance swimmer. Or a long-range goalmaker. Or a live-in-the-same-house-all-my-lifer.

You know how in Ocean's Eight and other movies about rakish confidence (wo)men it's all about the long con—the amazing heist that took months to plan and execute, resulting in fantastic wealth and revenge? In Ocean's Eight I'd be the ninth gal, the one who left before the movie started.

I'm great in a crisis, but lousy at the slow, tedious, persistent slog forward.

Unfortunately, God's plans often include seemingly endless swimming and long slogs.

God's watch runs on a different time system than mine.

So I get it when Saul decides the Philistines are too close for comfort. He sees his men are getting antsy. God's prophet Samuel doesn't show up on time, so Saul takes matters into his own hands and makes the offering to God. Which he's not supposed to do, because even though he's facing a huge battle that he's likely to lose, that's not what God's focused on.

Because of Saul's inability to wait and trust, God makes David king.

Saul, I see you, man.

God's watch is set to eternity, and Saul isn't a long-distance kind of guy.

Sometimes the most important spiritual practice you can do is to keep going, keep praying, keep showing up, trusting that even though you're bored out of your mind or anxious about the results, you're gaining points for the team.

—EOR

What long-haul goal are you pursuing these days?
What's your challenge in achieving it?

COMMON 62

So if anyone is in Christ, there is a new creation: everything old has passed away; see, everything has become new! —2 Corinthians 5:17

When I was a kid, I was reminded often in Sunday school that when God forgives our sins, they are removed from us as far as east is from west. Oh, and there's a Sea of Forgetfulness that God tosses them into as well.

I've never been able to get a handle on the idea that, after God forgives my transgressions, God forgets them.

Because I haven't forgotten them.

Even when our pasts are in the past, we still deal with things like trauma and addiction. We still have ideas that no longer serve us and ways of thinking that take real effort to reset. Then there's guilt and grief and shame that don't just go away. It takes work.

Becoming new in Christ doesn't erase where we've come from, and what we bring with us. So it isn't enough to just try to put the past in the past.

Living as new creatures means trying on new ideas, creating new habits, and taking on new spiritual disciplines. Transformation happens when we engage all our parts—mind, body, will, soul, spirit, and environment—in the work God is doing in us, around us, and through us.

We are made new when we commit to changing the course of our lives. Not just once, but again and again.

—BKS

What leftover from your history is keeping you from real transformation? What new practice could you put in its place?

COMMON 63

May I never boast of anything except the cross of our Lord Jesus Christ, by which the world has been crucified to me, and I to the world. —Galatians 6:14

When I was a kid, I played piano in church talent competitions. These shows were cute and cheesy—kind of like *America's Got Talent*, but with fewer wows and more taffeta.

I worked really hard at becoming a good musician. I spent least two hours every day at the piano. Nobody told me to practice all the time—I just understood that's what it takes to be really good at something. Well that, and I really loved playing.

When I was 14 or so, I worked up a really flashy arrangement of Andrae Crouch's My Tribute. If you don't know the song, it's really a prayer of gratitude and a commitment to humility. Here are some of the lyrics:

> Just let me live my life
> Let it be pleasing, Lord, to Thee
> And should I gain any praise
> Let it go to Calvary

At 14, I wasn't paying attention to the words, just the notes. I was playing to win after all.

It wasn't long before all those hours at the piano led to melody writing, then my first band, and my first complete, original song, which I wrote at 16. It was called The Giver.

Here's the chorus:
> To You, O Lord, the Giver of the gift
> I dedicate all that I am and ever hope to be
> My prayer, O Lord, cries out from within
> That You would take this life, let it be the key
> To sharing what You've given
> To caring and forgiving
> Because You gave the gift, I live

(I kinda think Andrae's song might've sunk into my bones more than I realized at the time.)

I worked hard after that to become a successful songwriter. I signed the deals, did the co-writing, tossed out hundreds of songs that missed the mark, and wrote some others that made it onto records and the radio. I don't think I ever became too full of myself—but feel free to disagree if you knew me in my twenties.

And it's not just about my music. Anything good that you see in me is a reflection of the God who created me. I give all glory and gratitude to God for all the good and beautiful things in my life. And there are a lot of them!

—BKS

What gifts do you have that comes from the Giver?
How are you sharing them?

COMMON 64

And the city has no need of sun or moon to shine on it, for the glory of God is its light, and its lamp is the Lamb. —Revelation 21:23

I'm fascinated by stories of people who've chosen to live off the grid. Like in an Airstream in the middle of Wyoming, with no internet, cell phone, mailbox, or debit card, and nowhere near a Target.

People live off-the-grid for lots of reasons. Some want institutions— governmental and otherwise—to get off their backs. Some do it out of a concern for the planet, using only renewable power and water or growing their own food. Others just like living independently of everyone for everything, like frontier people, or Libertarians.

I get the freedom in that. I sometimes daydream about a tiny house on a mountain, by a stream, with solar panels and a composting toilet.

But then I remember how I rely on internet and cell phone for all my communications except those that happen in person. I almost never have enough cash to fill my gas tank, or even buy a latte. In other words, without my debit card, PayPal, and bank drafts, I'm doomed. And almost my entertainment is internet-based too.

Sigh.

It's hard to envision a place where all that is needed is the glory of God to sustain a city. No cell signal, no wifi, no Target—just God. It's kind of like going off the grid, but instead of being self-reliant, you're God-reliant.

Honestly, isn't that the way we're supposed to live anyway?

I figure if we lived in ways that were God-reliant, we wouldn't abuse the planet like we do. Or have unhealthy preoccupations with social media. Or buy things we don't need from Amazon.

I'd probably read more, write more songs, pray more, sleep more, and consume less.

—BKS

What would a more God-reliant life look like for you?

COMMON 65

O that I were as in the months of old, as in the days when God watched over me; when his lamp shone over my head, and by his light I walked through darkness —Job 29:2-3

Job suffered mightily. He lost his kids, his wife, his wealth, his friends, and his health. He didn't understand why such awful things were happening to him. He felt like God was far away.

I've felt like that. I think most of us have.

Everyone suffers. My suffering may not look like yours—you can always find someone worse off than you are. But that doesn't minimize the fact that all of your struggles—and mine—are real and hard.

Maybe you lost a job you desperately needed.

Maybe your health took a troubling turn.

Maybe you lost someone very close to you.

Maybe you are depressed, or anxious, and life just feels like too much.

Even in the worst of his suffering, Job never blamed God. He didn't believe anything bad about God.

Sometimes we rush to pin our struggles on God, like we think we're being punished. God doesn't punish us. Instead, God grieves with us and offers hope, even when we feel hopeless.

Doubting God's goodness, faithfulness, and love deprives us of a close relationship with God when we most need it.

In the end, Job proved himself to be faithful to God. I want to be faithful to God too, even (and especially) when I'm suffering.

—BKS

When have you suffered?
How has God shown up in your struggles?

COMMON 66

And those who know your name put their trust in you, for you, O Lord, have not forsaken those who seek you. —Psalm 9:10

I was working 70+ hours a week. My business partner lacked empathy, frequently lied, and behaved irrationally. My personal finances were a mess. I was sinking in debt, and was falling behind on my bills. I was stressed out and exhausted.

I was in a long-distance relationship, that often left me feeling lonely and uncared for. I was emotionally spent.

I had trouble making even simple decisions. I was depressed.

In desperation, I prayed. A lot. When I was delivering pizzas. Between customers at my cafe. When I was falling asleep.

But was I seeking God?

I was seeking God's provision to fix my bleak financial picture. I was seeking God's attention to ease my loneliness and revive my spirit. I was seeking God's intercession in situations I felt I couldn't control.

But I wasn't getting to know God, because my prayers were so centered on myself. All I could see was me and the mess I was in. It wasn't until I stopped begging, and started listening, that everything started to change.

I found God to be kind, generous, forgiving, ever-present, and ever-the-same. It became easier for me to trust God, even when I knew I would have to change in order to see the changes I wanted to see in my life.

That tough season ended eventually, and I came out of it less fearful, more confident, and more trusting of God and myself.

We go to God with our needs, dreams, and longings, and we're invited to do that. But real, lasting change happens when we truly seek God, and we are changed in the process.

—BKS

What does seeking God look like to you?

COMMON 67

People will faint from fear and foreboding of what is coming upon the world, for the powers of the heavens will be shaken. Then they will see "the Son of Man coming in a cloud" with power and great glory. —Luke 21:26-27

Sometimes God calms the storm.

Your tests come back negative. A check shows up in the mail. Your kid passes math. Your circumstances change in the way you prayed they would. Balance is restored to the universe.

But sometimes, the storm keeps raging.

Your aging dad gets sicker. You don't get the job. Your partner leaves you. What then?

You wrestle with your questions, fears, and doubts. You prayed for a conquering hero to part the clouds and save the day, but you got ... crickets?

Jesus doesn't always show up in the clouds. But Jesus always shows up in the muck with us.

We've all had plenty of fear and foreboding since the beginning of COVID-19. Not even counting the hard stuff we brought into the pandemic with us. There were times I half-expected Jesus to come riding in on a white horse. But alas, not yet.

Still, there are answers to prayer, just not always the ones we ask for.

What if helping to care for your sick dad makes room for some understanding and healing for an old rift? What if a job opportunity, that you never would've gone looking for, finds you after the first (or tenth) one falls through? What if, after a year of WTF, you finally realize your partner wasn't the one after all?

Yes, one day Jesus will return to make everything right. Until then, we trust that, even if the storm keeps raging, God will hold us close till it blows over.

—BKS

When has God calmed you in the midst of a storm?

COMMON 68

Let the redeemed of the Lord say God is good, those he redeemed from trouble and gathered in from the lands. —Psalm 107:2-3a

God meets us where we are.

God may come to indigenous people as a mothering God of growth and harvest.

God may come to mechanistic thinkers as a reasonable mystery, the yet-unknown of the universe.

To exiles and the enslaved, God has often self-revealed as YHWH, the Deliverer. The Jewish people came to know YHWH when they were wanderers, former slaves seeking a safe home.

American slave songs dream of a land over yonder where they could steal away to Jesus and be rocked in the bosom of Abraham.

In our tradition, when God shows up and reveals God's nature and love, it is most often as Liberator.

On June 19, 1865, God showed up in Texas to proclaim and enforce liberation.

Two and a half years after the Emancipation Proclamation, human beings remained enslaved in southern Texas, largely because there weren't enough Union soldiers to enforce the new law.

Two months after the Confederate general Lee surrendered, a regiment came into Galveston and overpowered those who would have kept human beings enslaved.

It may have been soldiers who arrived in Galveston, but it was God who showed up.

Maybe you haven't been enslaved physically, but if you're anything like me you've spent seasons shackled to your own self-destruction, the demon voices of despair and hopelessness drowning out others' compliments and camaraderie. God has met me in those depths: one thin ray of light piercing the heavy darkness, guiding me to freedom.

And when I've been lonely, too conscious of my orphaned state, God has pulled me to Her breast, wrapped me in Her loving arms.

Our God delivers us from captivity, redeems us from trouble, rescues us from pain, and heals our broken hearts.

God gathers in the exiles and enslaved, making a home for us that isn't way over yonder, but is right here, and now.

—EOR

When have you been rescued and delivered?
How did God show up then?

COMMON 69

For they are holy to their God, and you shall treat them as holy ... for I the Lord, I who sanctify you, am holy. —Leviticus 21:7b, 8b

The church I grew up in believed in Christian perfection, also known as entire sanctification. In other words, I was taught that I could live a sinless life, if I were filled with the Holy Spirit, and if I no longer willfully disobeyed any known law of God.

The flip side was this: sin of any kind, without repentance, results in spiritual death. No oopsies, do-overs, or lapses in judgment allowed.

Holiness Christians believe it is vital to behave in ways that convey inner holiness. That's why they preach against drinking, smoking, or entertaining oneself with dancing or movie-going. They don't gamble or play cards. They don't use coarse language, and they dress modestly.

As a holiness teen, most of that list wasn't an issue for me. (Not getting to see Back To The Future in a theater was a bummer.) But it was the stuff going on in my head and my body that scared the bejeezus out of me. (Gee thanks, hormones.)

Anyway, some years later, I gave up on the idea of living a sinless life, as defined by my fundamentalist church.

But I did not give up on making life-giving choices, and worshipping a God who never intended for me to spend my days being defeated by sin.

Of course, living a Christian life has expectations. Being holy for me means pursuing God, following in the footsteps of Jesus, loving people, and sharing light. Yes, it means I look different, act different, and think different than other people. It also means I mess up sometimes. But I live my life energized by hope, not driven by fear.

—BKS

What does it mean to you to live a holy life?

COMMON 70

When Pharaoh saw that the rain and the hail and the thunder had ceased, he sinned once more and hardened his heart —Exodus 9:34

I forgive easily. At least I like to think so.

When I'm hurt or confused, I listen closely to the other's stories and longings. Empathy is my entrance into love and once I love, forgiveness is not so hard.

There are exceptions. I haven't forgiven a woman who destroyed my reputation in order to elevate her own. The man who raped my mother stands forever in my short if I ever get the power this one's going to hell queue.

Mostly, though, even a tiny glimpse of the world through the other person's eyes helps me release whatever wrong I'm clinging to.

That doesn't mean my heart doesn't get harder than Yosemite granite. It's very rare, but it happens. Maybe it's self-protection, or the drive to be right. All I know is that once stone forms around my heart, it's almost impossible to scale or tear down.

My hardened heart grieves me, and I work on it constantly, but I'm sure there are times it shows. Even when I really wish it would soften up for good.

Knowing that about myself makes me wonder about the whole plagues-on-Egypt story.

Pharaoh has the Israelites enslaved. God wants them to be free, so sends horrible plagues upon Egypt's land, livestock, and people. It's a show of force intended to let Pharaoh know he's outnumbered by the One True God. It works, for a while. Scared and worried, Pharaoh promises to let the slaves go. But once everything calms down, his struggle-softened heart hardens up again. Until he loses everything he loves.

I wonder whether Pharaoh was so used to having power and responsibility, erecting pyramids and monuments and winning wars, that the thick stone around his heart couldn't be cracked, even by God, until all that mattered was gone.

Though I go on my knees and beg God to soften my heart, I wonder: maybe Pharoah is me.

Maybe Pharaoh is you too.

—EOR

What will it take to finally unharden your heart? What will you have to lose?

COMMON 71

And the sun stood still, and the moon stopped, until the nation took vengeance on their enemies. —Joshua 10:13

In Joshua 10, we read about a battle between Team Joshua—the Israelites and the Gibeonites—and the kings of the Amorites. During the battle there is a terrible hailstorm, which kills more Amorite soldiers than the Israelites do. Then the sun and moon stand still at Joshua's command, while Team Joshua finishes off their foes.

I'm not a scientist or a Biblical scholar, but I think I can comfortably assert three ideas:

God can do anything God chooses to do.

Science and Biblical faith don't have to be at odds.

Reading the Bible as if it matters requires context.

To the first point, I think we can all agree that God can do anything God chooses to do. That said, God rarely chooses to break natural laws that were put into place at Creation. Though it might be fun to think about God pelting our enemies with softball-sized hail, those kinds of weather events are hardly supernatural, even if opportunely timed.

About the sun and moon standing still: we know that it is the earth that moves, not the sun and moon. If the earth were to stop rotating, or even slow down, the results would be cataclysmic.

There is no geological, meteorological, or historical record of such a thing ever happening.

We also recognize that God could choose to stop the earth without natural consequences. Because God can do anything God chooses to do.

To the second point, there are scientific explanations for many of the seemingly supernatural things in the Bible. Taking those explanations into account doesn't make us faithless Christians—it makes us thinking Christians. Science allows us a closer look at God's incredible imagination.

To the third point, some read the story of Joshua's victory literally—that is, they believe things happened exactly the way the Bible says they did.

Others read it figuratively, acknowledging that the Bible contains allegory, poetry, and other not-literal writing. The intent of each Biblical author— there are 40 authors and 66 books in the Bible, written over 1300 years— varies.

Whether we read Joshua 10 literally or figuratively, understanding what else was going on at the time is essential to learning anything from this, and frankly any, Biblical passage. Having cultural, historical, and scientific data to demystify what was happening can help explain why a Biblical event is significant.

Joshua 10 comes down to how you read the Bible, what you believe about God's nature, and what role (if any) you believe science plays in explaining the mysteries of the universe, including those in the Bible.

—BKS

Have you ever witnessed God breaking natural laws to suit a situation? If so, why do you think God made that choice?

COMMON 72

(But) David said to the Philistine, "You come to me with sword and spear and javelin; but I come to you in the name of the Lord of hosts, the God of the armies of Israel, whom you have defied. This very day the Lord will deliver you into my hand...so that all the earth may know that there is a God in Israel" —1 Samuel 17:45-46

You know the story. David was a skinny, young shepherd who toppled Goliath, a hulk of a man and an enemy Philistine, by hurling a rock at his head.

Did David have good aim? Good enough it seems. Was he able to sling a stone with such velocity as to kill a very large man? Apparently.

But this story isn't about David's physical strength, or his machismo, or the power of an underdog.

This very day the Lord will deliver you into my hand ... so that all the earth may know that there is a God in Israel"

What David had was confidence in God and a strong belief that God would come through for Israel. David jumped at the chance to be the instrument God would use to do just that, because he knew God would protect him a hand a win to the Israelites.

Not to diminish David's legendary victory, but we face Goliaths too. My list of past giants includes overwhelming debt, depression, coming out, and divorce.

In my experience, standing up to a Goliath takes more than my own strength or courage. Tackling a giant requires faith—faith in myself, yes, but also faith in a God who believes in me too. I can do mighty things when I know God has my back.

The Philistines were understandably shook and had no choice but to recognize the power of the God of Israel. When we overcome our own giants, giving God praise for the wins, we encourage others to trust God and overcome too.

—BKS

What's a Goliath in your life you've been afraid to face?

COMMON 73

There are six parts to each of us: mind, body, will, environment, spirit, and soul. Nobody has a livable, physical life if they're missing any one of them. Also—and this is important—none of our parts is inherently evil.

Mind, body, will, and environment are pretty easy concepts to grasp, but spirit and soul are a bit more ephemeral.

My spirit is my divine spark, created in God's image. It connects me to God, kinda like a cosmic USB cable of infinite length. Everyone's spirit is unique, sacred, and beautiful. When my spirit vibes with God's Spirit, I feel at peace. When it doesn't, I don't. That's when I'm more likely to mistrust myself, and doubt God's care for me.

So what can cause my spirit to get out-of-sync with God's? Lots of things, but most often, I look at what's going on with my soul.

Our souls stick to things. They aren't ever really satisfied by anything but God, but certainly will attach to other things if we let them. To keep my sticky soul from doing that, I have to be intentional about what I feed my mind, how I treat my body, and how I allow myself to be affected by my environment.

For example, if I choose to cyberstalk my ex, while eating a box of Little Debbie's, with Jerry Springer on the tv, then I'm giving my soul lots of unhealthiness to grab onto. Over time, any one of those things could have repercussions for my soul. And none of those things would ever satisfy it, causing me to consume more and more, while feeling increasingly empty.

Getting to a place of soul-satisfaction and true spirit-peace requires us to choose things like kindness, patience, and self-control (see verses 22-23). Spiritual disciplines, like fasting and prayer, help us get in the practice of being more self-sacrificial and loving.

—BKS

What is something your soul likes to stick to? How do you know when your spirit is out-of-sync with God's Spirit?

COMMON 74

You are not in the flesh; you are in the Spirit, since the Spirit of God dwells in you. —
Romans 8:9

How human are you, really?

I'm not talking about biology, not about this gene or that one, or whatever prevents us from having feathers.

And no, we don't think you're an android, cyborg, or zombie.

I'm talking about the full range of your humanity. All of it.

Your body.

Your soul.

Your mind.

Your will.

Your experiences.

Your divinity.

Wait. What?

Yes. Your divinity.

Here's how Christian novelist and essayist C.S. Lewis put it:

> It is a serious thing to live in a society of possible gods and goddesses, to remember that the dullest and most uninteresting person you talk to may one day be a creature which, if you saw it now, you would be strongly tempted to worship, or else a horror and a corruption such as you now meet, if at all, only in a nightmare ...

> There are no ordinary people ... You have never talked to a mere mortal ... it is immortals whom we joke with, work with, marry, snub, and exploit—immortal horrors or everlasting splendors.

If you believe in the Holy Spirit, and believe that the Holy Spirit lives in you, then you should believe that you have divinity in you.

You are, as Lewis put it, a possible god or goddess.

I know you won't let that go to your head.

We westerners have been taught that the body is separate from the mind, and that the mind is better than the body. (We call this dualism.)

We tend to either indulge our bodily desires or treat our bodies with contempt, which amounts to the same thing. Bodies are powerful things, but they are not morally bad because they have powerful desires.

In fact, Christ liked bodies so much he had to have one.

As a human being, you are not a mind inside a body, or a soul inside a body. You aren't separated that way.

When all your parts work together properly, you approach the wholeness of Jesus.

There are no ordinary people.

Especially not you.

—EOR

How would you live if you believed you were inhabited by the Spirit?
How would you treat others if you believed they were possible gods and goddesses?

COMMON 75

I am distressed for you, my brother Jonathan; greatly beloved were you to me; your love to me was wonderful, passing the love of women. —2 Samuel 1:26

The story of Jonathan and David is the longest and most detailed account of a human relationship in the Bible.

David was the heroic kid who killed Goliath and became Israel's second and most renowned king. Jonathan was the son of Saul, the crown prince, and David's protector and closest ally.

Jonathan and David had a deep love and admiration for each other.

When David learned that Jonathan had been killed in a battle with the Philistines, he was gutted. He tore his clothes, mourned, wept, and fasted for days. Then he sang a song a lament. In it he declared his love for Jonathan, singing, I am distressed for you, my brother Jonathan; greatly beloved were you to me; your love to me was wonderful, passing the love of women.

Based on what we know about David and his relationships with women, including Bathsheba and his many wives, it is likely true that his love for Jonathan was different.

Still, there is much we don't know about David and Jonathan and their relationship. The details we are given—their vows and their expressions of love to one another—tell us enough to know how deep their mutual love and devotion were.

The details we aren't given are debated furiously—especially the question of whether David and Jonathan had a sexual relationship.

I think the ambiguity around those details is an indicator that maybe they aren't actually all that relevant to the story. Nothing in the Bible, apart from Saul's shaming of Jonathan in 1 Samuel 18, is condemning of the relationship between the two men.

—BKS

Think about your closest relationships. What have you learned from them? Why are they important to you?

COMMON 76

The Lord shall be between me and you, and between my descendants and your descendants, forever. —1 Samuel 20:42b

Have you sworn forever to another person? Forever is a very long time.

Forever is eternity, and eternity never began and will never end. Eternity is now and beyond all nows. That's a long time for us humans who sometimes feel like waiting for a burger takes forever.

Even marriage vows don't pledge forever. "'Til death do us part" is about the longest promise you're going to get, and a lot of couples don't even use that anymore. The Apostle Paul used the expiration date of marriage to talk about how the letter of the Law no longer applied because he knew not much is forever.

Children swear forever to each other because forever is every day when you're six. When your every day is longer than you can imagine, forever is next Tuesday. The feeling of faithfulness, the overpowering affection: that is real and true for kids. But the concept of never-beginning, never-ending? That's a fairy tale phrase, a magical wish meaning can't imagine stopping.

That's why when the king's son Jonathan and the future king David swear their fealty, and that of all their descendants, it's a big deal. They are promising that no matter what comes, everyone in their families will have each other's backs. Period.

That moment is moving, though it's more like a Mafia pact than a wedding vow. It's childlike: two men with no descendants promising what their descendants will do displays how little understanding of forever they actually have. It's also literary foreshadowing, since Jonathan is about to die.

They know, like we know, that the only thing that is forever is God. That's one of the reasons the covenant includes the image of God standing between them. It is God who will bind them together, and only God who can make a promise of forever.

God's covenants of love and faithfulness are forever. And God understands forever. Unlike Jonathan and David.

—EOR

Is there anything in your present life you would count on as "forever"?

COMMON 77

I call upon the Lord, who is worthy to be praised, so I shall be saved from my enemies.
—Psalm 18:3

I have a few enemies. Sometimes I think they're conspiring together to end me.

They know my blind spots and my Achilles heel. They're pretty good with nunchucks. They're quick on their feet. They wear black.

They whisper lies to me about who I am and who my Defender is.

They gaslight me, catfish me, and try to throw me off my game.

They are doggedly persistent. They don't go down quietly.

So I work out. I build stamina by standing firm on what I know is true. I practice solitude, so that even when I feel isolated, I know I'm not alone. I listen for God's voice, so that I recognize it when other voices try to fool me.

And I pray, to the One who comes to my rescue, reminds me who I am, and encourages and empowers me.

My enemies may slow me down, but because God is on my side, they will never take me out.

—BKS

Who are your enemies?

COMMON 78

A belief is an idea you are willing to act on. If you say you believe something, you'd better be willing to put some action behind your words.

If you believe your son is a safe driver, then you'll get in the car with him. If you believe you have what it takes to be a good lawyer, then you'll pay the tuition and enroll in law school.

Belief requires you to do something. Otherwise, it's just an idea.

In this story from the Gospel of Mark, a father brings his son to Jesus. The boy has been possessed by a spirit since birth that causes him to harm himself and has left him without speech. When the boy's father says to Jesus, "If you are able, have pity on us and help us," Jesus replies, "If you are able? All things can be done for the one who believes!"

The father's responds, I believe … help me with my unbelief.

There are things I believe with every ounce of my being. Like the idea that this chair I'm sitting in can support me. I didn't hesitate when I put all my weight on it. That's probably because it has supported me before, many times.

It's easy to believe something that has been proven true over and over.

Here, this father has the idea that Jesus can banish spirits from tortured people. Jesus is asking him to believe that he can, and that he will, banish this spirit from his child. The father's request—help me with my unbelief—is an honest plea that Jesus honors. The boy is freed from his torment.

—BKS

When have you struggled to act on an idea you have about yourself? About God?

COMMON 79

When reviled, we bless; when persecuted, we endure; when slandered, we speak kindly.
—1 Corinthians 4:12b-13a

When you look at how Christians live in the world, do you think, by and large, our/their words and actions convey love?

When we are angrily criticized and insulted, do we ask God to look favorably upon our enemies? When we are caused to suffer because of our beliefs, are we made stronger by our suffering? When our reputations are damaged by someone's lies, do we answer their accusations with truth, delivered with kindness?

I'll speak for myself. It's difficult to will good things for someone who wants me to suffer. It's easier to stay a victim than to overcome. Being Jesus to a world that is antagonistic to Jesus is hard.

And ... that's what I am called to do.

It's not okay for me to go on attack with weaponized Scripture, even in the name of defending myself, or God—who doesn't need my defense.

It's not enough for me to pray for someone from a safe distance.

And though I am called to love my neighbor, I am not entitled to having my neighbor love me in return.

The love Paul is writing about is the love Jesus practiced. Loving like Jesus did requires us to practice too—by letting someone else have the last word, by always giving more than we take, by laying down our right to what we think we're due.

—BKS

What are some ways you can practice loving the way Jesus did?

COMMON 80

May he give you the desire of your heart and make all your plans succeed.
—Psalm 20:4

"Yo, let me tell you what I want, what I really really want."

The Spice Girls wrote and sang that in 1996 and I'm still no better at it than I was then. Oh, I can sometimes express my more fleeting desires— Thai rather than Italian, Monk not Davis—but the stuff that really matters? That's harder, and not just because I'm reticent and am afraid of getting told "no."

I just don't often know what the deep desire of my heart actually is. And I'm reasonably confident that the object of my plans is rarely the same thing as the desire of my heart.

My soul wants constant and deep connection with God.

My body wants healthy food, sufficient exercise, and restful sleep.

But what would truly satisfy my heart and release my spirit to joyful action? Beats me.

That's why this blessing in the Psalms is so perfect, so God-inspired: it wishes the reader both what you really, really want and the fulfillment of your plans.

The easiest way to get both of those is to align your will and spirit with God's will and Spirit. As hard as that can be, it just takes attention and practice.

Granted, most of us aren't very good at aligning fully with God, but it's a whole lot easier than plumbing your depths (including your more shadowy bits), naming your deepest desire, and then doing what you have to do to get it.

We know what God wants of us: justice, kindness, humility, love.

But that singing career that you never had and that probably wouldn't have made you happy or the world better? Might be just as well you didn't get that desire filled.

—EOR

Do you have a sense of the desire of your heart?
And if so, how well does it align with your current plans?

COMMON 81

If you are confident that you belong to Christ, remind yourself of this, that just as you belong to Christ, so also do we. —2 Corinthians 10:7b

Before the pandemic, I said yes to an invitation I received to an event that was attended by mostly evangelical Millennials. I have no issue with Millennials—some of my favorite people are Millennials. It's the evangelical part that's interesting.

They mostly came from one church in the Bay Area, whose brand you would likely know. I found myself feeling outside the group, not because I'm older, or even because I'm gay, but simply because I didn't belong to the group.

I've been on the other side of that kind of exclusivity. If someone unfamiliar showed up at church, I'd wait to see who—if anyone—made an attempt to make the visitor feel welcome. (But of course, if the visitor was attractive, it was a race to see who could make a new friend first.)

I get that most of this is simple sociology. I also get that Christians have a higher standard to live up to.

It is not up to me to determine who belongs to Christ and who doesn't. I don't decide who belongs in my church, and who doesn't.

It is simply my job to be welcoming, accepting, and kind to anyone who shows up, and to everyone I meet, especially if I'm representing myself as a follower of Jesus.

If you visit—or even attend regularly—a church where you feel like an outsider, hear this: God loves us all the same, which means there is a place at God's table for you. But maybe you need a new church.

—BKS

When have you felt less loved, accepted, or acceptable because of someone's exclusive behavior?

COMMON 82

Steadfast love and faithfulness will meet; righteousness and peace will kiss each other. —Psalm 85:10

Sprawled across the ceiling of the Sistine Chapel in the Vatican is Michelangelo's image of God creating the first man, Adam (or earth). I'm sure you've seen it: God lies atop a dozen or so cherubs, a few of whom look very uncomfortable, with his arm reached toward Adam, while Adam lounges on a grassy knoll, languidly extending his hand toward God as if inviting a suitor's kiss.

God is stretched out, barely anchored in the heavens by angelic force, the tip of his finger just millimeters away from Adam's hand.

Adam is making no effort to reach God. In fact, Michelangelo's Adam is so fully leaning into the earth that it's a wonder his hand has the strength to escape gravity, bless his heart.

I'm sure Adam feels like he's doing all the work: praying, tithing, attending church from 10-10:55 almost every Sunday morning. He's been baptized, for Heaven's sake. He's supposed to have a personal relationship with the Almighty, isn't he? Can't God just put out a little effort for a change?

From our perspective it's clear that all creation effort is God's.

Re-creation mostly depends upon God, too, even when we feel like we're trying so darned hard to change.

When the Bible talks about the eventual happy ending it's always a meeting of God and humanity, rather than a ticketed trip to heaven. God accompanies the Israelites through the Red Sea and beyond. God shows up in Palestine as a Jewish kid from a good family. God comes running to grab up the prodigal son. God brings the new city to earth and welcomes all the nations in.

Here's how the Psalmist puts it: God's steadfast love and our faithfulness meet up, joining in a kiss between righteousness and peace.

God's love needs our faithfulness—our effort—for new creation to happen, especially if the new creation is us.

—EOR

How are you participating in God's re-creation?

COMMON 83

For you were called to freedom, brothers and sisters; only do not use your freedom as an opportunity for self—centeredness, but through love become slaves to one another. —Galatians 5:13

There are many kinds of freedom, and many more kinds of incarceration.

We can be physically free without being mentally free. Spiritually free without physical freedom.

Uncaged while shackled by addiction.

Free from toxic churchgoing while believing in a brute of a God.

Free under the law of the land but denied the protection, justice, and provision it takes to enjoy it.

The Israelites and their God cared less about physical freedom than religious. In Egypt, Pharaoh was not only king but God. Served. Worshipped. The Israelites wanted to be able to worship YHWH, erect a temple, install their priests, offer sacrifices to the God who had chosen them and whom they had chosen in return.

YHWH could not be freely celebrated as The One God above all others as long as God sat on the throne in Memphis.

Out of Egypt they had something like sociopolitical freedom until they decided they wanted a human king.

Later, under Roman rule, they had a temple where they could worship their God. That didn't solve all their servitude problems. Jews were taxed without representation. They also held slaves, and their women and children were legal property.

Oh, and Jews could be killed by Romans, and tortured. Freely.

Which is why when the Jewish Roman citizen Paul wrote to his fellow Jesus-followers that freedom wasn't about personal liberty but loving, protecting, and providing, it struck a nerve for some and a chord for others. Paul was calling them to choose: a king (Christ or themselves), and utilize their freedom well, as loving, justice-seeking Kingdom-citizens.

On that day that many American Christians celebrate escaping a king and becoming Romans, let us recall that we can be enslaved to patriotism, nationalism, king-worship, wealth, process, color-blindness and profit, among other things.

And that the King we worship demands no other gods before him. Not even ourselves.

—EOR

To what kings are you enslaved?
What are you doing with the freedom you have in Christ?

COMMON 84

And David became greater and greater, for the Lord, the God of hosts, was with him.
—2 Samuel 5:10

God created us humans with the ability to make choices. I guess God trusted that we would occasionally make good choices, all while knowing we would sometimes choose paths that would harm us and others.

David made some questionable choices. He had many flaws, but God remained faithful to him. And in spite of—or maybe because of—his human failures, David became a man after God's own heart.

I've made some questionable choices too. Not to sound like a Sinatra song, but regrets—I have a few. To be honest, I don't trust myself easily, partly because of those past missteps.

But I can honestly say, even (and especially) at my lowest moments, God has remained faithful to me. God reminds me who I am when I can't see it or don't feel it. God helps me make amends, choose differently, and grow from my judgment lapses. God shows me that I was not born a screw-up, and that I have never been beyond the reach of God's heart.

I relate to David more than I'd care to admit.

I recognize that I am becoming the man God hoped I would become. Sometimes I get it right.

But because of my freewill, I'm still a wild card. I'll probably choose the hard way now and then. I'm certain I'll take the long way around to get there. And God will continue to be with me, in spite of—and because of—my humanity.

—BKS

When have you been able to relate to David and his flaws? How did you experience the presence of God in those times?

COMMON 85

Do not swear, either by heaven or by earth or by any other oath, but let your Yes be yes and your No be no, so that you may not fall under condemnation. —James 5:12

Once when I was a kid, I remember my dad and I took my go-cart to some property that was being developed near our house. It had dirt piles and rough terrain that was great for off-roading. Dad said that if there were security guards watching the property that, obviously, we'd have to find somewhere else to go.

When we got there, it seemed the coast was clear, so we freewheeled all over the dirt dunes and were having a great time when a policeman approached us. The officer asked if we knew we were on private property, and stated that trespassing was a crime. Dad, who is always friendly and disarming, played dumb and said he didn't realize the property was off-limits. The officer probably knew Dad was lying, but he allowed us to leave without consequence.

I was surprised and confused as to why Dad didn't just fess up. I learned that day that there are circumstances when it's okay to lie a little.

Except that it isn't.

Christians fudge the truth sometimes. To get out of a speeding ticket. Or to make their tax liability less expensive. Or to save face when embarrassed or humiliated.

Some even do it under oath—a criminal offense, and an indication of even bigger issues.

But as Jesus-followers, a baseline expectation is that we are honest, speaking truth in love. (I will say, some of us can be a little too honest, and a bit lacking in love, but that's a topic for another day.) When it comes to truth, either you're being honest or you're lying, whatever your reasons.

—BKS

Think of a time when you've told what felt like an acceptable lie, just to have it bite you later. How did it make you feel when your untruth was discovered? What did you do to rectify the situation?

COMMON 86

For godly sorrow produces a repentance that leads to salvation and brings no regret, but worldly sorrow produces death. —2 Corinthians 7:10

I replay the past way more than I like to admit. Old mistakes and failures mostly. I ask the what ifs and how comes, and then watch all the alternate outcomes play out like an episode of *Lost* (season 5).

Sorrow is painful. Part grief, part regret.

Godly sorrow leads us to repentance—a recognition of our life-destroying behaviors and a commitment to changing course. That may mean making amends, forgiving ourselves and others, and then choosing to leave the past in the past, independent of what others choose.

Even though there are countless books about letting go and moving on, there is no one foolproof way to get to the other side of sorrow. Prayer and self-reflection help. Time heals some wounds. But there comes a point when we have to choose to move on.

I think the death Paul is talking about in 2 Corinthians 7:10 is the endless spinning in place we do when we don't move on. The condemning self-talk, the replaying of events and conversations, the tornado of emotions. I'm certain that isn't a fate God wants for any of us.

Moving on isn't easy for me. I hold onto things longer than I wish I did. I'm working on engaging more fully in the present, which means facing forward, and looking back a lot less. I'm learning to trust God and myself.

—BKS

Are you sorrowful?
Is it time for you to move on?
What does moving on look like for you today?

COMMON 87

The earth is the Lord's and all that is in it, the world, and those who live in it;
—Psalm 24:1

I have a friend who is very generous with his time and money. When someone comments on his generosity, I've heard him respond many times with, It's all God's.

He's 70-something and still works all the time, something he credits God for. In his work, he schleps his sound equipment all over the Bay area every day, setting it up and tearing it down multiple times a week. He'll probably never choose to retire, because he sees his continued ability to work as a gift.

It's all God's.

On Sunday, he brings his gear to church, arriving hours before the rest of us and leaving long after the service ends. I never hear him complain. He's glad to share the mics and audio equipment he's collected over 50 years in broadcasting, as well as the stories that go along with each piece.

It's all God's.

A couple days after I arrived in San Jose in 2019, he called and offered me a spare ticket he had to the Monterey Jazz Festival. I accepted his invitation (because: Diana Krall) and we spent the entire day together.

Somewhere late in the day, our conversation led to my mentioning offhandedly that I am gay. I'll never forget his reaction. He looked me in the eye and said, "It means a lot that you would trust me with that. Thank you."

It's not just money and microphones, or even time and opportunities. People, all kinds of people, belong to God too.

—BKS

What would happen if we all saw our livelihoods, our bank accounts, our stuff, as God's?
What if we treated the earth like God's backyard?
What if we heard God's voice when someone shared their story with us?

COMMON 88

Devote yourselves to prayer, keeping alert in it with thanksgiving. —Colossians 4:2

Is prayer a part of your daily routine, like brushing your teeth? Do you pray when you're enjoying your morning coffee? What about when you're walking your dog? Maybe you pray when you're driving to work, or while you're waiting on your kid in the car riders' line. Do you pray as you're falling asleep at night, or before you open your eyes in the morning?

Do you pray in solitude? Do you set aside time to be by yourself so you can pray without interruption or distraction?

Is prayer something you turn to when there is a need? When money is short? When you have a new ache or worry? When someone you love is in trouble again?

Do you pray for your kids, your partner, your parents, and your friends? How about your enemies?

Do you confess to God the things you've done—or haven't done—that might've hurt someone else? Do you admit to your own unhealthy habits and behaviors, and ask God to help you overcome them?

Is praise a part of your prayers? Do you remind God—and yourself—that God is awesome and worthy of all your praise and more? Do you thank God for what you have?

Prayer is an act of trust, believing that God wants to hear from us, wants to answer our prayers, and shares our concerns. There is no right or wrong way to pray. God simply wants to hear from us.

You've probably seen that bumper sticker that says Prayer changes things. The truth is, prayer does change things. Because consistent, earnest prayer changes us.

—BKS

Why, how, when, and where do you pray?

COMMON 89

A scribe said, "Teacher, I will follow you wherever you go." And Jesus said to him, "Foxes have holes, and birds of the air have nests; but the Son of Man has nowhere to lay his head." —Matthew 8:19-20

Jesus wasn't homeless.

Well-meaning liberals have used these verses in Matthew's Gospel to draw attention to the needs of unhoused people. That's a good goal: the US's lack of care for the poor, unhoused, mentally ill, addicted, and children (plus anyone who cares for them) is appalling.

Instead of being angry at homeless encampments we should be ashamed.

Instead of griping about syringes in parks we should be angry that getting help is so hard.

Shame and anger aren't enough, of course. Voting for those who will boldly advocate and allocate for the least of these as well as giving freely to those in need (and those who serve them) is vital.

Talking the talk is irrelevant when you choose to stand still, which was Jesus' point.

When the scribe proclaimed his fealty to Jesus, promising to follow Jesus and his Way, Jesus made it clear: talk without action is nothing.

Jesus wasn't claiming to be homeless—itinerant rabbis had places to stay and could choose a less peripatetic ministry. Instead, he was letting the scribe know just what he was signing up for if he called himself a follower of Jesus.

Following Jesus means actually doing what he says, choosing his Way of living with God and others. Praying the sinner's prayer or professing the One Lord in front of your church is great, but it's the beginning of the path, not the end.

Following Jesus means you won't know where you're going. You will lose your comfort, your habits, your home.

Following Jesus is learning to be like Jesus—treating other people as if they matter, being in conversation with God, training yourself to give up your claims, aligning yourself with the Spirit's movement, being kind.

All of which is a long Way from what most of us call success. Or heaven.

—EOR

How far are you willing to go to follow Jesus?

COMMON 90

Let me hear what God the Lord will speak, for he will speak peace to his people, to his faithful, to those who turn to him in their hearts. —Psalm 85:8

I've been grieving a loss I suffered some time ago. And as grief goes, I've cycled through denial, anger, bargaining, and sadness over and over, in no particular order.

I've told myself all the things you tell yourself when you're trying to get to the other side of a loss. Things like:

It wasn't meant to be.

I'm better off without _____.

God must have something (or someone) better for me.

Eff this! I'm moving on with my life.

All those things might help in a moment. But honestly, the only thing that has brought me peace when I've been hurting is this:

I am with you.

That's what I've felt in my spirit every time the grief has been more than I think I can handle. That's the peace God has spoken to me when I've felt lonely, sad, angry, restless, hopeless, and defeated.

I've gone to God with those prayers that have no words. You know the ones. Where you don't know how to verbalize what you're feeling or thinking, so you trust that God knows, and will respond.

And every time God says to me, I am with you, the truth of it sinks a little deeper into my bones. Until I believe it.

—BKS

Have you heard God speak peace to you?

COMMON 91

David danced before the Lord with all his might —2 Samuel 6:14

When is the last time you looked foolish and didn't care?

I work part-time as a barista. It's a job that gets me out of the house and gives me some structure. And it's fun.

I enjoy my co-workers. And together, we enjoy music. All kinds of music. But mostly, we play upbeat, feel-good music in the coffee shop to keep the mood light. And you know what feel-good music leads to? That's right ... dancing!

I find myself dancing every shift. To Earth Wind & Fire. To Carly Rae Jepsen. To The Monkees. Spontaneous dance breaks occur while steaming milk, mopping floors, and chatting up customers.

Dancing is a by-product of joy.

Listening to danceable music gives me joy. Pulling shots and pouring lattes gives me joy. Making customers happy gives me joy. Doing all those things with friends gives me joy.

When I'm doing things that give me joy, I can get lost in them. I might start dancing, and I might look foolish. But I don't care.

David looked foolish sometimes when he got lost in his exuberant love for God. And he didn't care.

I wonder what would happen if all of us God-worshippers started dancing in the streets, because of the joy we feel and can't contain.

—BKS

What if going to church was more like a dance party? Would you dance?

COMMON 92

Look on my right hand and see—there is no one who takes notice of me; no refuge remains to me; no one cares for me. —Psalm 142:4

The same David who danced before the Lord also had moments of despair.

Reading many of the Psalms is like reading David's prayer journal. Throughout, he expresses to God both soaring highs and crushing lows. He shakes his fist, rends his clothes, cries for help, weeps in sorrow, comes to realizations, and seeks forgiveness. He also expresses his love and devotion to God, sometimes with abandon.

Next to Jesus, no one in the Bible gives us a better example of how to pray.

As a kid, I was taught to be reverent and submissive in prayer—to say things like if it be your will as Jesus did in Gethsemane. Prayers were to be polite and to the point, as to not waste God's time, I suppose.

When I became an adult, I found that polite prayers didn't cut it for me. As I navigated marriage, parenting, career—and later, coming out, I learned to be transparent with God, sharing my fears and sorrows, as well as my joys and self-discoveries.

What I've come to believe about prayer is that it's more about us than it is about God.

Taking things to God is an act of trust. That trust is grounded in the idea that God does not, in fact, have more important things to do.

God cares about the things we care about. That includes our feelings, our anxieties, and our frustrations.

A few lines from my song *Confessions Of A Lesser Me*:

> Blessed is the man who knows himself
> Who can yell at the sky, beg to know why
> And still manage to make his peace
> That's who I wanna be

—BKS

When have you yelled at the sky, aloud or silently?

COMMON 93

The Son of Man has come eating and drinking, and you say, "Look, a glutton and a drunkard, a friend of tax collectors and sinners!" —Luke 7:34

Ever been found guilty by association?

I am a gay Christian. I know those two words side-by-side cause some to have heart palpitations. But if you know me at all, you know that I am at peace with the coexistence of my faith and sexuality. Most everyone in my life seems to be too.

I have great friends. Many are straight, and of those, many are Jesus-followers of various stripes. Hanging out with my straight Christian friends is never a problem for me. I also have gay friends who aren't Christians. They are cool with me too, but they'd rather I not proselytize. (Understandable.)

But in most circles, Christian and LGBTQ+ don't mingle so easily. Don't ask, don't tell is how many families, and congregations, avoid having difficult conversations that lead to inclusion or exclusion. It keeps things copacetic on the surface, but at what cost?

I come from Nashville. I hate how gay-and-Christian is still an uncomfortable, if not downright offensive, idea there. (I love you, Nashville, but please catch up.)

In liberal Silicon Valley, it's easier to openly be yourself. Many of you don't know what that's like, and I understand that feeling well.

Jesus liked outsiders. He hung out with people the Jewish elite thought were trash. His disciples were crude, uneducated, and some were unlikable. (Looking at you, Matthew.) But Jesus saw in them what others didn't see. Those were the people he built his church on. And those are the people he continues to build *his* church on.

—BKS

Be honest: Who is someone you'd like to know better, but hesitate because they are _____?

COMMON 94

He is the image of the invisible God, the firstborn of all creation —Colossians 1:15

Picture yourself at a family gathering. Lots of people are there, some you haven't seen in a long time, and some you don't even recognize.

An older woman—maybe your father's aunt on his mother's side—comes up to you and says something like, "You look just like your father did when he was your age," and then starts pointing out things like, "You have the Stokes nose," or some other thing you can now be self-conscious about.

Then you start noticing how your cousins look or act like their parents. It's uncanny really. Even their voices sound the same.

Then you ask yourself, "Am I just like my parents?!"

I mean, you like your parents and all, but they can be pretty annoying. What if you have all their annoying traits and no one's ever told you?

As panic starts to set in, you hear your dad's laugh from across the room. Then you think about his terrible (aka hilarious) dad jokes, his goofy facial expressions, his attempts at cheering teenage-you up, and his off-to-the-side comments to you (at events just like this) that make you both snicker.

So you follow the laugh, and you spend the rest of the afternoon being reminded that resembling your dad isn't such a bad thing after all.

Jesus resembled his Dad. He had the DNA of his heavenly Father. He also spent his life watching and listening to his Dad, becoming more like him as he grew. So much so that, if we want to know God better, we can look at Jesus, God's spitting image.

—BKS

What are some things you have—your nose aside—that you can credit your parents for?

COMMON 95

The God who made the world and everything in it, he who is Lord of heaven and earth, does not live in shrines made by human hands, nor is he served by human hands, as though he needed anything, since he himself gives to all mortals life and breath and all things. —Acts 17:24-25

I used to think God needed me to be a pastor, and that to choose a different vocation would be disobedient. I was 16, eager to please God, and mostly oblivious to all the ways my gifts and passions were better suited for other careers. I thought God needed me to serve a specific purpose in a Divine Plan and if I didn't, I'd be messing up everything.

But God doesn't need me that way.

God doesn't need me to do things the way a boss needs his employees to complete their assigned tasks. Because I make choices, I would be a constant eraser to the Master Architect's perfect plans.

However, God does want me to choose to do things that bring light to my world. Things that matter in that Kingdom kind of way. Things that I'm equipped to do and impassioned about.

The Great Creative gave me a love for music and a songwriter's spirit, so I write songs. God doesn't tell me what to write or how to write. In fact, God never asked me to write songs at all. But I think God enjoys the fact that I do.

When I write a song, the process gives me joy. And sometimes, listeners are moved by what I write—moved to dance, sing, cry, pray, rethink, or hope. God uses my songs, and my willingness to write them, in ways I'll never know.

If I were to stop writing songs today, God wouldn't think less of me. If I were to write every waking moment of my life, God wouldn't love me more.

The fact is, God doesn't need us in the way we think. Instead, God delights in us, loves watching us find purpose and joy, and excitedly uses what we do, and who we are, to change the world.

—BKS

Where do you find purpose and joy? How has God has equipped you to change your world?

COMMON 96

You have turned my mourning into dancing; you have taken off my sackcloth and clothed me with joy, so that my soul may praise you and not be silent.
—Psalm 30:11-12a

When my ancestors emigrated to North America from various parts of Britain they settled mostly in New England.

They were, in a word, stoic.

Visible emotions were frowned upon in my family, particularly if the emotion was sorrow.

My ancestors also didn't dance much.

Coincidence? I think not.

So when church services eschew confession and lament, favoring only the happy-clappy songs of Christian contemporary radio, I'm not surprised when they neglect spiritual joy as well, or clap on the wrong beats.

The capacities for joy and sorrow are connected, in ourselves and in God.

In the Bible mourners rip their clothes. They wail. Write long laments. Repeat stories about their despair and defeat.

Those same biblical characters also dance, particularly if they're portrayed as spiritually close to God.

The closer you are to God, the more likely you are to both mourn and dance, because sorrow and joy emerge naturally from paying attention and from love, both of which God excels at.

And how your soul loves to be connected to God!

Around here we try to express how we're feeling, even when we're embarrassed by it. There's not a lot of clothes-ripping, but we know grief and loss, which can mean tears coming from nowhere.

And spontaneous dance parties in the kitchen.

—EOR

How comfortable are you with the depth and range of your emotions? Which do you express easily? Which are harder?

COMMON 97

Go and tell my servant David: Thus says the Lord: Are you the one to build me a house to live in? —2 Samuel 7:5

There are places many people experience as sacred—Notre Dame, Joshua Tree, Stonehenge. Places where the distance between heaven and earth seems to collapse. Where the presence of the Divine is almost touchable.

You may know of a sacred place or two, where you often encounter God. A favorite bluff that overlooks the ocean. A tree you climbed as a kid. A hillside that overlooks your hometown.

The Israelites had a holy mountain. It was their sacred place, where they would go to meet with God.

But the thing is, God didn't want to live on a mountain. The Almighty can live, or be, anywhere and everywhere all at once. What God wanted was to be with the Israelites. To dwell with them.

And God wants to dwell with us.

For 40 years, the Israelites carried the Ark of the Covenant around with them as they wandered the desert, much the way Egyptians would've carried a pharaoh. They believed the Ark contained the holy presence of God, and treated it that way. When they rested, they placed the Ark under a tabernacle, or tent, but God wanted more than a temporary home.

God posed the question to David, "Are you the one to build me a house to live in?" God wasn't talking about a temple. The house God wanted to inhabit was David himself.

God wants to inhabit us too.

We make ourselves a home for God when we make ourselves available to serve others, to be light when darkness prevails, and to yield our kingdoms to God's Kingdom.

—BKS

How have you offered yourself to be a dwelling place for God?

COMMON 98

So then you are no longer strangers and aliens, but you are citizens with the saints and also members of the household of God, —Ephesians 2:19

My friends Joel and Twila wrote a really great song several years ago called *Orphans Of God*. It's been recorded a few times over the years, first by a Christian vocal group called Avalon, and recently by a country artist named Ty Herndon, who happens to be gay.

Here's the chorus:

> There are no strangers, there are no outcasts
> There are no orphans of God
> So many fallen, but hallelujah
> There are no orphans of God

Some of us have a hard time reconciling who we are, or who we love, with the God we were introduced to earlier in life. Some of us can't fathom reentering a church building, or trusting Christians, because of the abuse we suffered in the name of Jesus.

That anger, mistrust, and fear are warranted.

Some of us have spent years tearing down and rebuilding our ideas about God, just to get to the place where we can believe we are not condemned to hell for things we can't change about ourselves.

That fragile hope is not misplaced.

Hearing Ty sing a song about the inclusive nature of God (it also features Kristin Chenoweth—both are professing Jesus-followers) puts a spin on its message that I find irrepressibly hopeful.

None of us is rejected by God, for any reason, ever.

—BKS

What ideas about God are you holding onto that keep you from seeing yourself as loved, accepted, and embraced by God?

COMMON 99

Ask rain from the Lord in the season of the spring rain, from the Lord who makes the storm clouds. —Zechariah 10:1

If it matters to you, it matters to God.

I used to think that God had more important problems to tend to than mine. Even though the things I wanted to talk to God about were big to me, I knew there were other people suffering more than me.

For example, I remember feeling guilty asking God to help me with my financial debt. I thought that, because it was a problem I created, it was something I should find a way out of myself. But at the same time, I was suffering from all the anxiety that trying to manage my money was causing me. I found myself asking God for relief from the stress, which led me to earnestly pray for answers regarding my finances.

If I'd kept the mindset of I got myself into this, I'll get myself out, I probably never would've actually found solutions for both my anxiety and my financial issues. Treating my suffering as if it was something I deserved was creating distance between me and God.

Learning to go to God with everything—our joys, frustrations, fears, doubts, pains, everything—teaches us that we can trust God.

Entrusting God with everything broadens our view of who God is and helps us see ourselves the way God sees us.

At the end of the day, prayer is about us, not about God.

—BKS

When (and why) have you hesitated to ask God for something you needed or wanted? What was that about?

COMMON 100

Which one of you, having a hundred sheep and losing one of them, does not leave the ninety-nine in the wilderness and go after the one that is lost until he finds it?
—Luke 15:4

Sheep aren't the smartest creatures. They need a shepherd who looks out for them. I've been the sheep and I've been the shepherd.

Being the sheep means you wander off sometimes. You get into trouble, not because you're bad, but because you're a sheep. You're curious, or maybe bored. You've forgotten what happened the last time you strayed from the flock. Or maybe you get a buzz from being unsupervised. It's understandable. At least until a wolf spots you from a nearby hill.

Being the shepherd means you keep your sheep safe. You know how many you have and you count them almost constantly. You've probably named them, and you know who the troublemakers are. (Kenneth, I'm looking at you.)

When Kenneth, or Francesca, or #100 wanders off, the shepherd leaps into action. He doesn't hesitate, because hesitating could mean life or death for a sheep. You can't call a sheep and expect it to respond like a dog would. You have to go get it.

If you're the sheep, and the shepherd comes for you, there's a sense of relief, and the reminder that, even when you're stupid, the shepherd still cares about you, and won't let you die if he can help it.

If you're the shepherd, you shake your head, breathe a sigh of relief, and hoist the scoundrel on your shoulders.

Not everyone is a shepherd, but all of us are sheep. Sometimes, we're the lost sheep.

Thank God for shepherds.

—BKS

When is the last time you were a lost sheep?

COMMON 101

May you be made strong with all the strength that comes from his glorious power, and may you be prepared to endure everything with patience —Colossians 1:11

I've heard it said that praying for patience is asking for trouble. Because when you pray for patience, God will put things in your path that require patience. Things like traffic, slow internet speeds, and long checkout lines. Not to mention downright difficult people.

We all know patience is a virtue. We also know that it is something many of has in short supply. Or maybe that's just me.

Webster's defines patience as the capacity to accept or tolerate delay, trouble, or suffering without getting angry or upset. Biblically, patience is more like self-restraint, or not giving way to anger, even when provoked. It's like long-suffering, or endurance.

In some ways, I'm more patient than I was when I was younger. That's because I've learned that there are often reasons why difficult people are difficult.

A woman who used to come into my cafe was a difficult customer. Always complaining that we didn't have what she wanted. Usually unhappy before she ever ordered anything. I sometimes grumbled to myself when she left, and secretly hoped she'd buy her bagel somewhere else.

I learned after a while that she was battling cancer. And that her only daughter had moved from Nashville to Seattle.

Chemo + missing your kid will make anyone cranky. Once I knew that, I was able to engage with her differently. I became more patient.

Truth is, everyone has stuff going on we know nothing about. Hard stuff. So a little patience might just go a long way with them. I know there've been times I've needed people to be patient with me.

—BKS

When is a time when you've needed someone to be patient with you?
How did you ask for a little understanding?

COMMON 102

> Bear with one another and, if anyone has a complaint against another, forgive each other; just as the Lord has forgiven you, so you also must forgive. —Colossians 3:13

Forgiveness—the kind that brings lasting peace to both the forgiver and the offender—is a process. It isn't as easy as saying I'm sorry, hugging it out, and forgetting anything ever happened.

To forgive someone is to release your right to revenge or repayment. Before you can do that in a way that brings healing, you must first understand what it is you are forgiving.

Say your neighbor borrows your lawn mower, then breaks it. The neighbor apologizes, but never offers to fix or replace it—which is, of course, what you are owed. Sure, you can say to yourself, and to your neighbor, It's no big deal and go buy a new lawn mower.

But what if buying another lawn mower causes you financial stress by adding something else to your nearly maxed-out credit card? What if you start to feel resentment toward your neighbor, believing he can't be trusted anymore? What if you start feeling like you want to break something of his to even the score?

You haven't actually forgiven your neighbor, because you haven't ruled out revenge or released him from what he owes you.

Before you forgive someone, you have to consider all the ways you were wronged—materially, emotionally, physically—so that you can address each of them individually. It's not until you've considered all the ways you've been harmed, and forgiven each of them, that you can say that you've forgiven the person who wronged you.

The process of forgiveness can take a long time. But remember that it actually has very little to do with the person who wronged you. Forgiving someone is for your own peace and healing.

—BKS

When was the last time you forgave someone?

COMMON 103

You will be in the right, O Lord, when I lay charges against you; but let me put my case to you. —Jeremiah 12:1a

"It's not fair!"

When a 4-year-old says this what they really mean is I don't understand or that's not what I want.

For us, it usually sounds something like this:

"I worked for years at that lousy place and I didn't get a severance package. Ungrateful S.O.B.s"

"My husband got the same medicine that woman did but HE got sick. They must have messed up."

"My darling little Beauregard is twice the spaniel that Priscilla is. The judges are SO biased against him!"

When you're a parent and your 4-year-old says, That's not fair! and stomps her size 4T foot, you might want to respond, "Life isn't fair, Genevieve. Get used to it" but you don't. Or you might want to give her perspective: "I know it seems like you got the smaller piece of cake but Mommy had a really hard day at work and it's all she can do to not hit the bottle, dearest." You refrain, because kids don't start having perspective until they're 10 and why waste your breath when there's cake?

To God, we're all 4-year-olds. 6, max. So when the prophet Jeremiah, who is at his wit's end because he's killing himself trying to turn things around and the bad guys keep winning, he turns to God and says "I know you're right, God, but hear me out, please?" God listens.

God never says "life isn't fair" or "Mommy had a hard day" or "shut up—you don't know what you're talking about." God knows how deeply you hurt, and how little you truly understand.

It's not just okay to yell at the sky, "It's not fair!" God wants you to. Because when you finally cry out that you've done everything you can and there's nothing left to do but wait and weep, that's when you might realize that God's arms are wrapped around you.

And when you finally stop sobbing long enough to take a breath you might just hear that soft steady I love you like a holy heartbeat that will never, ever leave.

—EOR

Have you ever felt God's arms around you? Try describing the feeling.

COMMON 104

I pray that you may have the power to comprehend, with all the saints, what is the breadth and length and height and depth, and to know the love of Christ that surpasses knowledge, so that you may be filled with all the fullness of God.
—Ephesians 3:18-19

As a kid, I would draw maps of places that only existed in my imagination. Small towns with cute main streets and country churches. Big cities with gleaming towers and suspension bridges. They were inspired by places I'd been—only better.

As a teen, my imagination moved to creating and drawing superheroes. I used to read a lot of comic books and, no doubt, my characters were amalgams of heroes I already knew and loved. Just more awesome.

Now, as a songwriter, I know that I'm inspired by songs that move me. My writing draws from classic influences like Elton John and Billy Joel, as well as modern writers like Sara Bareilles and JP Saxe. I know my brain rearranges bits of things I've heard when I write something new. And knowing how much I admire the writing of my influences gives me faith in my own.

That's the way an imagination works.

There's a germ of something we've experienced in the things we dream up. It's how we know they're believable, or maybe even do-able.

Understanding God's love for me works like that too. It started with the love I received from my parents. It continued as I learned to love others. Over time, I got the notion that God's love for me is even greater than any love I've known, as hard as that is to imagine.

I may never fully grasp the depth of the knowledge-surpassing love of Christ for me as long as I'm breathing. But the more I strive to be like Jesus, the better I understand what it means to love the way Jesus did. And that's the best picture we have of what God's love looks like.

—BKS

Who in your life has helped you imagine the way God loves you?

COMMON 105

For I have learned to be content with whatever I have. I know what it is to have little, and I know what it is to have plenty. —Philippians 4:11b-12a

I used to work most all the time. I owned and managed a cafe, I was on staff at a church part-time as a worship leader, and I delivered pizzas four nights a week. Almost all of my income was going to debt, living expenses, and child support.

I was also living in a basement apartment in my parents' house. I'd bought and sold three houses of my own in the ten years before. I might've resented my living arrangement a tiny bit.

I would daydream about owning a downtown loft, or a bungalow in East Nashville, or an atomic ranch in Donelson, the suburb where I grew up. I'd get salty with God occasionally about it, which was deserving of a divine eye roll.

But after a while, the allure of a house, and things to put in it, started to dim for me. I got comfortable in my little in-law space, and made it a place I liked hanging out in. I stopped thinking so much about things and, when I'd save up for something, I'd plan for experiences instead.

Pretty soon, I started to believe that having things was like dragging baggage around. I began to feel relieved that I didn't have a house to pay for and furnish and maintain and keep comfortable. And my increasingly minimalist heart became incredibly grateful for what I did have—which was, of course, more than enough.

Contentment is something we all think we want. I'll admit I still struggle with it sometimes. But then I remember that I began finding contentment when I practiced—you guessed it—gratitude.

—BKS

Would you say you are content? Why or why not?

COMMON 106

The wicked draw the sword and bend their bows to bring down the poor and needy, to kill those who walk uprightly —Psalm 37:14

Who are the wicked?

Psalm 37 says the wicked are those who draw their swords on the poor and needy. But since we live in a society where people don't go around drawing (literal) swords, I'd say the wicked are those who do all in their power to keep poor, needy people in poverty.

Poverty is perpetuated by things like underfunded schools and teachers, a lack of access to even basic healthcare, and insufficient investment— both public and private—in struggling communities. It is made worse by legislation that weakens the rights of the poor—most specifically, women's rights and voting rights.

These are things the wicked could change to improve the lives of the poor if they chose to.

Psalm 37 also says the wicked kill those who walk uprightly—aka those who seek and follow God in the way of Jesus. I'd say what they kill (or attempt to kill) is the spirit of a God-seeker.

Enemies of God-seekers are those who profit from guilt and shame. By telling people they are condemned by God because of something they've done, or because of who they are.

The wicked effectively kill hope for those who most need it. They work to keep people down and defeated. That's where their power comes from.

—BKS

In the world where you live, who are the wicked?

COMMON 107

Then the Lord God will wipe away the tears from all faces —Isaiah 25:8a

My grandfather recently turned 96 years old. Four generations of McManuses gathered to celebrate at his house in rural Alabama. My Uncle Darrell prepared the Boston butt, my Aunt Barbara brought all the sides, and my mom, who always makes sure there's dessert, brought four kinds of home-baked cookies. (Everybody talks about the food for days after.)

There were tears and I-love-you's, mostly from my Papa Mac, who gets emotional at such occasions. He treats each family visit as if it is likely his last.

My grandmother passed away a few years ago. In almost every conversation I've had with Papa Mac since her passing, he has mentioned how badly he misses her. He married her when they were both teenagers, and they lived together for over 70 years.

Many of those years were tough. My grandmother suffered from depression. They both had their share of physical issues—heart disease, stroke, diabetes. There are other struggles they endured that I'll never know about. But I do know they endured them together. And I believe he would say that those times drew him closer to her, and closer to God.

I have no doubt that a long, full life is a blessing. But I can also imagine feeling like it's a curse when you're grieving or suffering. An eternity without tears or pain starts to sound really good.

When God wipes the tears from my grandfather's face, I wonder if it will erase all the pain and sorrow he's felt throughout his life. I wonder if he'll forget the hard times, and only remember the best times.

Or I wonder if maybe it's the hard things that will make seeing God all the more beautiful and peace-giving.

—BKS

What is one of the hard things you've endured that has drawn you closer to God and to those closest to you?

COMMON 108

> Whoever, therefore, eats the bread or drinks the cup of the Lord in an unworthy manner will be answerable for the body and blood of the Lord. —1 Corinthians 11:27

In the church where I grew up, there was an older married couple—we'll call them the Clairs—who always declined taking Communion.

At my church, whenever it was Communion Sunday, a big deal would always be made about whether or not any of us was worthy to participate—that to take Communion when there was sin in one's heart was an even bigger sin than whatever was already lurking there.

As a kid, I assumed there was sin in the Clairs' hearts. I mean, what other reason could there be?

But as I grew older, it made me sad to see the Clairs sitting in their pew while the rest of us went forward for Communion. I knew them to be upstanding folks. Mr. Clair served on the church board, and Mrs. Clair was always in attendance for worship. They actively shared, even led, in our community.

I started to question why such seemingly committed Christians would be excluded from the Lord's Table.

When Paul is instructing the church at Corinth, he is helping the young Jesus-followers there become a church. And New Testament churches, like the one in Corinth, were built on community—making sure everyone was fed, that the sick were cared for, that children were taught, and the like. On top of that, they were Greeks (aka Gentiles), without the frame of reference for set-apart-ness that the Jews had.

Paul is insisting that, to partake of the Body and the Blood, one must follow in the ways of Jesus by being part of the community. He is teaching the Corinthians to ask themselves, "Am I feeding the hungry? Am I tending to the sick?" Not "Am I a sinner?" because by that measure, no one, not even Paul, would be worthy.

The Clairs were justified to take Communion. And so are the rest of us when we have faith—no matter how small—and a desire to know God and to follow in the ways of Jesus.

—BKS

What does receiving Communion mean to you?

COMMON 109

One of you puts to flight a thousand, since it is the Lord your God who fights for you, as he promised you. —Joshua 23:10

One of my favorite worship songs of the last couple of decades is *Whom Shall I Fear (God Of Angel Armies)* by Chris Tomlin, Ed Cash, and Scott Cash.

The chorus:

> I know who goes before me
> I know who stands behind
> The God of angel armies is always by my side
> The One who reigns forever
> He is a friend of mine
> The God of angel armies is always by my side

It's one part battle cry, one part "my God is bigger than _____."

I need to be reminded sometimes that God is bigger than _____. My blank has been filled with things like debt, coming out, depression, and divorce, among other things. As I faced each of them, I knew our really big God was with me, which gave me hope and a vision for what my life could look like on the other side.

Joshua, on his death bed, reminded the Israelites that just one of them can send a thousand enemies packing when God is fighting for them. So can we.

No matter what defeats you have faced in the past, you can overcome the thing you're staring down right now. The God of angel armies is by your side.

—BKS

What is some thing (or things) you could fill your blank with? Say it aloud: My God is bigger than _____!

COMMON 110

It tastes like chicken.

Isn't that the joke about foods we're squeamish about trying? We finally eat the snake or alligator or whatever and because we have no other way to describe it we say it tastes like chicken. Which is about the blandest, least distinctive meat there is.

If you've ever been really, truly hungry, nothing tastes like chicken. Even chicken doesn't, because there's nothing bland about the food that finally fills that giant emptiness where your stomach used to be.

I think we've all been starving at one time or another.

Starving for acceptance. Starving for interior peace. Starving for love.

When the Israelites were out in the desert, starving for security and familiarity as much as for food, God sent them manna to eat. A lot of manna. They got far more than they needed, at which point the Israelites started to complain: Too much manna! Enough with the manna! Send us meat!

Apparently the manna tasted like relief but not enough like chicken.

To fill their giant emptiness that had nothing to do with food and everything to do with despair and fear, God sent food that could feed their souls as well as their bellies, if they let it. But as soon as their bellies were full they didn't notice their longing for God.

I've done that: fed my stomach, gotten the job, had sex, binged tv ... whatever filled the craving for acceptance or peace or love, for a moment. Our souls are sticky and latch onto spiritual junk food when they can't find manna.

The bread of angels is what feeds hungry souls.

Angels are never hungry, because they are always full of God.

—EOR

Are you hungry? When have you chosen spiritual junk food over the bread of angels? How long did it satisfy?

COMMON 111

The gifts he gave were that some would be apostles, some prophets, some evangelists, some pastors and teachers, to equip the saints for the work of ministry, for building up the body of Christ —Ephesians 4:11-12

Most of the work of ministry isn't done by vocational ministers—that is, people who get paid to preach, teach, or lead worship. Most of it is done by volunteers, who give time, money, and know-how to enable ministry to happen.

At the church where I used to lead worship, we had terrific volunteers. Bill—who I've written about here before—shared his trove of mics and assorted audio equipment with us, and gave hours each week to making sure we sounded our best. Diana, an experienced seamstress, created a cover for our grand piano from fleece-lined vinyl tablecloths, and when I left was working on one for the organ. Louann, a retired chaplain in the prison system, did all kinds of things, including assembling our monthly newsletter, serving on a number of committees, and moderating our Zoom room.

Without volunteers, most of the work of the church wouldn't happen. Not just at that church, but at every church. That goes for nonprofit ministry too.

God has given us all gifts, talents, and passions. God also opens doors of opportunity for us to use what we've been given, and what we've cultivated, in the service of the Kingdom. It is all of us working together that builds up the body of Christ.

So whether you teach toddlers in Sunday school, clean the restrooms of a community center, drive senior adults to the grocery store, or pack lunches for unhoused folks, everything you do in the name of Jesus matters.

Seriously. Thank you.

—BKS

Whose volunteer ministry has made a difference in your life?

COMMON 112

> You were taught to put away your former way of life, your old self, corrupt and deluded by its lusts, and to be renewed in the spirit of your minds, and to clothe yourselves with the new self, created according to the likeness of God in true righteousness and holiness. —Ephesians 4:22-24

I've been feeling the need to refresh my closet. Some of my clothes are really old. Like the blue-and-maroon striped button-down that my former brother-in-law gave me on my birthday in 1999. And the drawer full of t-shirts I haven't worn in three summers. Some of my things just don't fit my body or my style anymore, so it's time for them to go.

Sometimes we outgrow things—and not just jeans.

I have a good friend who came out last year. He is finding that many—maybe most—of his ideas about God don't fit him anymore. For him, putting away his former way of life includes discarding old notions of who God is, and what God expects from him.

The condemnation that his old beliefs would've sentenced him to isn't consistent with the God he's been getting to know.

As a result my friend's begun the process of sorting through those ideas he's held onto, and committing to a new walk with God, even though he's still figuring out what that looks like.

If we are growing spiritually, it only makes sense that we'd have some ideas or beliefs that don't serve us anymore. Like an itchy sweater that used to fit, but if you're honest, that was a long time ago.

We hold onto these beliefs longer than we probably ought to because we are afraid of what will happen when we let them go.

New ideas sometimes lead to new friends, a new church, new ways of spending your time or money, or new clothes in your closet. Because when you think differently, you'll make different choices—choices that suit your ideas about God now.

—BKS

What are some ideas you still hold that you've outgrown?

COMMON 113

Take care that you do not forget the Lord your God, by failing to keep his commandments —Deuteronomy 8:11a

When I was a kid, I memorized the Ten Commandments for Sunday school. I understood most of them—except for the one about coveting—and proudly recited them. I also understood that they were important, and that I was supposed to obey them.

Seems simple enough, but it turns out they aren't as easy to follow as I thought.

It wasn't easy for the Israelites either. They were a forgetful bunch, even though they were often reminded by their prophets, leaders, and kings that God had expectations they needed to meet. Chief among them was the command to only worship the Lord their God.

One might think that worshipping God alone wouldn't be a big ask. After all, it was God who led them out of Egypt, from slavery to freedom. It was God who provided food and safety for them in the wilderness. It was God who chose them, and intended for them to be set apart from everyone around them.

Still, the Israelites melted gold and made idols, like the ones their adversaries had. They resisted being different, complained about God's provision, and essentially did everything the hard way.

Kinda like we do.

We admire other people's idols—sometimes claiming some as our own. We fail to seek the mind of Christ, and instead, we acquiesce to our culture. Turns out, it's a lot easier to blend in than to stand out.

We know God leads each of us from captivity to freedom. God provides everything we need to thrive. God keeps choosing us, even when we are wishy-washy in our faith, and determined to assimilate, when we were meant to shine.

—BKS

God's love for us is tenacious. God's grace is abundant. God is with us persistently and patiently. So why do you think it is that we Christians so easily forget?

COMMON 114

For as the heavens are higher than the earth, so are my ways higher than your ways and my thoughts than your thoughts. —Isaiah 55:9

I'm a pretty smart guy. I know stuff.

Some of what I know I learned from going to school. Things like how to multiply fractions, when to use "who" and when to use "whom," why Abraham Lincoln was important, and what a mitochondrion is.

I learned other things from my parents and mentors, like how to drive a stick shift, and how to play a G♭ scale.

I learned even more things from experience.

Like what to do when your Karmann Ghia's distributor cap breaks in half. (Hint: Wedge it together with a piece of gravel. It'll get you home.) Or where the best view of Nashville is. (Love Circle, hands down.)

Somewhere along the way, I discovered my voice, formed opinions, and found convictions. I got better at sharing what I know, and what I believe. And as I learned more about God and what it means to follow Jesus, I realized how little I actually knew.

I learned that God's ways are higher than my ways.

Even so, I can become more like Jesus by practicing things like patience, humility, and generosity. And I can trust in God's infinite wisdom, and the leading of God's Spirit, when I have questions, doubts, and fears.

—BKS

When have you trusted that God's ways were higher than yours? What did you learn?

COMMON 115

May the God of steadfastness and encouragement grant you to live in harmony with one another, in accordance with Christ Jesus, so that together you may with one voice glorify the God and Father of our Lord Jesus Christ. —Romans 15:5-6

I love learning about church history. It's a weird, winding road that's brought us here.

The capital-C Church has always dealt with disharmony. There've been schisms over huge things like the priesthood of all believers, and rifts over seemingly small things like whether women should wear pants.

Even Christians who attend the same local church have disagreements, some that cause lasting damage. That's because small-c churches are made up of people, who have kingdoms that bump into each other, and sometimes even go to war.

True unity among Christians seems nearly impossible to achieve. And it's nothing new.

Jesus taught that we should strive to live in peace with one another. His gospel was much simpler than we make it out to be. All of our doctrines and dogma make it harder for us to see eye-to-eye. Our often-public arguments distract from who we are called to be.

Conversely, being one in spirit does not mean being the same. We each bring our experiences of God and the world to the collective—and it doesn't have to result in chaos and contrariness. We can respect, even admire, our uniquenesses as individuals while yielding our kingdoms to the One True God.

—BKS

What does it look like for Christians to be different, yet unified?

COMMON 116

Be angry but do not sin; do not let the sun go down on your anger —Ephesians 4:26

"Don't make me angry. You wouldn't like me when I'm angry."

Physicist Bruce Banner was socially withdrawn, physically weak, and emotionally reserved. When he was accidentally exposed to gamma rays while trying to save his friend from a detonating bomb, Bruce was given the ability to transform into someone completely different—someone who was both physically powerful and driven by rage.

The shocking transformation happens whenever Bruce is emotionally stressed or angry, and he has no power to stop it. The Hulk's impulses and actions are also outside of Bruce's control.

The Hulk is what happens when Bruce's anger literally takes over.

Anger, which is usually rooted in some kind of fear, pain, or frustration, is not a negative emotion. even though many of us have been taught to believe it is. But when we approach the anger we feel with curiosity—not judgment, it can teach us a lot about ourselves.

Imagine you're on your daily commute. You control the car you're driving, the lane you're in, what music you're listening to, and what route you're taking.

When someone cuts you off in traffic, your sense of control has been taken away. Your will has been thwarted. You get angry.

You experience the fear that you narrowly missed being in an accident. Or the pain caused by spilling your Starbucks on your lap when you hit the brakes. Or the frustration that this bozo is driving ten mph under the speed limit, and now you're gonna be late.

At my best, the thing that keeps me from becoming the Hulk in that situation is trust. Trusting that whatever fear is expressing itself as anger will not kill me. That I am cosmically okay. That there are bigger hands than mine that control the things I can't.

Letting the sun go down on my anger really means letting fear reign my thoughts, shape my decisions, and rule my life. Dealing with anger, and what is behind it—in the moment, is how I keep that from happening.

—BKS

What are some underlying fears that may cause you to feel persistently angry? How might you combat your anger and fear with trust?

COMMON 117

There's a country gospel song I love called *The Moon And I*.

The chorus:

> We are much the same, the moon and I
> We are both reflections of a greater light
> Despite the phase we're going through
> When we rise or when we fall
> The truth is we know without the Light
> We'd never shine at all

As we become more like Jesus, we reflect the light of Christ. Kinda like the moon is just reflection of the sun.

Becoming like Jesus takes work. It requires us to live like he lived, denying ourselves and serving others. It means we practice spiritual disciplines like prayer, solitude, and fasting. It takes intention, commitment, and devotion.

Becoming like Jesus doesn't happen because of a single decision we make, but because of many, many decisions we make to continue following in his footsteps—when it's hard, when it's painful, when we don't want to. And understanding that we can't embrace both light and darkness.

Another great song about light is Charlie Peacock's *In The Light*.

The chorus:

> I wanna be in the light as you are in the light
> I wanna shine like the stars in the heavens
> Oh Lord, be my Light, and be my salvation
> All I want is to be in the light

When we live as children of light—pursuing God in the way of Jesus—we shine. And the darkness has no choice but to step aside.

—BKS

What are you doing to be a light in the darkness?
How do you reflect Jesus?

The Moon And I—Words & music by Wendy Wills and Joe Beck. Recorded by Jeff & Sheri Easter.

In The Light—Words & music by Charlie Peacock. Recorded by dcTalk and by Charlie Peacock.

COMMON 118

Therefore, beloved, while you are waiting for these things, strive to be found by him at peace, without spot or blemish; and regard the patience of our Lord as salvation.
—2 Peter 3:14-15a

Most everyone says they want to live in peace—with God, with neighbor, and with oneself. The trouble is, living in peace takes real work.

To live in peace with yourself, you have to make the effort to really get to know you. It means approaching yourself with curiosity (not judgment), while looking closely at your thoughts, beliefs, and actions. Getting to the bottom of what you actually believe about God and everything else—that is, the ideas you have that you are willing to act on—is an important place to start.

To live in peace with your neighbor means approaching them with compassion, assuming the best about them, and striving to find common ground. That doesn't mean compromising the things you hold most important, but it does sometimes mean letting go of things that aren't really important. Making peace with others is easier to do when you've made peace with yourself first.

Living in peace with God means lowering your defenses, holding a little less tightly to the things you have some control over—that is, your kingdom—and striving to live in peace with others. A growing, life-giving relationship with God is one that aims for peace in all our relationships, including the one with ourselves.

Just as we hope God will be patient with us as we make peace with our neighbor and ourselves, we must choose to be patient with everyone else as they do the same.

—BKS

What are you doing to live in peace with yourself, with your neighbor and with God?

COMMON 119

Jesus said to them, I am the bread of life. Whoever comes to me will never be hungry, and whoever believes in me will never be thirsty. —John 6:35

The soul is the part of us that longs for deep satisfaction, peace, and joy. It yearns for connection with God. A healthy soul integrates all the other parts of us—body, mind, will, spirit, and environment.

The trouble is our souls don't stay satisfied. They are drawn to ideas, relationships, impulses, and indulgences. The soul has an itch, and a lot of things can scratch it—at least for a while.

The crowd Jesus was addressing was peppering him with questions. He knew their souls were restless. He also knew what would bring them peace.

"I am the bread of life."

The people understood manna, the food God sent to their ancestors from heaven when they were wandering in the desert. Jesus tells them that even manna can't satisfy the longings of a hungry soul.

"Whoever comes to me will never be hungry."

When I'm hungry, I can be placated with chips, cookies, bread—most any carb will do. But my appetite returns as soon as my brain realizes that my body still needs nourishment.

Even though I like snacks, they only curb my cravings for a short time.

A satisfied soul is one that lives on more than snacks. Though other pleasures may soothe our souls for a season, only God brings us the deep peace we all long for.

—BKS

How are you feeding your soul today?

COMMON 120

Stephen, full of grace and power, did great wonders and signs among the people. Then some of those who belonged to the synagogue of the Freedmen ... stood up and argued with Stephen. But they could not withstand the wisdom and the Spirit with which he spoke. —Acts 6:8-10 *excerpted*

Stephen was one of seven men appointed by the apostles to care for widows who had been neglected. He was essentially a servant, but he was also full of grace and power, doing great signs and wonders among the people like the apostles were doing.

The establishment Jews (think Pharisees) were threatened by Stephen. They staged arguments with him, trying to put him in his place. But his wisdom, and the Spirit with which he spoke, were too much for their weak rhetoric. He only gained popularity with the people.

So the Jews began spreading lies about Stephen, claiming that he was blaspheming against God and Moses. The elders and scribes were appalled and popular opinion started to turn on him. Soon, he was arrested and brought before the council and the high priest, to explain and defend himself.

But they could not withstand the wisdom and the Spirit with which he spoke.

When the Spirit speaks—however She chooses to do so—Her words can be hard to hear, especially when they threaten our understanding of what we think we know. Like those who accused Stephen, we can become self-righteous, pulling out all the stops to discredit the messenger because we're challenged by the message.

But as Jesus-followers, we are called to be openhearted and teachable, listening for the Spirit and willing to go where She leads.

—BKS

When has the Spirit spoken to you and challenged your way of thinking? How did you respond?

COMMON 121

For such people do not serve our Lord Christ, but their own appetites, and by smooth talk and flattery they deceive the hearts of the simple-minded. —Romans 16:18

When I was a kid, there were tv preachers who scared the bejeezus out of me. They were loud, angry, and wore ill-fitting suits. One of them would put his hand on a person's forehead, then knock them to the ground while screaming at them to be healed in the name of Jesus. Yes, it was horrifying.

The message I got was clear: God is powerful and mad, and it's a good thing I'm here to warn you. Now buy me a jet so I can warn more people.

Another similar phenomenon is celebrity pastors. They hang out with superstars like Justin Bieber and Chris Pratt. They wear ridiculously expensive sneakers (there's an Instagram account). They have lavish lifestyles, thanks to the financial support of their parishioners, followers, and fans.

Their message seems pretty clear too: I'm cooler than you.

Then there are those who claim faith in Jesus for the credibility it gives them with his followers. Politicians and media types leap to mind. Some Christians swoon over people who are powerful or influential and occasionally nod to Jesus. Never mind that they are, generally speaking, terrible in lots of other ways.

Their message is more insidious: Stick with me and you can be powerful too. (I hear nothing remotely Jesus-like in that message.)

We must not get caught up in the hype, celebrity, or perceived influence of those who would steal our attention away from what is actually important: participating in the life-giving work we are called to do in the name of Jesus.

—BKS

Why do you think it is that we Christians fall for influential people who claim Jesus, but serve themselves?

COMMON 122

The fear of the Lord is the beginning of wisdom. —Psalm 111:10a

There are days I wish my kid were just a little more afraid of me.

Home is a safe place. My daughter has plenty to eat, surplus clothes, and an extremely patient mother who has sometimes taken 37 deep breaths and counted to 10 in five languages to avoid exploding into a thousand shards of sarcasm or a hearty slap.

I'll be honest with you: When I've made sure the cupboards are full, her laundry is clean, and the internet is up, only to have her snipe at me because I haven't found the missing earring that I didn't lose in the first place, it's all I can do not to smite her silly.

Maybe you were raised in an unsafe place, neglected or hungry or abused. If so, "the fear of the Lord is the beginning of wisdom" may rub you the wrong way.

Or if you still feel, deep down, that God is just waiting for you to fail so that He can finally wash his hands of you, you may think you don't need any more fear in that relationship.

That kind of fear—the kind that makes you tiptoe around, or hide, or feel ashamed—that's not what the Psalmist is talking about.

The good kind of fear, the healthy kind, is what you have of gravity on most days. Most days you don't have to think about gravity, and you really don't have to tiptoe around it. Instead gravity keeps you from flying off the planet and prevents your hot coffee from leaping out of the cup into your face.

About the only time you have to be afraid of gravity is when you're leaning out a high window or walking on the edge of a cliff. In those times, you'd best be afraid.

When my kid is walking on the edge of a cliff, real or metaphorical, I want her to be just afraid enough to watch what she's doing and consider the natural consequences of her actions.

That's the kind of fear that leads to wisdom.

The good news is that God is infinitely more patient than I, so when I'm moaning about some hardship that's tiny compared to everything God has given me and done for me, God doesn't have to count to 10 even once.

Remembering that God could smite me silly, and doesn't, can make me just a little more grateful for what I have, including my kid.

— EOR

What are your healthy fears?

COMMON 123

Be filled with the Spirit, as you sing psalms and hymns and spiritual songs among yourselves, singing and making melody to the Lord in your hearts.
—Ephesians 5:18b-19

When I was 15, I was invited to play a short piano piece I'd written at a praise gathering for a charismatic church. I'd never been to a charismatic church before.

Now, I was no stranger to people lifting their hands in worship, or shouting amen in agreement with a sermon. But in this service, there were people dancing in the aisles, and praying in tongues. It was a little weird for me. Still, I knew enough about the Holy Spirit to know that She sometimes makes her presence known in unexpected ways.

Churches like this one are described as (Holy) Spirit-filled. People who have spiritual gifts like healing, prophecy, or tongues are described as Spirit-filled too.

But the Spirit fills and gifts people in many ways. And anyone who pursues God in the way of Jesus can be filled with the Spirit.

I spent years in Christian music, collaborating with Spirit-filled people from all kinds of faith traditions. Contemplatives, charismatics, and everything in between. I learned a long time ago to not make assumptions about what the Holy Spirit might be doing in someone's life.

Truth is, the Kingdom of God is made up of all of us, using what God has given and what the Spirit has inspired to make a difference wherever we are.

So let's sing our psalms and hymns and spiritual songs. God loves the sound of our hearts.

—BKS

What does being Spirit-filled mean to you?

COMMON 124

Now therefore thus you shall say to my servant David: "Thus says the Lord of hosts: I took you from the pasture, from following the sheep to be prince over my people Israel. I will be a father to him, and he shall be a son to me."
—2 Samuel 7: 8a, 14a

Is Jesus the only son of God?

The ancient statement of faith, known as the Nicene Creed (because it emerged from a big meeting called the Council of Nicaea during the 4th century CE), asserts this: "...Jesus Christ, the only begotten Son of God, eternally begotten of the Father..."

If it's true that Jesus is the only begotten Son, does that mean that he was the only son? Not according to the Bible.

God tells the prophet Samuel that David, little David the shepherd, will not only rule Israel but will be God's adopted son.

Adopted kids aren't less part of the family than biokids.

And David's not the only one. The Christian scriptures state that those who trust Jesus are adopted into that family too.

You are a son, a daughter, a child of God, as much as David or Jesus or anyone else.

Where Jesus is quite different from me or you or David is that he "looks" just like our Father. Oh, not in the physical way, but the divine DNA is so strong in him that knowing him is like knowing our Dad.

We can get there. Having been adopted and having the Spirit pitch a tent in us means that when we choose to learn from Jesus how to live, and choose to live that way ourselves, more and more we come to be like him. Which means that more and more we resemble our Father. And Jesus'. And David's.

You are God's child, just as if God had birthed you Themselves. The only question is: how will you live that out?

—EOR

Do you want to resemble Jesus more? What do you want to do about that? Where can you get help?

COMMON 125

Because the Lord your God is a merciful God, he will neither abandon you nor destroy you. —Deuteronomy 4:31

In Deuteronomy 4, Moses addressed the people of Israel, challenging them to obedience and warning them (again) of the dangers of disobedience.

Israel had a history of being unfaithful to God. In this moment, as they were about to face a formidable foe in order to occupy the Promised Land, Moses reminded them of their many rebellions against God in the wilderness. He was making himself crystal clear that only obedience to God would keep them safe. Their lives would depend on it.

But after all the painful reminders and cautionary warnings, Moses declared this:

"Because the Lord your God is a merciful God, he will neither abandon you nor destroy you" -Deuteronomy 4:31

Have you ever been told that God would abandon you or destroy you? In other words, that God would send you to hell because you did something bad...or *are* something bad?

Maybe a preacher, a pious pewsitter, or a Facebook "friend" has made you feel like God would rather end you than embrace you because of something you've done, or just because of who you are.

Well, it just isn't true. No one is unloved or forsaken by God.

Sure, some of us have regrettable histories, like the people of Israel. But no matter what we've done, or what we've been told, God loves us all and seeks to reconcile with each of us. That reconciliation begins with a recognition of the life-destructive choices we've made, and a commitment to seek God and to choose differently.

—BKS

If you worry that God doesn't love or accept you, for any reason, contact us (*info@schoolforseekers.com*) and let's chat.

COMMON 126

At Gibeon the Lord appeared to Solomon in a dream by night, and God said, "Ask what I should give you…" [Solomon replied] "I am only a little child; I do not know how to go out or come in… Give your servant, therefore, an understanding mind…"
—1 Kings 3, excerpted

In 1 Kings, we read that Solomon—son of David, King of Israel, writer of the Book of Proverbs—made a sacrifice to God. To honor his sacrifice, God appeared to him in a dream and asked him what he desired most. Solomon's answer was wisdom. God answered his prayer, in large part because his request wasn't self-serving like a long life or the death of his enemies.

I want wisdom too.

I want to be the friend who gives the best, most-right advice. I'd like to be the go-to guy for all kinds of useful information and direction. I wish I could solve the world's big problems, or even some of the small ones.

I'm not that guy, at least not all the time. But I am some of the time. And so are you.

What if we all took seriously Solomon's admonition in Proverbs 1:7: "The fear of the Lord is the beginning of knowledge; fools despise wisdom and instruction"?

We'd probably all be a little (or a lot) wiser, wouldn't we?

There've been seasons of my life when I thought I knew everything. But life had a way of saying "Bless your heart" right before I got put in my place. After several of those experiences, I started to get it.

Being smart, talented, and successful aren't the same as being wise. Wisdom comes from seeking God, and being humble, observant, and teachable.

—BKS

What are you doing to seek wisdom?

COMMON 127

> When Gentiles, who do not possess the law, do instinctively what the law requires...They show that what the law requires is written on their hearts.
> —Romans 2:14a, 15a

Children first learn through don'ts.

Don't touch the stove. Don't pull your sister's hair. Don't walk out into the street. Don't say that word. Don't pick your nose in public.

Those don'ts give them the guidance they need to stay safe when their grown-ups aren't around to protect them. And as they grow older, they don't have to actively think about the don'ts because they've become second nature.

Children who want to please their grown-ups extrapolate other don'ts that aren't spelled out. They also understand that there are do's that make their grown-ups happy. This combo of do's and don'ts becomes the basis for safe, socially acceptable behavior as adults.

In the early church, Gentile Jesus-followers (aka non-Jewish Christians) had no history with following Jewish law. There was no expectation for them to even know the laws that God had enacted to keep Israel safe, set apart, and devoted to God.

But here in Romans, Paul is pointing out that Gentiles can instinctively follow those laws because they are written on a Jesus-follower's heart.

If I want to be like Jesus, then practicing spiritual disciplines like prayer, gratitude, service, and fasting are how I retrain my thinking. Over time, those Jesus-like behaviors become more second-nature. So even though I'm not following a list of do's and don'ts, I am living within the boundaries that such a list would provide for me.

P.S. Jesus didn't come into the world to replace or erase the law, but to fulfill it. Following Jesus in this way keeps us safe, set-apart, and devoted to God, just as the law did for the Israelites.

—BKS

In what ways are you practicing living like Jesus?

COMMON 128

The Lord created me [Wisdom] as the beginning of his work, the first of his acts of long ago. —Proverbs 8:22

Indiana Jones, selecting a common clay cup as the true Holy Grail—the cup from which Jesus drank at the Last Supper—among a visual clamor of gold, silver, and jeweled goblets, proclaimed, "THAT'S the cup of a carpenter."

"You have chosen wisely," replied the ghostly Grail Knight.

Wisely? Really?

Shrewdly, yes. Archaeologically appropriately, okay. Cinematically satisfying, for sure. But wisely? Isn't wisdom more than realizing that one of these things is not like the others?

Indeed. Wisdom is said to be the first of God's creations. She (and in Scripture Wisdom is a She) was there when everything else was made. Having emanated from Godself, Wisdom accompanies God in that pouring forth of imagination and love that is the created world.

When God spun out stars and trees, mountains and mankind, Wisdom rode shotgun.

Wisdom "delighted in the human race" as we were made.

She delighted in *you* when *you* were made.

Whether you were planned or a surprise, whether you got A's in school or struggled to get by, whether you had to learn to accept yourself as you are (even when no one else was like you, it seemed), your coming-into-being was surrounded by Wisdom.

Beloved child of God, when you despair of this broken world, when it seems like everyone is selfish and the worst among us wins, when you cannot imagine why God would tolerate our being so far off the mark, remember this:

Wisdom was there at the beginning of all of it. She is old, and favors maturity. She still cries out, calling to us in the hope that we will know Her and love Her, and having loved Her, keep choosing well, and slowly become wise.

When you don't know what to do and despair is far too close, ask Wisdom to accompany you (as She has God, for so very long), helping you to make good (not shrewd) choices, and in Her presence, discover delight.

—EOR

When have you encountered Wisdom?

COMMON 129

So faith by itself, if it has no works, is dead. —James 2:17

I believed the COVID-19 vaccine would protect me from the virus. So when it was made available to me, I made an appointment, drove to Levi's Stadium at the appointed time, stood in line, asked the nurse which arm I should get it in, took the shot, sat for the required 15 minutes to make sure I had no immediate adverse reaction, and set my appointment for the second shot (which I got a few weeks later).

My belief in the COVID-19 vaccine motivated me to do all of those things. I believed it would keep myself, those in my household, and everyone I come into contact with, safe from the virus. And so far, it has.

I also believed that the carnitas taco I had for lunch wouldn't poison me, so I ate it. And that the couch I'm currently sitting on wouldn't collapse under my weight, so I sat on it.

We believe lots of things.

Beliefs are ideas we are willing act on. But without action, those "beliefs" are just ideas.

We get bent out of shape when someone espouses a belief in a person or a cause, but then doesn't stand up when the rubber hits the road. The truth is we can say we believe anything, but until we've put some skin in the game, it's just words.

Our faith is proven when we act on the beliefs we say we have. That's why James says a living faith comes with actions. For instance, if you believe God cares for the poor, then your faith might compel you to volunteer at a food bank, or to donate to a coat drive. Your actions say you believe that God cares about the poor.

We always behave in concert with our true beliefs. Our beliefs about God are no exception.

—BKS

How does your faith in God express itself?

COMMON 130

Therefore, since we are surrounded by so great a cloud of witnesses, let us also lay aside every weight and the sin that clings so closely, and let us run with perseverance the race that is set before us —Hebrews 12:1

My Aunt Frances was a saintly woman. She was my grandfather's sister and she and her husband, my Uncle Breland, were a Godsend for my parents when they were young and newly wed.

See, the town where Mom and Dad grew up was poor, and opportunities were few. Uncle Breland owned a tool-and-die business in Nashville (250 miles away) and offered to pay for my dad to go to night school to learn the skills necessary to make a living working for him.

My parents bravely made the decision to move (thank God) after they'd been married only a few short months.

My dad retired from my Uncle Breland's business after working there for over forty years.

If it hadn't been for the kind and generous hearts of my Aunt Frances and Uncle Breland, my parents would probably have never left Alabama, which would've meant a very different future for my sister and me. They were like grandparents to us.

When I was in high school, navigating my adolescent faith, I remember often asking myself "What would Aunt Frances do?" She modeled a Jesus-trusting life for me all through my childhood. I still sometimes ask myself that question.

I'm incredibly grateful for everyone God has placed in my life to teach me how to live a faith-filled life. I won't start naming them because there isn't space for that. But they (and you may be one of them) are my cloud of witnesses. They started me on my journey, and they continue to cheer me on.

—BKS

Who is in your cloud of witnesses?

COMMON 131

All your works shall give thanks to you, O Lord, and all your faithful shall bless you.
—Psalm 145:10

Have you ever heard a Kudzu weed say thanks? How about a tick?

Are mountains, in your experience, generally grateful?

I was taught to formally thank a benefactor with a handwritten note. Does a spider weave a "thank you" into her web?

A lot of Christians were brought up to believe that God is revealed in the Bible, period, as if God needed Hebrew, Greek, Aramaic, and English to be noticed and understood.

Nature is God's first self-revelation. All that creativity spun out from God's words and hands shows us what kind of person God is.

The Psalmist says that God's works are thankful. The spider and the mountains, the ticks and the weeds: all expressing thanks, all the time, for God's god-ness.

That means that we are literally surrounded by gratitude.

Perhaps if we pick up a stone and listen very carefully we can hear it shouting, "Appreciate it!" to the biggest benefactor of all.

—EOR

Here's a new spiritual practice for you to try on during this summery season of Pentecost:
Next time you go to swat a fly, imagine it singing praises.

COMMON 132

> Now, discipline always seems painful rather than pleasant at the time, but later it yields the peaceful fruit of righteousness to those who have been trained by it.
> —Hebrews 12:11

My parents never had to discipline me much. I was a compliant kid who craved their attention. Plus, I was a firstborn with perfectionist tendencies (aka a parent's dream).

When they did discipline me, however, it was soul-crushing. I felt like I'd failed them and that I wasn't a good son or a good person.

I projected parental disapproval onto God a lot as a teen. Whenever I noticed a girl or boy and felt aroused, I could see my heavenly Father shake his head. If I felt ungrateful, or doubted that God's will was what was best for me, I could hear His correction.

But God wasn't doing that.

I took years for me to realize that discipline isn't punishment, it's training. Without discipline, our minds and bodies follow whims that can be self-destructive and life-destroying for other people. Discipline is how we learn to behave in ways that are socially acceptable and, in the case of spiritual discipline, more like Jesus.

Looking back, I can see that I was more self-disciplined than I realized as a teen. I read my Bible daily and prayed regularly to be the person God desired me to be. I created strict boundaries for myself, so my parents didn't have to. My practices and boundaries kept me safe and helped shape my thinking and behavior as an adult.

The other thing I didn't realize at the time was how much my parents, and my heavenly Parent, delighted in me. When they did discipline me, it was to prepare me for the life in front of me, not to punish me for something I'd done wrong.

—BKS

What role does discipline (of any kind) play in your life today?

COMMON 133

If you have faith the size of a mustard seed, you will say to this mountain, "Move from here to there," and it will move; and nothing will be impossible for you.
—Matthew 17:20b

In the verses leading up to Matthew 17:20, we read about a man whose son has epilepsy. He had previously brought the boy to the disciples to be healed, but they could do nothing for him. So he brings his son to Jesus and tells him just that. Jesus' exasperated response is something like, "Do I really have to do everything myself?" Then he heals the boy.

When the disciples ask, "Why couldn't we heal him?" he replies with that well-known verse about faith and mustard: "If you have faith the size of a mustard seed, you will say to this mountain, 'Move from here to there,' and it will move; and nothing will be impossible for you."

That is not how faith has ever been for me.

Sure, faith begins with believing something. Belief, as we know, is an idea that we're willing to act on. But then, faith takes work.

I can envision a mountain of debt being moved out of my way, but then I spend years living in my parents' basement, eating oatmeal and Lean Cuisines, and working three jobs to make it a reality. I picture myself living in California, doing (mostly) music and ministry, so I take (what feels like) a risky leap and it pays off.

Mountains move by inches—sometimes millimeters. And you have to put your back into it.

That is not to discount the mustard seed of faith it takes to get the ball rolling. Everything worth doing starts there.

—BKS

What have you done, or overcome, that required that tiny seed of faith to begin?

COMMON 134

Return to your rest, my soul, for the Lord has been good to you. —Psalm 116:7

I prayed for peace today. Not for the world, though it certainly needs it. I prayed for interior peace. For rest. For myself.

Lately, I've been feeling anxious, irritable, unsatisfied, and melancholy. Like I'm stuck in an emo pop song, or an itchy sweater. I can't seem to control my thoughts as they drag me to my past, linger on my what if's, and get riled at my how come's.

I could blame depression, grief, unresolved endings, the state of the world, even interference from the dark side, and they may all play a part. But knowing the cause doesn't necessarily point the way to peace.

So I've been reminding my restless soul that God has been—and still is—good to me. This helps center me, until my feelings (eventually) catch up.

I also have a best friend (and ministry partner) who gives amazing spiritual direction, as well as a terrific therapist. Both help.

I don't have a tidy ending for you with sunny advice and renewed perspective. But I will say this:

If you're feeling the way I feel today, you're not a bad person, partner, parent, or Christian. Try and be kind to yourself, looking at your emotions and thoughts with curiosity—not criticism or condemnation. Talk to someone you trust. Pray for rest.

—BKS

Be gentle with yourself in your hard times. After all, who are you to condemn what God doesn't?

COMMON 135

The king's heart is a stream of water in the hand of the Lord; he turns it wherever he will. —Proverbs 21:1

Is there anyone who captures your attention? Someone in your daily life you spend time watching, or whom you notice without trying?

New lovers are attentive to each other's words as they try to discern hidden meanings, and to their actions: how often they call, give gifts, remember dates.

New parents attend to their infant as they learn its cries and habits and watch for distress.

As time passes we become less aware. We get comfortable, less worried about making mistakes. We know the other better, making prediction easier. Or we get used to them, our relationship running on habit rather than desire or love.

Being comfortable with others is good: anxiety is miserable to feel and annoying to live with. Anyone the child of a helicopter parent? The subordinate of a micromanaging boss? Living with volatility? I see you.

Developing habits of useful or loving behavior is also good, not only because it makes life better for others but also because it shapes our inner beings into better people.

Often our lack of attention isn't due to comfort or good habits, but to self-centeredness and apathy.

Whether you're unaware of your spouse or kid or housemate or dog or God (and yes, I might be talking about myself here), your lack of attention says a lot about where your heart actually lives.

To be responsive to someone's else's soft or unspoken needs you have to pay attention as well as want to respond. To be part of their joy, or experience the enfolding of their affection for you, you have to both notice and take it in.

If you want to be the kind of person the Spirit of God can use for good in the world (me again. And you.), your own spirit must align with The Spirit and your soul pay attention to God. That attention, coupled with the desire to do what God wants, is what makes it possible for God to turn your heart, and mine, toward need and joy.

—EOR

When have you felt seen and attended to?
How might you cultivate that goodness in yourself and share it with others?

COMMON 136

Therefore no one will be declared righteous in God's sight by the works of the law; rather, through the law we become conscious of our sin. —Romans 3:20

In Romans 3, Paul talks about how no one is righteous, everyone has turned from God, and that Jews and Gentiles are alike under the power of sin.

Yeah, I don't see much hope in that either.

But then, in verse 20, he says this:

"Therefore no one will be declared righteous in God's sight by the works of the law; rather, through the law we become conscious of our sin."

In that verse Paul points to the real problem, which has nothing to do with the law. It's sin—life-destroying actions and attitudes that cause pain for ourselves and others, and create distance between us and God.

The problem isn't whether we are obeying a list of rules. Truth is, we like rules. They make it easy to know if we're doing okay or if we're screwing up. It's also clear who the rule-breakers are so they can be judged and dealt with.

But living life as a Jesus-follower is not about rules. Sure, there are two commandments that Jesus gave us: Love God and love your neighbor. But Jesus doesn't define *how* we are to do that. At least not with a list of do's and don't's.

Churches and denominations tell us how to be good Christians by creating doctrines—ideas interpreted or extrapolated from Scripture, accepted as gospel, and then practiced as if they are law.

Many (most?) Christians go to these churches, know the rules, and choose whether or not they want to live within them, understanding the consequences.

But when it comes to whether our actions are life-destroying or not, the real bottom line is how much our choices look like those of Jesus. His life (the fulfillment of the law) is what we can measure ourselves against in order to—as Paul puts it— "become conscious of our sin."

—BKS

What are some ideas you have about sin—what it is, why we do it, and how we can conquer it?

COMMON 137

Set your minds on things above, not on earthly things.—Colossians 3:2

Science says we have over 6000 thoughts every day. That's a lot of thinking.

Our thoughts allow us to make sense of the world around us. They underlie our all actions and interactions. And though the way our thought processes work has been studied forever, there is still so much we don't understand about the way our brains and minds operate.

Practically (and spiritually), we do know that what we allow our minds to drift to, or dwell on, has a big hand in shaping us. That's because thoughts are the basis of emotions, decisions, self-image, and ultimately, the quality of life we have.

In other words, we are what we think.

Because Jesus was human, he would have had negative thoughts occasionally—about his parents, his disciples, random people approaching him in the street, even about God. No one can keep negative thoughts out of their head completely.

But sitting with those thoughts can lead us to form negative ideas, which lead to life-destroying beliefs. Those beliefs lead to actions that hurt others and ourselves.

Since everything starts with our thoughts, training our minds is vitally important.

I try to manage my negative thoughts by practicing gratitude, getting rid of shoulds, assuming the best in others, and giving grace to myself. I don't do any of these perfectly—I have bad days too. But the more I practice thinking in these ways, the more they become second-nature over time.

—BKS

How do you practice setting your mind on things above?

COMMON 138

> [The exile] occurred because the people had sinned...had walked in the ways of the nations and ... the ways their kings had introduced. —2 Kings 17:7-8

I have an uneasy relationship with stuff. I enjoy beautiful things and really appreciate a well-designed tool, like the laptop I'm using, but having nice stuff can be a problem.

When the quantity of nice stuff I have reaches a certain indeterminate level I stop enjoying it. I just want More.

It's the same with politics, or entertainment. I am fascinated by the workings of human beings, and can be vigilant about justice or compassion, but too much justice work or too much of the news or Netflix-binging and I don't feel well. I have to shut it all off.

My inner world can healthfully handle only a portion of the outer world. Too much information or sorrow, or beautiful glassware and books, and the constant craving make my soul frantic. It cries out, "I don't feel well. Help me!"

Craving stuff and feeling overwhelmed are my symptoms of soul-sickness. Maybe they are yours too.

Here's the real problem: I develop a kind of tolerance. If I gradually increase the amount of stuff in my place or news in my head, I don't really notice. And if I also gradually decrease my time in worship and charity, over time my tolerance for stuff and news increases. I can handle more things, more money, more righteous indignation, more immorality, more sin, without even noticing.

Over time my soul seems to lose its voice. It's not well, but when I reach the point of TOO MUCH. my soul's sweet voice is drowned out by all the other noise. Which feels great...because I don't have to listen to its whining anymore.

I'm not alone in this. The Israelites started out attending to their souls, focusing their eyes on God, learning to be comfortable with being different from the surrounding culture, and living by rules that helped their souls be healthy.

So did the early Christians, and so did many small communities of supportive seekers.

Over time, the Israelites and Christians obeyed their human kings rather than their heavenly one, accepted the greed and injustice of the culture, and built up their tolerance for soul-sickness until those things overtook them.

My soul gets overtaken by my tolerance for things and noise.

To get my soul well again, and to keep it that way, takes paying attention, saying no, and resisting the lure of both media and More.

—EOR

**When do you realize that your soul health needs attention?
What do you do to help it out?**

COMMON 139

You have searched me, Lord, and you know me. —Psalm 139:1

Is there someone in your life who knows you? Like really knows you?

I am, by nature, a fairly guarded person. I like having friends, but I also tend to keep them at a safe distance. My family knows me, but we aren't deep sharers, and nobody asks deep questions.

Add a fear of abandonment and a dislike of goodbyes and you get me waving at you from behind a moat.

Still, it is nice to be known sometimes. Like when someone knows how you like your coffee, or how you'd most likely choose to spend a free day, or what makes you feel better when you're going through a rough patch.

If you have that person in your life, consider yourself pretty darn lucky. (Thanks, Elane.)

Psalm 139 reminds us that we are seen, known, protected, and cherished by God. We have no greater Champion and no closer Companion than our Creator.

—BKS

If you feel unseen, unheard, or unvalued, read Psalm 139, slowly and aloud. Sit with the idea that you are a treasured child of the Divine—sacred, beautiful, and loved. How does that feel?

Psalm 139 (NRSVUE)

O Lord, you have searched me and known me. You know when I sit down and when I rise up; you discern my thoughts from far away. You search out my path and my lying down and are acquainted with all my ways.

Even before a word is on my tongue, O Lord, you know it completely. You hem me in, behind and before, and lay your hand upon me. Such knowledge is too wonderful for me; it is so high that I cannot attain it.

Where can I go from your spirit? Or where can I flee from your presence? If I ascend to heaven, you are there; if I make my bed in Sheol, you are there.

If I take the wings of the morning and settle at the farthest limits of the sea, even there your hand shall lead me, and your right hand shall hold me fast.

If I say, "Surely the darkness shall cover me, and night wraps itself around me," even the darkness is not dark to you; the night is as bright as the day, for darkness is as light to you.

For it was you who formed my inward parts; you knit me together in my mother's womb. I praise you, for I am fearfully and wonderfully made.... In your book were written all the days that were formed for me, when none of them as yet existed.

How weighty to me are your thoughts, O God! How vast is the sum of them! I try to count them—they are more than the sand; I come to the end—I am still with you....

COMMON 140

[King Solomon] then gave an order: "Cut the living child in two and give half to one and half to the other." —1 Kings 3:25

My favorite book was *The Children's Bible* and my favorite story in my favorite book was the one about the baby and the two women. You may know it: they live together; both give birth; one baby dies so its mother steals the other's baby; they go to Solomon, each claiming to be the mother. Solomon says to cut the baby in half. The baby-thief agrees; the other one cries out and begs for the child's life. She gets the baby, of course.

In *The Children's Bible* some details alluding to class and character were omitted: the women were prostitutes; the baby died because its mother laid on him in her sleep; the baby-thief agrees to the halving so that neither woman would get the baby.

It's not a pretty story, right? As an adult I've tried to figure out why I loved that story. All the other kids liked Noah's Ark with its cute giraffe illustrations while I preferred Moses' Levite (i.e. not Jewish and not Egyptian) mom putting him in a basket on the river and hoping for the best.

From my current vantage point it's obvious why I liked these stories: both have a poor mother who so desperately loves her child that she's willing to do without him.

I wonder whether those two babies ever realized how much they'd been loved. Especially Moses, whose mother loved him so much she gave him up.

I wonder whether they *felt* loved.

As the mother of an adopted child, I've aimed to show my love and affection while acknowledging the sacrifice the birth mother made.

As a daughter with a complicated origin story whose mother chose to not give her up, I've recognized the pain of that decision, regardless of what one chooses.

As an adopted kid of an eternal Parent, I try to realize, and remember, just how loved I was, and am, and always will be.

—EOR

370

As a child, did you feel loved? Do you now?

COMMON 141

But all this gives me no satisfaction as long as I see that Jew Mordecai sitting at the king's gate. —Esther 5:13

Some mental habits destroy your life or diminish your joy. These thoughts can be so deeply ingrained that you don't notice them (like unconscious bias), or they can be ideas that you have repeated to yourself so often that they feel true.

Mental habits that are life-destroying are known as "sin." The famous list of sins: envy, greed, gluttony, lust, wrath, sloth, and pride.

My two "besetting" sins—the ones I am tempted by regularly—are envy and pride.

I can be having a perfectly wonderful life when out of nowhere I'll be struck with the fact that I'm Not making my living doing spiritual work (like fill-in-writer-here) and Not getting acknowledged in various media (like fill-in-teacher-here).

When envy strikes, that "What about Me? I deserve what She has!" can turn my own successes and blessings into dust that swirls up and blows away in the hot wind of my feelings.

My other tempting sin, pride, usually takes one of two forms: not wanting to appear (or be) weak, and feeling like I'm stupid/fat/lazy/a terrible mom. Both destroy: the one keeping me from closeness and care, the other reinforcing my shadow sense of unworthiness.

In the book of Esther, the king's right-hand-man Haman hates a particular Jew named Mordecai because Mordecai didn't bow to him. His hatred of Mordecai flames into a hatred of all Jews, so Haman tricks the king into decreeing all the Jews should be killed.

That sin is obvious, right? Having people killed is obviously life-destroying and a morally big no-no. Even Haman's pride (hating someone for not bowing) is clearly a problem.

But to me, Haman's worst sin is this: though he brags about his power and status, he cannot enjoy them because Mordecai exists. Everything Haman has seems like dust as long as his enemy lives.

Talk about life-destroying. And familiar.

The way to temper these thoughts is to notice them, call them out as false, and speak back to them gently but firmly, over and over and over again.

—EOR

Which of your persistent thoughts is destroying your life or diminishing your joy? Are you willing to resist that particular sin?

COMMON 142

There is neither Jew nor Gentile, neither slave nor free, nor is there male and female, for you are all one in Christ Jesus.—Galatians 3:28

There is neither Baptist nor Catholic.

There is neither immigrant nor native.

There is neither weird nor normal.

There is neither black nor white.

There is neither Marvel nor DC.

There is neither liberal nor conservative.

There is neither wealthy nor poor.

There is neither Star Trek nor Star Wars.

There is neither housed nor unhoused.

There is neither educated nor uneducated.

There is neither Madonna nor Gaga.

There is neither Millennial nor Baby Boomer.

There is neither married nor divorced.

There is neither LA nor SF.

There is neither Pepsi nor Coke.

There is neither homo nor hetero.

While God appreciates our differences, and enjoys our uniquenesses, God doesn't feel the need to label us. Nor does God exclude anyone on the basis of anything.

That's right. Anything.

You are not dirty, unworthy, or beyond hope. In fact, every one of us is sacred, beautiful, and loved—where we are and as we are.

There are no hoops of fire you are expected to jump through. There are no secret handshakes or magic words to recite.

All of us may come to God, with whatever faith we have (little or much), and find hope, healing, and wholeness. Full stop.

—BKS

Go ahead and fill in the blanks for yourself: There is neither _____ nor_____, for we are all one in Christ Jesus.

COMMON 143

O house of David! Thus says the Lord: "Execute justice in the morning and deliver from the hand of the oppressor anyone who has been robbed, or else my wrath will go forth like fire and burn, with no one to quench it, because of their evil doings."
—Jeremiah 21:12

Fire scares me. I learned early on that it could destroy everything, painfully, and that the slightest breeze could send it in a new direction. I've seen miles of hillside blackened by fire, and watched trees and houses burn uncontrollably.

While it's smart to be wary of fire, and to take precautions when using it, I don't need to base my way of living on fear of destruction by fire. I've learned to cook with fire, light candles with fire, and warm our living room with fire.

My fear of fire needn't control my life, but a healthy respect for its power should inform how I live. I move fragile things out of fire's way, and make sure I keep an eye on it. Knowing what fire is, and what it does, and why, allows me to behave rightly around it.

But imagine if I thought fire's destruction was caused by evil spirits, or by other people's skin color, or by their affections and affinities. Suppose I believed that everything else was flammable except me, or that poor people deserved to have fire destroy their homes, but that rich people were immune.

If you misunderstand fire, or are cavalier about it, it will destroy you.

When the prophet Jeremiah compares God's wrath to fire, he also says that God's wrath will destroy those who do not act justly, or oppress others, or refuse help to the abused and the poor.

How you behave toward others, not who you are or whom you love, determines the consequences of your actions.

If you respect the power of God's wrath, you can avoid its destruction by doing justice, loving kindness, and walking humbly with God.

—EOR

What are some ways you could practice being childlike in the presence of God? And in the world?

COMMON 144

I said, "I will watch my ways and keep my tongue from sin" … So I remained utterly silent, not even saying anything good. —Psalm 39:1-2

You ever gone through a period in which you were so cranky, so out of sorts, or in so much spiritual-mental-physical pain that every word that emerged from your mouth had ugly behind it?

Me neither. (How I wish that were true.)

Here's the real truth: Eventually someone would snap at me for being so damned negative and I'd suddenly realize I was miserable. Or anxious, which is its own kind of misery.

Because I couldn't pull myself out of my pain I would simply shut up. Retreat. Hide. Still do, sometimes. It's a habit: avoid hurting others … avoid having to face my own desolation.

Through lots (and lots) of work, and by the power of God, I don't lash out or disappear very often. But the "sin is in my body" as the Apostle Paul would say, meaning that bad habits are deep.

Training out bad habits and training in good ones is never about simply saying "No! Don't do that!" to yourself. Sharp rebuke simply shames, never grows something beautiful.

To change what you do, you have to change what you think (and especially what you think when you don't realize you're thinking it). That's where spiritual, mental, and physical disciplines come in. You develop a practice that's life-giving, which, over time, replaces other habits that destroy.

Meditation, prayer, reading, celebrating, gratitude: all these can be used to retrain our minds and bodies. So can more mundane, daily things.

Noticing when you feel like shit and turning toward a friend or therapist is a good practice. It feels terrible the first thousand times: deliberately exposing your vulnerability. Around the thousand-and-first time, you're able to take in a little bit of others' care, which in turn makes it easier to say good things—about yourself, about others—and build the cycle of love that can, slowly, change everything.

—EOR

How do you gently and honestly face yourself? What practices could you develop when you don't feel bad that will help you out when you do?

COMMON 145

Therefore let us move beyond the elementary teachings about Christ and be taken forward to maturity. —Hebrews 6:1

If you call yourself a Christian, or ever have, what was the marker for you?

Did you grow up under the assumption that you would take the faith, the way that some families presume the next generation will take over the family business?

Did you say some special words, perhaps tearfully, that ended your old life and began a new one? And if that, did your new life look much different than the day before?

The writer of Hebrews insists that all the focus on repentance, sin, proper ways to do church, resurrection, even eternal judgment, is "elementary." That's all the baby stuff, the words and worries that get you to the starting line.

In other words, if your daily life —your habits, the way you treat others, whether you care for the poor and imprisoned, help the sick and prevent the sickness, the way you make and spend money —if that doesn't change, you can repent all you like, but you'll be missing the point.

Salvation is not the natural consequence of baptism, or the sinner's prayer, or confirmation, and it's only barely about anything like heaven.

Salvation is a process of discipline, work, love (I'm quoting here), and imitation of those who exercise faith and patience. Salvation is an ongoing activity, not a one-and-done. The process of being saved — which does not end —results in a deepening maturity, demonstrated through behavior: wisdom, kindness, patience, service, hope, and joy, to name a few.

The end result is the person you become, not a particular place you arrive at.

And whether you are aiming for maturity or gratification or the apocalypse or pleasure or the land "way over yonder", you are still becoming the person you will be forever.

For good or ill.

The question for those of us who call ourselves Christian, or Jesus-followers, or even "good people" is this:

Am I becoming wise, kind, patient, full of hope and joy, ready to serve? And if not, what is my faith for?

—EOR

COMMON 146

> The fear of the Lord is the beginning of knowledge; fools despise wisdom and instruction. —Proverbs 1:7

In 1 Kings, we read that Solomon—son of David, King of Israel, writer of the book known as Proverbs—made a sacrifice to God. To honor his sacrifice, God appeared to him in a dream and asked him what he desired most.

Solomon's answer was wisdom.

God answered his prayer, in large part because his request wasn't self-serving like a long life or the death of his enemies. Solomon got wisdom. And then he shared it liberally.

Wisdom is something most of us achieve through experience. We can learn from mistakes that we have made or observed. That's why the wisest people are, by and large, the eldest among us: they have the most experience.

While wisdom is a perfectly fine thing to ask God for, generally we don't instantly become wise. All that knowledge and understanding doesn't instantly morph into good actions. God responds to our desire for wisdom with insight, clarity, discernment, even common sense.

Seems to me there are two ways we can actively pursue wisdom. One is to seek God for the purpose of knowing God better. When we do that, we get better acquainted with ourselves and more perceptive of what's going on around us. The other way is to be teachable and humble, understanding that as we learn and grow, we realize how little we actually know.

No matter where you are in life—young or old or in-between—you have some wisdom to share. Your history is unlike anyone else's. There is value to your perspective and experience that could benefit someone else. I mean, what good is wisdom if we don't share it?

—BKS

Who in your life would you consider to be wise? What could you learn from them, either by observing or asking? For whom could you be a source of wisdom?

COMMON 147

My beloved speaks and says to me: "Arise, my love, my fair one, and come away;
for now the winter is past, the rain is over and gone. The flowers appear on the earth;
the time of singing has come, and the voice of the turtledove is heard in our land. The
fig tree puts forth its figs, and the vines are in blossom; they give forth fragrance.
Arise, my love, my fair one, and come away." —Song of Solomon 2:10-13

It's a sunny Saturday morning in June. Your eyes aren't even open yet when you hear your phone buzz. You think, "It's Saturday, for Pete's sake! I'm obviously trying to sleep! Blarrgh!"

But you put on your glasses anyway and squint as you read: "Good morning, sunshine! Get dressed! We're going on an adventure!" It's a text from your favorite co-pilot for all things adventurous.

A day full of errands, laundry, leftovers, and some reality tv just became something way better. All thanks to somebody who loves you and loves spending time with you.

What if I told you that's how God approaches every day with you?

Back when you were in a winter, God walked with you, listened to your (mostly legitimate) complaining, and heard your longing for a new season. Spending time with God was like survival.

Now that you've weathered the worst of it, there are hydrangeas blooming and hummingbirds buzzing outside your window. Hope persists. Life continues. You might just as soon sleep the day away, but God is saying, "Let's go play!"

The Almighty may not show up to your house in a convertible, ready to get brunch at the beach. But God does love spending time with you and is leaving invitations all around for you to be in life-giving communion with the Divine.

—BKS

What are some invitations God may be leaving for you to notice? How will you respond?

COMMON 148

My beloved is mine, and I am his. —Song of Songs 2:16a

What would it be like to feel absolutely secure in an intimate relationship?

"How intimate?" you might ask.

So intimate that the events you don't like to remember and the wordless self-doubts can be spoken, safely, and with both grief and hope.

So intimate that you're not afraid to say, "I miss you."

So intimate that all your needs—from being held to getting the trash taken out—can be spoken and attended to without your feeling like *too much*.

So intimate that "vulnerability" isn't a four-letter word.

That intimate.

Intimacy isn't about sex, though we call sexual relationships "intimate." Even when there's no intimacy at all.

I've heard people try to explain away the Song of Songs as a description of the relationship between Jesus and His Church. (Can we just not, please?)

I've also heard the Song praised as exquisite erotic poetry: sexual impulse and attraction poured out onto the page. Which it is, even if "your teeth are like a flock of shorn ewes" (4:2) isn't your kind of tribute to beauty.

But reading it just now I heard something new: security in intimacy.

That kind of safety in vulnerability I've experienced only in my relationship with God. *That* Beloved is mine, and I am Theirs. I have no fear of ruining that, or being left, or forgotten, or being too much for God.

"I will seek him whom my soul loves" is a repeated refrain in the Song. In times of my deepest loneliness, I remember that my soul reaches out eternally for God.

Most times, God is enough.

—EOR

How intimate do you want to be with another human being, really? With God?

COMMON 149

Your throne, O God, endures forever and ever. Your royal scepter is a scepter of equity; you love righteousness and hate wickedness. —Psalm 45:6-7a

Kings, queens, presidents: they come and go.

Sure, royal families can lead monarchies for generations. But eventually the lack of an heir or the loss of a war results in handing authority over to a new line of succession.

In democracies, elections are won and lost. Power is transferred between people and ideologies. It can be scary, especially when incoming leaders don't regard your rights or share your concerns. Or value your life.

But God's reign isn't like that.

First of all, God doesn't come and go. God will always be God. While our experience of the Divine may evolve, the Unchanging One will remain essentially the same. God isn't moody, capricious, populist, or wishy-washy. God's ego doesn't get in the way of God's wisdom.

Secondly, God is both just and kind. While we may live with injustice in our manmade kingdoms, inequity doesn't jive with God. While our leaders can make decisions and act in ways that hurt people, God does not.

We can always trust that all is well in the Kingdom because God is both awesomely great and truly good.

Yes, we live in uncertain times. Evil is evident in the world. It's tough to be a fearless Jesus-follower if we fixate on what we read in the news. I often have to remind myself of Jesus' words in John 16:33: "In this world you will have trouble. But take heart! I have overcome the world."

And then I have to live as if I believe it.

—BKS

How will you remind yourself that God is always God, especially when the world around you seems to have gone off the rails?

COMMON 150

Eat, friends, drink, and be drunk with love. —Song of Songs 5:1b

There is nothing—no thing—like the powerful giddiness of attraction. That's what "drunk with love" is about. Not love—chosen, thoughtful, other-focused love—but attraction that makes you a little loopy.

And while I hate to be a killjoy, the less whole and balanced your mind, body, spirit, and soul are, the more exalted that feeling (and the bigger the drop from the mountaintop is when something isn't as you want it to be).

That doesn't mean attraction isn't good, or that if you're strongly attracted to someone (sexually or emotionally or intellectually or whatever) you're living in the shallow end of wellness.

Attraction is factual, and it's mostly not sexual. There are people to whom we are drawn, and people whom we don't notice at all. We can all guess at why, or why this one and not that one, but all those questions point to the reality of attraction.

Perfect world: we love the people we're attracted to, and we love the people we're not attracted to, and we don't mistake attraction for love. (Or love for attraction, which probably happens but not as often.)

If you're regularly attracted to cads who treat you as an object, or as disposable, that's worth looking at.

If you find yourself drawn to someone—you're curious about them, you are mostly at ease around them—enjoy that. Close friendships are based in attraction and develop into love: you are pulled toward each other, committed to the other's good, and choose to maintain that connection.

I can be in the same room with my best friend paying absolutely no attention to each other, or talking about something so important we both wind up teary, or laughing so hard that...well...the tears are different then.

And sometimes the *affection* you have for someone—a lover, your child, a friend, a mentor—can be so strong that the joy of their presence is intoxicating.

In those times, when your soul is satisfied and your spirit is alive, may you find yourself full, your cup running over with joy.

—EOR

Who attracts you? Why do you think that is?

COMMON 151

> So now, Israel, give heed to the statutes and ordinances that I am teaching you to observe, so that you may live to enter and occupy the land that the Lord, the God of your ancestors, is giving you. You must observe them diligently, for this will show your wisdom and discernment to the peoples, who, when they hear all these statutes, will say, "Surely this great nation is a wise and discerning people!" —Deuteronomy 4:1, 6

We humans don't like being told what to do. Rules restrict our freedom. They cramp our style. I mean, who likes being told they have to eat their broccoli? Or to be in bed by 10:00? Or to follow the speed limit on the 101? Not this guy!

The Israelites didn't like rules either. They tended to be defiant, whiny Lawbreakers. Granted, they had a whole lot of rules (*just read Leviticus*), but it was because God wanted to teach them how to live in community.

Notice that the Ten Commandments are more about how to treat others, including God, than they are about the person who is either following or breaking the rules. The Ten Commandments aren't about you: they're about how your relationship with others.

In giving the Israelites the Law, God wasn't interested in stifling their individuality, ending their personal expression, or just getting under their skin. God was shaping a bunch of individuals into A People.

The Israelites had to survive in a very hostile world. If they were ever going to take the land God had promised them, they would have to stand out as the favored people of the One True God. Learning to live within God's rules would make them a disciplined, devoted people that no one could ignore or overtake.

While Christians are not "under the Law"—that is, we don't adhere to the statutes followed by Jews—we benefit when we live within life-giving and life-preserving boundaries. We become better neighbors, better bosses and employees, better family members and friends, better citizens, and better pursuers of God.

We thrive, and the world benefits, when we follow God's rules.

That famous Jew Jesus lived a disciplined life of self-denial, centered on his relationship with his Father and his heart for humanity. When we discipline ourselves as Jesus did, we become more like him and more attuned to the needs of the world around us. And become part of A People of God.

—BKS

What is a spiritual discipline you could put into practice to prepare you to live in a hostile world?

COMMON 152

Happy are those who live in your house, ever singing your praise.—Psalm 84:4

Today my often-surly teenager spontaneously hugged me. Multiple times.

Light flooded the house. Flowers sprang up from the carpet and bloomed. Birds sang light opera.

Okay, so none of that happened, but her embraces and whispered "I love you's" transformed my corner of the atmosphere. I'd been tired and a little blue; those simple acts of affection and respect revived my soul.

In those moments when your home feels filled with love and affection, you're happy.

I say *moments* because that feeling of being loved and wanted isn't constant, is it? I live with three people I *know* love me—will my good—and often express affection for me. That doesn't mean I *feel* it consistently.

When you factor in those times that we *don't* have mutual love and care going on, like when we're squabbling or distracted, that could be a lot of feeling unloved.

That's one of the reasons that learning to experience God's tender affection is so valuable: it never fades or fails. God is never distracted. God doesn't get pissy or start a fight. God's house is wherever God is, and when God is there, love is too.

One way to practice feeling God's love is to sing God's praises. Just like with any other cheerful love song you really like, singing along can make you more aware of your own good feelings. (*If you need suggestions, I recommend practicing with Benton Stokes' "Love Is Like."*)

Don't wait for a teenager's hug to appear. Practice feeling loved, and see if technicolor gardens pop up in your heart.

—EOR

What's your go-to praise song (whether it praises God or someone else lovable)?

COMMON 153

O Lord, who may abide in your tent? Who may dwell on your holy hill? Those who walk blamelessly, and do what is right, and speak the truth from their heart; who do not slander with their tongue, and do no evil to their friends, nor take up a reproach against their neighbors; in whose eyes the wicked are despised, but who honor those who fear the Lord; who stand by their oath even to their hurt; who do not lend money at interest, and do not take a bribe against the innocent. Those who do these things shall never be moved. —Psalm 15

God has a (mostly) open tent policy. As long as a single requirement is met, anyone may come in, regardless of religious affiliation (or lack thereof), race, ethnicity, socioeconomic standing, gender and sexual identity, or education.

The single requirement isn't to claim some particular name as the right one for God, or to claim you know someone who is already in the tent.

The single requirement: Tent-dwellers must strive to do the right thing all the time.

That means always seeking out the right thing — the just, kind, loving, life-giving thing — and when necessary, asking God for the courage to do it. It also means making things right when we know we've failed.

When there is an ethical or moral issue that needs to be addressed, we must speak truth in love, recognizing that the person we're talking to is a treasured child of God. It is never okay to bully, ridicule, or humiliate, no matter what the offense.

We must treat our neighbors with respect, and not engage in petty arguments that can escalate into full-blown wars, forever burning the hope of a bridge.

When we see injustice, we must call it out and work to make the world a more equitable place, even when it makes us less comfortable, less privileged, or more vulnerable ourselves.

Living honestly and standing by our commitments is expected.

We must not take advantage of those in need or kick anyone when they're down.

Assuming you may enter God's tent simply because you know somebody (yes, Jesus) isn't reason enough. No matter what your church tells you.

The bottom line is this: God cares about how we live among each other. Our relationships with God are not meant to be private and nobody's business. God wants us to live out our faith in the world. Not tell it; live it.

Seriously, if our faith in God doesn't lead to life-giving activity, is it faith at all?

—BKS

How are you living out your faith at home, at work, and in your community?

COMMON 154

You were blameless in your ways from the day that you were created, until iniquity was found in you. —Ezekiel 28:15

If Adam caused us all to be filled with sin, when does that "filling" happen? When the two cells collide and create a zygote? How about the day we're born: is that when the sin pours in?

According to the doctrine of original sin, we inherit the stain of Adam's guilt, as well as his propensity for evil. We can't help it; we're born that way. Since *someone* had to be punished for all the bad we're bound to do, God killed his (obviously) sinless son, so we'd better cling to Jesus so we can be rescued from eternal punishment.

[If you're realizing how this way of thinking makes God a tyrannical father, you should know our Only Rule: Never believe anything bad about God. If God has to be a celestial child abuser to make sense of a doctrine, rethink the doctrine, because that's not God.]

Instead of Adam's disobedience ruining each of us forever, the Bible repeatedly states that we are blameless in our ways from the day that we were created (Ezekiel 18:15). We are innocent from the beginning, just as Adam was, and we make choices, just as Adam did.

When we make choices that have life-destroying outcomes, or that separate us from God and each other, we "sin." But sin isn't a part of who we are, like some aberrant chromosome. Sin is the result of how we choose to behave.

You weren't born a sinner. You were created in the image of God; the two of you share cosmic DNA. With the power of the Spirit's indwelling, and by learning from Jesus how to be good, you can overcome the iniquity— the unjustness—that's like a bad habit trained into your daily life.

—EOR

What do you *really* think about your basic nature? Deep down, are you good and holy? Bad and doomed? Something else?

COMMON 155

Every generous act of giving, with every perfect gift, is from above, coming down from the Father of lights, with whom there is no variation or shadow due to change. In fulfillment of his own purpose he gave us birth by the word of truth, so that we would become a kind of first fruits of his creatures. —James 1:17-18

Much of the theology I grew up with centered around how depraved and sinful I was. I thought God was disappointed in me most of the time, not because I had done anything wrong, but because I *was* something wrong. There was nothing I could do but try to make good choices and constantly ask God for forgiveness.

While my church kept reminding me of my hopeless state, they were also teaching me a very clear and ugly view of God.

That version of God was obsessive about my behavior, always judging, and never satisfied. Like a parent who is never happy with his kid. Or a deity completely self-absorbed and out of touch with his creation. Or that cranky neighbor who is always mad at everybody and cackles when things go wrong for them.

It's a wonder I didn't give up on God, since it seemed apparent God was always giving up on me.

Thankfully, I learned to think for myself, read the Bible for myself, and experience God for myself. And what I discovered was that God was and is a very different Person, Someone who is magnanimous with Their love and kindness. God: The Giver of every good and perfect thing.

From the start, we were the infinitely creative God's wild imagination come to life. And just as God delighted in humanity then, God delights in us now.

You and I are treasured and beloved by our Creator—who is not, in fact, a cranky old so-and-so waiting for us to fall on our faces.

—BKS

What are ideas you have about God you've been carrying around since you were a kid? Do you think maybe it's time to take a look at those?

COMMON 156

But you, brothers and sisters, are not in darkness, for [the day of the Lord] to surprise you like a thief; for you are all children of light and children of the day... So, then, let us not fall asleep as others do, but let us keep awake and be sober...
—1 Thessalonians 5:4-6

I like going to the symphony. I enjoy orchestral music and admire the players' skill in making it. And every time I doze off for a couple of minutes (*yes, only a couple—I know the music well enough to tell)*, I think it's because I'm relaxed and sitting still: I don't have to be on alert.

It's a little like being in the same job or the same relationship for a while: you get into a habit that makes it easier, but you're less attentive too.

The meticulous proofreading of the first few months? They're not going to fire you, right?

You didn't notice she was angry? Eh, she'll either talk to you or get over it.

We get used to things. Bad or good, life-destroying or life-giving, we adjust, or go into denial, or simply form habits of doing whatever it is.

It's the same with our spiritual lives. Or our church lives (those aren't always the same). We might notice if something disturbs our routine (*did they REALLY change the carpet?)* but unless our routine is shaken we just can just mosey through it, half asleep.

When we're asleep, we miss the Spirit doing Her thing. We miss divine interventions of peace when we're with people who don't like us.. We don't notice the little miracles that happen constantly.

Keeping spiritually and emotionally awake requires a combination of habit and diligence, as well as the occasional switch-up.

Maybe journal instead of meditating. Try praying to Mary (*don't panic: prayer isn't worship*) or a different member of the Trinity than usual. Make that overdue gratitude list, or take someone flowers.

You don't know when Jesus will be here with you, but you sure don't want to miss it.

—EOR

What is one thing you could do to shake up your spiritual life? (You might start by answering this question in writing.)

COMMON 157

You must understand this, my beloved: let everyone be quick to listen, slow to speak, slow to anger; for your anger does not produce God's righteousness. —James 1:19-20

Spend ten minutes on Twitter or Facebook and chances are you'll see quite an array of knee-jerk reactions to all kinds of things. People have opinions, y'all, and they are not afraid to share them. At least not when they're hiding behind their technology.

Social media has made it possible to criticize, attack, harass, harangue, bully, and belittle strangers, "friends," family members, celebrities, politicians—just about anyone—from a safe distance. We've all seen the posts and read the comments. Everyone has a virtual pulpit from which to preach whatever point-of-view they espouse about anything from favorite cocktail recipes to the climate crisis.

We are quick to speak, slow to listen, and there's a conclusion to be drawn just a short leap away. We vigorously seek out like-minded people to validate our positions, closing our minds even more to differing views. Online news sources and vlogs spread misinformation, conspiracy theories, and outright lies.

I'll admit I'm not immune to doom-scrolling. Christians of all stripes are caught up in the melee, and we're becoming angrier and angrier because of it. Including me.

But James has some important perspective for the Christian-identified: Anger does not produce God's righteousness.

There is a time and place for righteous anger. (*See Matthew 21:12-13 for a rare example.*) But Jesus-followers are becoming less empathetic, less able to disagree civilly, and less willing to seek reconciliation with those who don't see things the way we do. Our actions and attitudes are antithetical to the Gospel.

So what do we do about it? Here's my challenge to all of us:

As a spiritual discipline let's try limiting our online time, particularly the time we spend consuming social media, news, and opinion. Like kindergarteners, let's count to ten before we type a comment responding to someone we disagree with. Let's seek out differing opinions from even-tempered sources, not to pounce on them, but to learn from them.

You and I don't have to agree to learn something from one another's experiences.

—BKS

Do you feel angry when you surf the web or check your Facebook feed? Why is that? What can you do about it?

COMMON 158

Now concerning love of the brothers and sisters, you do not need to have anyone write to you, for you yourselves have been taught by God to love one another, and indeed you do love all the brothers and sisters throughout Macedonia. But we urge you, brothers and sisters, to do so more and more. —1 Thessalonians 4:9-10

God has no interest in a plastic-wrap kind of love.

You know the kind: it's that feeling that seems transparent and sturdy, but it's flimsy. Easily torn. You'd poke a hole in it if you looked at it too hard.

That kind of love is based on affection or attraction, both of which are fickle. Lose the attraction and all you've got left is a sticky wadded up ball of plastic that goes into your spiritual landfill.

Love is willing the other's good. Love is wanting what is good for another person, while not deluding yourself into thinking that you know or can dictate what that good is, and then being willing to act on its behalf.

It's hard work, that kind of love, especially when it's love for someone you don't like. Like yourself.

Love like that is a decision, made over and over again until you're in the habit (and then sometimes after that).

Like most life-giving habits that go against the grain of the material world, training to love takes the Spirit to give you the strength to make it happen.

Now, no one but God loves constantly, unconditionally. That means we can always get better at it. Wiser, more consistent, more active, until our kind of love is no longer destined for the landfill, but for eternity.

—EOR

Think of someone you're attracted to. Now think of someone you continue to choose to love. What's the difference in your feelings? Try to describe it.

COMMON 159

I will heal my people and will let them enjoy abundant peace and security. I will bring Judah and Israel back from captivity and will rebuild them as they were before. I will cleanse them from all the sin they have committed against me and will forgive all their sins of rebellion against me. —Jeremiah 33:6b-8

When I was a kid, I believed that all my sins were covered by the blood of Jesus the moment I accepted him as my Savior. Which meant that a gracious (but unsatisfied) God sent Jesus to earth—and eventually to the cross—to take on the consequences I deserved for my sins, saving me from after-death punishment.

My church also taught that my salvation (*whatever determines whether I go to heaven or hell when I die*) was not finalized when I accepted Jesus as Savior, so I would still have to earn my way into heaven by keeping clear of sin.

Yes, these are contradictory ideas. Many Christians accept both.

In the book of Jeremiah, written generations before Jesus was born, we read that God is ready to do the heavy lifting for the restoration of the Hebrew people. That *God* will heal God's people, restoring Judah and Israel, cleansing and forgiving them of sin.

Nothing is said about God being angry or needing to be appeased. Nothing is said about the Israelites having to do anything to receive God's forgiveness and restoration.

That's because it is in God's nature to forgive and restore. That's just how God is.

It doesn't mean we don't put in the effort to make things right.

It does mean that God isn't vengeful, happy to put Jesus through hell (*maybe literally, depending on your theology*) to save us. And it doesn't mean God is petty, keeping tabs on our every thought, action, and impulse on some cosmic spreadsheet.

When we believe bad things about God, fear motivates our service to God, not love. We are more concerned about our own eternal outcome than we are about caring for the world around us. My faith becomes about me and me alone, which is the opposite of what God was instilling in the Israelites.

—BKS

What do you think God thinks of you? What do you think of God? What do you think God is asking of you?

COMMON 160

Since we belong to the day, let us be sober and put on the breastplate of faith and love and for a helmet the hope of salvation. —1 Thessalonians 5:8

There were years when I wandered around the city at night, not looking for trouble, but also not avoiding it. Those were heady nights, dressing in what felt like gutsy girl-drag, or maybe armor, my emotions running hot and unpredictable, flipping from one to another when my girlfriend looked away, or didn't. Or when a stranger followed me at 3 a.m. up the long blocks between the subway and my apartment...to make sure I got home okay.

Those were not sober times. I don't mean chemically per se, but I wasn't clearheaded. I had personal demons screaming in my heart—Loneliness, Unworthiness, Arrogance—and a strong desire to be someone's savior. Sometimes I wanted to save myself.

Those nights were very different from my days, which were spent with work- friends, doing activism and the work of social justice, planning and cooking good meals with better ingredients, listening to every piece of music I could get my hands on.

You ever had that night-and-day life? In your head, maybe?

So whenever the Apostle Paul contrasts night and day, I get it. And when he says "we belong to the day," I can almost sense a flood of light, and openness, and trust, and ease, because I remember what the opposite is like.

When you belong to the day, clearheadedness is easier, and the only armor you might need is awareness, faith, love, and hope. When you belong to the day, breathing is easier, even in hard times, and the possibility of better is just a nighttime away.

John the Revelator wrote of the eternal kingdom of God, "and the city needs no sun or moon for the glory of God is its light."

May you live in that city, today and every day, and may you know you belong.

—EOR

What does living in the day feel/look like to you? What about living in the night?

COMMON 161

If any think they are religious, and do not bridle their tongues but deceive their hearts, their religion is worthless. Religion that is pure and undefiled before God, the Father, is this: to care for orphans and widows in their distress, and to keep oneself unstained by the world. —James 1:26-27

Religion is a difficult concept to pin down. The word is confusing, even to many who are technically religious. If you look up "religion" in the Oxford Dictionary, it reads: "A state of life bound by religious vows; the condition of belonging to a religious order." Well, what makes vows "religious?" What exactly is a "religious order?" (*scratches head*)

The Amplified Bible says the religious person is "scrupulously observant of the rituals of his faith" (James 1:26). Well, what are "rituals of faith?" Are they in a pamphlet you get when you join a church? (Usually, no.)

When I think of the word "religion," I think of churches governed by antiquated ideas and rules, filled with joyless people. The word is often paired with "organized" and coupled with a wince or a grimace. Even Christians don't want to be associated with it.

I also have a greater concern: What happens when the words "Christian" and "Christianity" get similar grimaces? Not the organized part or the joyless religion part, but the people and beliefs themselves.

They already do. What do we do about *that*?

I think we do what James says. We learn to rein in our tongues, but more than that, we retrain our thinking, paying attention to the way Jesus did and doing that. We also choose to be proactive in helping those in need, paying attention to the way Jesus did and doing that, too.

Maybe by living what Jesus taught and lived will rebuild the trust Christians have lost, one opportunity at a time.

—BKS

Think of someone you know who has a negative view of religion and Christians. What are some ways you can change their opinion by the way you live?

COMMON 162

See that none of you repays evil for evil, but always seek to do good to one another and to all. —1 Thessalonians 5:15

I wasn't always a good public speaker. When I was in college I gave a waaay overlong and off-point presentation. I'd done a lot of research, but it really wasn't good. When I finished, the instructor started screaming at me, berating me for what seemed like hours. He was so loud that other students shrank down in their chairs and I cowered in a corner wishing it would end.

For months thereafter I contemplated retribution. Setting his car on fire. Starting ugly rumors in his department. Locating a medieval crossbow, climbing to the roof of our gothic building, and shooting him as he strolled out for lunch.

I never actually did anything except get through the course and avoid him when I could. But I hated him—did not wish him at all well—and spent far too much time focusing my mind on that hate and humiliation.

Repaying evil for evil is life-destroying. If you do take evil action—even if they "deserve" it—you sin. And even if you don't take action, your mind is connected to your soul and your spirit, neither of which benefits from your dwelling on the harm you'd like to incur.

Sometime after that jerk screamed at me I heard he was being divorced, a rare thing in our college. At first I sneered, enjoying his hurt and embarrassment. But after a while, I remembered that dogs in pain often bite. My thoughts somehow slowly shifted from visions of revenge to moments of understanding.

As I forgave (some) of his behavior, my own healing began, which made me kinder, which helped me forgive more, and so on.

All these years later, I'm not completely over it. I still experience deep shame and embarrassment when I think about it. But I think I have forgiven him, and hope that in the rest of his life, he experienced kindness and love.

—EOR

Have you wished evil or revenge on someone who's hurt you? How did that feel? Did it bring you closer to God or push you farther away?

COMMON 163

[Jesus] said to them, "Isaiah prophesied rightly about you hypocrites, as it is written, 'This people honors me with their lips, but their hearts are far from me; in vain do they worship me, teaching human precepts as doctrines.' You abandon the commandment of God and hold to human tradition." Then he said to them, "You have a fine way of rejecting the commandment of God in order to keep your tradition!"
—Mark 7:6-9

The Jewish leaders Jesus is speaking to are seriously preoccupied with ritual cleansing, such as the practices of washing oneself ceremonially after sex, exile during menstruation, and avoiding contact with dead things like carcasses and corpses.

Jesus isn't saying there is anything wrong with ritual cleansing, but he is saying that to stress the practice is to minimize other things that God considers important.

Jesus is also saying that those who don't ritually cleanse—a "human tradition" —-are being rejected by those in leadership for reasons that aren't justified by God. Reasons that exclude rather than include.

We Christians do that too.

We make our table smaller when we draw lines around who can and can't participate in things like Communion, or even who's allowed to hand out programs at the door.

When we make our human traditions and precepts important, we push the things God cares most about to the background. We replace God's ideas about the value of every person with our own.

Interestingly, in the original Greek, the word translated as *hypocrite* means "actor" or "one wearing a mask."

A common example: Church people can wear the mask of "everyone is welcome," while simultaneously rejecting the person in front of them. Ask a queer person who's been catfished into visiting a non-affirming church just to be told—with words, actions, or both—that they are actually unworthy to be there.

Hypocrites say one thing and do another. So how do we guard against becoming hypocrites ourselves?

By making Jesus' life and teachings the foundation we build our Christian lives and churches upon, rather than on traditions that draw attention away from the life-giving Gospel of Jesus.

—BKS

Do you think hypocrisy is an issue inside your church's doors? Is it being dealt with or ignored? How can you help make sure everyone is welcome in your faith community?

COMMON 164

Pray without ceasing, give thanks in all circumstances, for this is the will of God in Christ Jesus for you. —1 Thessalonians 5:17-18

Please hear me: Paul is not giving a commandment. He is providing spiritual guidance that will draw you closer to God. That—being close to God, living in God's eternal presence now—is the will of God in Christ Jesus for you.

God is not your middle-management boss, reviewing your timecard and clocking your bathroom breaks.

God's will for you is wholeness—body, soul, mind, spirit, will, and environment—working in concert, plus (and it's a big plus) the awareness, comfort, joy, and peace that come from constant, intimate relationship with God.

Prayer is communication with God. The more you are in constant, intimate, communication with God, the better.

Giving thanks is consciousness and gratitude for what you have. For some reason, cultivating gratitude expands our lungs as well as our hearts: we breathe more deeply, even in horrible circumstances.

Giving thanks in all circumstances does *not* mean giving thanks for those horrible situations. There is no world in which giving thanks for your being abused fulfills God's will. (And if you've forgotten what God's will is, back up a couple of paragraphs.) Learning to experience gratitude for the tiniest morsel of hope or sustenance? Life-giving.

How do you learn to pray without ceasing? Try this: set an hourly timer. When it goes off, close your eyes, breathe, and focus your attention on the Divine Presence. Or try this: Find a very short prayer (like "*Come, Lord Jesus*") and repeat it when you're trying to draw strength, or meditating, or doing dishes. Praying that way sinks into your bones. It becomes part of you, so that even when you're not consciously thinking those words, they're a neurological habit.

You were built for connection to God. You were made to live easily in God's will. You are Beloved.

—EOR

Write this out and put it where you cannot help but see it: You were built for connection to God. You were made to live easily in God's will. You are Beloved.

COMMON 165

Remember me, Lord, when you show favor to your people, come to my aid when you save them, that I may enjoy the prosperity of your chosen ones, that I may share in the joy of your nation and join your inheritance in giving praise. We have sinned, even as our ancestors did; we have done wrong and acted wickedly. —Psalm 106:4-6

There's an old gospel song called *Pass Me Not, O Gentle Savior.* It was written by Fanny Crosby in 1868. That's old. I remember singing it during altar calls at my church when I was a kid. The lyrics are quite beautiful:

> *Refrain:* Savior, Savior, hear my humble cry.
> While on others Thou art calling, do not pass me by.
> Pass me not, O gentle Savior, hear my humble cry.
> While on others Thou art calling, do not pass me by.
>
> Let me at Thy throne of mercy, find a sweet relief.
> Kneeling there in deep contrition, help my unbelief.
> Trusting only in Thy merit, would I seek Thy face,
> Heal my wounded, broken spirit, ave me by Thy grace.

I have felt like the Psalmist, who felt like Ms. Crosby, I suspect. Unworthy, and longing to belong. Anxious over the state of my soul. Concerned that others *knew* something I didn't, or *had* something I didn't, that gained them favor in the eyes of the Almighty. Wounded. Broken. Contrite.

When I meditate on the words of the Psalm or the song, I understand my need for God and why confessing that need matters so much. It isn't about what God requires of me; it's about what I seek from God. And what God is most happy to provide.

—BKS

Think of a time when you've prayed for God to heal your wounded spirit, or to help you bear your grief, or to strengthen your faith and ease your doubts. How did God answer your prayer?

"Pass Me Not, O Gentle Savior" Words & music by Fanny Crosby. Public Domain.

COMMON 166

> But Ruth said, "Do not press me to leave you, to turn back from following you! Where you go, I will go; where you lodge, I will lodge; your people shall be my people and your God my God."—Ruth 1:16

"Would you move to a strange land to be with someone you loved?" Sure. I would—and have.

"How about the whiny mother of your recently dead husband? With neither of you having jobs or a place to live?" Umm, well, maybe?

"If you had to worship her gods, value what she valued, live with her, adopt her people as your own?"

Want to talk about love? Ruth proclaims her devotion to her self-pitying, grieving mother-in-law, begging Naomi to not cast her aside, because Ruth will make Naomi's life her own.

Ruth's act is a little self-serving: she's already in a foreign land and at least Naomi has family in the next place. But that's all she knows, except that Naomi is worth sticking with, and caring for, through this difficult time.

What interior strength inspires Ruth to make her pledge? What makes us act out of love when we don't necessarily see any benefit to ourselves?

Trust. We are able to make the sacrifices of love because we trust in something bigger than the situation or the acts themselves.

When I've made a big "leap of faith," it's never been because I could see a clear outcome, or because I was secure in another person's devotion and care for me, regardless and forever.

To do a big audacious thing, either you have to be in such a dark and hopeless place that it's change or die, or you have to believe (even if you don't realize you do) that God or Fate or Goodness or something universal and powerful will take care of you somehow.

When Ruth turns to Naomi's God, and lets the older woman guide her, things turn out really well.

But Ruth couldn't have known that when she threw her lot in with Naomi. She trusted Providence, and leaped.

—EOR

When have you done something out of love without any guarantee of success? Looking back, where had you placed your trust?

COMMON 167

Only be careful, and watch yourselves closely so that you do not forget the things your eyes have seen or let them fade from your heart as long as you live. Teach them to your children and to their children after them. —Deuteronomy 4:9

On my birthday several years ago, I stood alone in the pouring rain with a goofy smile on my face. I was waiting for the weather to pass so I could ride Diamondback, a roller coaster with a 210-ft drop and a top speed of 80 mph. I didn't mind the soggy sneakers. In fact, I had no concerns at all. It was like I was 14, excited to be waiting in the rain to ride a coaster. The anticipation that lived in a memory deep inside me came rushing right back as if no time had passed at all.

Some things we just never forget.

Like the moment each of my kids was born. And when their mom and I told them we were divorcing.

Like hearing my first cut on the radio while delivering pizzas to make ends meet.

Like holding my grandmother's hand as she was having a massive stroke.

Like walking up to an altar with my friends from youth group to become a Christian.

I've been shaped by the heartbreaks, the milestones, the embarrassments, the near-misses, and the homeruns. They make me *me*. They make me the dad I am, the friend I am, and the Jesus-follower I am. All of them have taught me something important, about myself and about God.

—BKS

What are the memories that are shaping you?
How have your experiences shaped those closest to you?

411

COMMON 168

After thinking it over, I contended with the nobles and the officials; I said to them, "You are all taking interest from your own people." And I called a great assembly to deal with them. —Nehemiah 5:7

As a queer woman who spent half her life in social justice work of one kind of another, I have real trouble imagining a society in which a major religious leader could critique the dominant economic system and be taken seriously.

God's prophet Nehemiah points his finger at the people in financial power, "Dudes, what's this with charging people interest? How can you take money you don't need from people who desperately do?"

Can you imagine a society in which that even makes sense? Where Elon Musk "loans" money to the poor and expects nothing in return?

It's a tough one for me too.

When I take off my Justice Hat and put on my What Does This Mean For Me Hat (bigger, and with feathers) two things stand out: as a man of faith, Nehemiah calls out the powerful people doing the unjust thing; and as a woman of faith, I need to make sure that I'm not using the dire situations of others to my own benefit.

Uh oh.

Like the clothes made by children in really poor countries that are cheap for me to buy.

Like how the chips in the computer I'm using to write this are full of toxic chemicals that someone else is breathing.

Like being able to exceed the speed limit and not fear getting shot at when I'm pulled over.

I guess as someone who thinks of herself as a lover of God and people—a woman of faith—social justice can't really be part of "what I used to do." It has to be part of the way I live my life every single day.

Whether God's prophet is pointing the finger at me or not.

—EOR

How does the call to love God and neighbor affect your financial decisions?

COMMON 169

Train yourself to be godly. For physical training is of some value, but godliness has value for all things, holding promise for both the present life and the life to come.
—1 Timothy 4:7b-8

When I was a kid, I played the piano competitively. I practiced for hours a day, memorizing scales and perfecting pieces. It took self-discipline to practice when I really just wanted to ride my bike or read my comic books. But because I trained, I didn't just win trophies, I also became a good musician. And music has remained a huge part of my career and my life because of it.

When you really want progress or success in an activity, training gets it out of your head and into your bones.

If you want to make progress in living spiritually—if you want to be more like Jesus—train your spirit like you would your body, getting all you know about love and God out of your head and into your bones.

Take patience, for instance. To become a patient person, you have to practice patience. That could mean taking the long way to work, through school zones and irritating traffic lights, until you no longer feel annoyed by speed-limit drivers and pedestrian crosswalks. After you've worked at becoming patient for a while, you'll find that impatience doesn't rear its head nearly so often.

How about prayer? If you discipline yourself to pray three times a day—focusing once on the specific needs of others, once on the state of the world, and once on your own personal growth—then eventually praying will become something you do without prompting. And as a result, you will become more attuned to the needs of others and to your own spiritual health.

Jesus didn't become *Jesus* without studying, asking questions, observing, trying-and-failing, and spending time alone with his Father. It took training: intention, effort, and discipline. We won't become more like him without being disciplined too.

—BKS

What is a spiritual practice you could use to train yourself into being more godly (or Jesus-y)?

COMMON 170

If the peoples of the land bring in merchandise or any grain on the Sabbath day to sell, we will not buy it from them on the Sabbath or on a holy day, and we will forego the crops of the seventh year and the exaction of every debt. —Nehemiah 10:31b

The first time I went to New York City, I was appalled to discover that I could not buy a bottle of wine on a Sunday. In the heathen West, the day of the week was irrelevant; was Manhattan more religious?

Or a better question: what are the "Blue Laws" that regulate Sunday commerce about? It varies from place to place, but historically they're about one of three things:

1. Ensuring Christians went to church on Sunday mornings, rather than sitting about drinking.

2. The idea that Sunday is inherently holy, alcohol is inherently sinful, and never the twain should meet.

3. No one should work on the sabbath day (which for most Christians is Sunday) because God decreed it a day of rest.

That last one is actually biblical. The 613 laws of the Hebrew Scriptures have a clear rhythm of rest and restitution. On the 7th day, everyone (including slaves) should not labor. In the 7th year, farmers forego both planting and the usual payment on their land as all debts are forgiven.

Imagine a world in which all debt had an expiration date. Or one in which everyone had a real day off, together.

In the nominally Christian USA, economic productivity and easy acquisition hold far more value than biblical mandate. That doesn't mean that as Christians we can't follow a sabbath schedule.

You may not have control over your workdays, but you do have a say in what *rest* means, and whether you maintain a rhythm of rest.

You may have debts that last far longer than 7 years, but you can aim to regularly forgive what you believe others owe you.

Even if you don't have an active faith community, you can make sure that once a week you count your blessings and give thanks to the One who makes life possible.

Over a glass of wine, if you like.

—EOR

What do you do to keep a sabbath rhythm of rest? If that doesn't feel sufficient, what could you do differently?

COMMON 171

Do not put your trust in princes, in human beings, who cannot save. When their spirit departs, they return to the ground; on that very day their plans come to nothing. Blessed are those whose help is the God of Jacob, whose hope is in the Lord their God.
—Psalm 146:3-5

We like our kings. They're easy.

Do what they say and all goes well. Kings punish those who don't follow the rules. Kings protect us from enemies abroad and among us. Even Israel wanted a king, so God gave them Saul.

I saw the musical *Hamilton* recently. It's based on two historic conflicts: one between the American colonies and England, and one between Aaron Burr and Alexander Hamilton. King George, who ruled England during the American Revolution, was depicted as pretentious and out-of-touch with reality, finding the uprising of the colonists hilarious. (I admit that his recurring song *was* hysterical.)

In reality the king was quite surprised by the separatists' tyranny and reacted strongly. In the end though, the soon-to-be-American people pushed against a monarchy and won independence, establishing a republic-style democracy in its place.

Even so, at moments throughout American history—particularly now—Americans have liked having a king. The problem for American Christians is we can't give both our Divine King and an earthly king the same devotion. Either we trust the God of Jacob and place our hope in the Lord, or we don't.

No matter how enticing it is to give power and allegiance to someone who says exactly what we want to hear, punishes those who disagree with us, or flips the script on the course our country is moving in, it is not wise to trust monarchs—even elected ones—who cannot save.

Only one King is eternal and his name is Jesus.

—BKS

Who is your king? How can you tell?

COMMON 172

O that my ways may be steadfast in keeping your statutes! —Psalm 119:5

Very little is achieved by sheer strength of will: our wills simply aren't that strong.

The difference between success and failure is usually vision+habit. Explicit, clearly defined vision of what we could gain is what motivates action. Habits reinforce whatever direction we're headed. To change direction, we have to change both our vision and our habits of mind and body.

If you want your "ways to be steadfast in keeping God's statutes," you have to develop the habits that reinforce that. Going to church on Sunday can be useful, but simply getting your body into a particular building may not be part of the habit cluster your "ways" really need.

Tending to your habits of mind and soul is as important as those of your body. Your soul hungers for God; feeding it junk food (sex, food, tv, distraction) isn't healthy for it. And you already know how destructive, self-and-other-loathing thoughts can become habitual, shaping your view of everything else.

It gets tiring, this monitoring of thoughts and behaviors, and it's really hard not to slide into a spiral, like "I've already missed my meditation time, and now my kid wants dinner, and WTF anyway?" Or "I'm already working 50 hours a week and living on cheese puffs. There simply isn't room in my brain or my life to make real changes in my habits. God's gonna have to take me as I am."

But that's the thing. It's not about whether God takes us as we are. It's whether we can love ourselves, and God, and others a little bit better every other day.

That's all being steadfast means: the tiny-but-consistent movements toward the vision of a joyful and manageable life fully in real and satisfying relationship with God (sometimes described as "keeping your statutes").

Tiny-but-consistent movement. Very little strength of will required.

—EOR

What is one tiny action of mind or body you could do that would be life giving? (Now, cut that aspirational action back again and again until it's do-able.)

COMMON 173

Then the eyes of those who see will no longer be closed, and the ears of those who hear will listen. The fearful heart will know and understand, and the stammering tongue will be fluent and clear. No longer will the fool be called noble nor the scoundrel be highly respected. For fools speak folly, their hearts are bent on evil: They practice ungodliness and spread error concerning the Lord; the hungry they leave empty and from the thirsty they withhold water. Scoundrels use wicked methods, they make up evil schemes to destroy the poor with lies, even when the plea of the needy is just. But the noble make noble plans, and by noble deeds they stand."
—Isaiah 32:3-8

We American Christians say we love Jesus. We even preach that Jesus is the Answer to everyone's problems. We insist that without Jesus, there is no way to approach God.

We put up billboards on the interstate that tell people to "repent" because "the time is near." We say anyone is welcome in our churches, but we don't really want someone in the pew next to us who doesn't look and think and act like us. We sing worship songs about our individual devotion to Jesus, but we don't confess our unfaithfulness, or show concern for humankind.

We refuse vaccines in a pandemic because we doubt the minds and reasoning God gave scientists. We prioritize our personal freedom over the lives of our vulnerable neighbors.

We restrict abortion because we say we must protect unborn children, but we don't insist that our elected leaders restrict guns, even though guns are responsible for more child deaths than anything else.

We know Jesus said we should care for the poor and the outsider, but we don't like what immigrants are doing to our country, and we punish the poor by denying them a meaningful voice at the polls and limiting their access to health care.

We've have little respect for our planet, leaving certain cataclysm for our kids to deal with. We consume indiscriminately, use our resources unwisely, and refuse to be inconvenienced for the greater good.

We American Christians are the fools and scoundrels Isaiah is talking about. Our plans and deeds are not noble. Until we allow God to soften our hearts and change our perspectives, we do not deserve respect from God or anyone else.

—BKS

How are you a part of the solution, as well as the problem, in one of the areas I just mentioned? (*Yes, I ask myself these questions too.*) And if you're not an American Christian, how are you helping solve the problems wherever you are?

COMMON 174

I waited patiently for the LORD; he inclined to me and heard my cry.—Psalm 40:1

Are you patient? I'm not.

I have areas of patience. Smatterings of patience. The occasional dewdrop of patience. But would I describe myself as *patient*? Um, no.

(I'm going to blame this on being an Enneagram 1, but that's because I don't have the time and inclination to think it through.)

What does it mean to be patient, anyway? Being patient with the well-dressed woman in front of me at the grocery slowly counting out pennies and nickels is not the same thing as being patient with loved ones on their own journey who don't move along as quickly as I'd like them to.

Which is also different than trying out a skill I don't have and sticking with it until I do.

What makes patience possible for me? A long story arc and real investment in the outcome.

I have multiple advanced degrees because I could see why I enrolled and the ego investment I had in finishing. That kind of patience is more like persistence.

Patience with people has to have an outcome that matters to me. If I don't tailgate the driver in front of me when he's going 20 miles under the speed limit, it's because the outcome of tailgating can be death. When I take deep breaths and count to 100 because my child is being rude, it's because my calming down will lead to a more desirable outcome.

I'm patient with God when I know I'm not the one in control of the situation. Like when my mom was dying of cancer and I prayed for her comfort. I trust God's guidance when I feel deeply insecure but accept that I can't control others' responses. Not too long ago I applied for a job I really wanted but prayed God would get in my way if it wasn't right for me.

In all those cases, and countless others, when I've chosen a path of patience, God has leaned in to listen to both my complaints and my sorrow, then carried me through.

—EOR

Does patience come easily to you? When do you find it easy to be patient with others? With God? When is it the hardest?

COMMON 175

O Lord, by these things people live, and in all these is the life of my spirit. Oh, restore me to health and make me live! Surely it was for my welfare that I had great bitterness, but you have held back my life from the pit of destruction, for you have cast all my sins behind your back. —Isaiah 38:16-17

Hezekiah was the 13th king of Judah. His father, Ahaz, was, by all accounts, a truly bad person. He ordered the doors of the Temple of Jerusalem nailed shut. He burned his own children as sacrifices to pagan gods. He halted the worship of God and shut down the Levitical priesthood. Even being King David's son couldn't save him in the eyes of God.

But when Hezekiah took the throne, though he had his work cut out for him, that all changed. He reinstated the priesthood, reinstituted Passover as a national holiday, restored temple worship, and the people of Judah returned to God.

Then Hezekiah became deathly ill.

Remembering Hezekiah's faithfulness and commitment to making right the sins of his father, God gave the king fifteen more years to live. Because God spared him, Hezekiah responded with humility and gratitude, like most of us would, and continued to be the loving, responsible ruler of Judah.

Like Hezekiah, we sometimes find ourselves at a crisis point. We stare at a wall we don't know how to knock down, climb over, or get around. What then?

God never wants to see us cower in defeat at the sight of an obstacle, even one as daunting as terminal disease. That's why, in the case of Hezekiah, God does the heavy lifting—places Hezekiah's sins behind Their back. Nowhere in the story does Hezekiah beg for God to save him, deliver him, or heal him. God does it anyway.

God does that for us too. The burden of salvation is not on us. It isn't about praying the right words, or even doing the right things.

—BKS

When have you been rescued, somehow, from a situation you couldn't handle?

COMMON 176

Sacrifice and offering you do not desire, but you have given me an open ear.
—Psalm 40:6a

It's the next-to-last scene of dozens of romantic movies: "I've done everything I can! Tell me what you want from me!" (Cut to long-suffering lover's pitying face as she turns and walks out of the house forever.)

It's why the 10 Commandments or the 613 laws of the Hebrew Scriptures are so enticing. They appear to require no attention or interpretation. Yes, no, black, white. Yet repeatedly God says to the law-keepers, "I don't want your sacrifices and your rule-following. I want you to listen to the cries of the needy. I want you to love."

Listening and loving are a lot harder than checking off tasks.

Here's the crazy twist on those old romantic movies: God doesn't turn and walk out the door. Instead, God calmly replies, "Forget about doing more. That's not what I want. I just want to hang out with you, hear what's on your heart and mind."

God's not your long-suffering lover, or your guilt-inspiring parent. God really, truly doesn't need *anything* from you. Does God want you to love, do justice, be humble? Sure! But *need*? God's immensely creative and pretty darned self-sufficient.

God loves you. God cherishes you. And like anyone who cherishes another, God wants to hear from you. No pressure. No guilt.

Just joy from the One who will never turn and walk out the door, and will always welcome you home.

—EOR

How are you still trying to earn God's love?

COMMON 177

Jesus replied, "Very truly I tell you, everyone who sins is a slave to sin." —John 8:34

Who would willingly become a slave?

In America, as elsewhere, slaves were people who were bought and sold like property. They did whatever their owners asked of them. If they complained or disobeyed they were punished, often severely. So slaves generally served their owners without question or hesitation.

Slaves didn't ask to be slaves. But sometimes we do.

We give authority and control over our lives to sin when we choose life-destroying actions and attitudes instead of life-giving ones.

We give sin control little by little. Sharing one piece of gossip. Entertaining a lustful thought about a co-worker. Seething with envy over a rival's accomplishments.

My sticky soul will adhere to whatever gives me a thrill or comfort or satisfaction in a moment. That is, if it isn't sticking to God and at peace with what God has given me.

We may not realize the hold sin has on us until we have hurt people, stained our own reputations, and created distance between ourselves and God. Jesus' warning isn't about an eternal outcome; it's about here and now and the damage sinful behavior can do.

We can refuse to be slaves to sin by intentionally pursuing God, following in the way of Jesus. We can train our minds to see people as subjects and not objects. We can teach our bodies to wait for gratification. We can find contentment in what God has provided for us. And we can ask God to help us when our trust and resolve are weak.

—BKS

Name a life-destroying behavior that you know you are susceptible to. How are you going to make sure you are not enslaved by it?

COMMON 178

> Now Balaam saw that it pleased the LORD to bless Israel, so he did not go, as at other times, to look for omens but set his face toward the wilderness. —Numbers 24:1

We God-watchers can tie ourselves in knots looking for some sign that we're Doing It Right. You might call it "discerning God's will" or "seeking a sign."

How many times have you watched for some signal that you were making a good decision? That signal-seeking can be a way of putting off taking action. I used to work with someone who would never make a big decision until he'd had three sure signs that it was the right one. What counted as "sure" was unclear.

I know I'm procrastinating when I'm either a) tied up in knots over the needed action, or b) so totally focused on doing something else (hello, clean refrigerator!) that I forget everything else.

God frequently guides us through both whispers and stop signs, and not only on those decisions that feel big, but in the little things too. It's a matter of listening for God's voice, learning to recognize its timbre and tone.

When you're regularly practicing tuning your heartstrings to the Spirit, listening for Her song is just part of what you do. There's very little hand-wringing or sign-seeking. You just go.

That's what happened for Balaam. Once he realized that God was going to do good, he stopped frantically looking for signs and headed into the wilderness.

The wilderness isn't a forest, or a desert, or a dangerous part of your town. A better word for wilderness is *wildness*: those situations you can't control.

One he's convinced of God's love and care, Balaam stops looking for signs and heads straight into the uncontrollable unknown, trusting that he's doing it right, and that if he's not, God will whisper and guide him to wherever he needs to go.

—EOR

What current practice do you have that you could use to listen for the Spirit's song?

COMMON 179

Where can I go from your Spirit? Where can I flee from your presence? If I go up to the heavens, you are there; if I make my bed in the depths, you are there. If I rise on the wings of the dawn, if I settle on the far side of the sea, even there your hand will guide me, your right hand will hold me fast. If I say, 'Surely the darkness will hide me and the light become night around me,' even the darkness will not be dark to you; the night will shine like the day, for darkness is as light to you. —Psalm 139:7-12

Sometimes God's Spirit is a comforting presence. She comes alongside us when we're lonely or grieving or confused and offers hope, peace, and perspective. She sits with us, even when we don't want the company, and waits until we're ready to talk. Then She reminds us that we are, and will be, okay.

Sometimes, though, She drags into the light things about ourselves we don't want to see. She points out the times we're self-absorbed or we hold grudges. She shows us our jealousy, our pettiness, and our greed. She reveals where our current path is leading. She can be like a Divine Therapist, opening old wounds to get us to healing. She can make us feel, think, and squirm.

I think most of us want to be in the light most of the time. But sometimes we want to curl up in the darkness. I've been there—when I was feeling overwhelmed by debt, beyond stressed in my business partnership, lonely in my relationship, and uninspired to write or create anything. The result was depression, anxiety, and a serious shortage of hope.

In those seasons, the Spirit will do whatever She can to pull us out of our darknesses and into God's self-revealing (and us-revealing) light. Because that's where hope is.

—BKS

How has the Spirit brought light and hope into your darkness?

COMMON 180

> When you reap the harvest of your land, you shall not reap to the very edges of your field or gather the gleanings of your harvest. You shall not strip your vineyard bare or gather the fallen grapes of your vineyard; you shall leave them for the poor and the alien: I am the LORD your God. —Leviticus 19:9-10

Prosperity gospel makes me crazy. If you think Jesus did life right, and believe the Bible when it says he didn't die rich (and none of the apostles did either), then it doesn't seem likely that God rewards faithfulness with a winning lottery ticket.

In fact, the God of the Bible repeatedly emphasizes how important it is that all of us who have some (or much) take care of those with little or none. That's what blessing looks like for God: the ability to do more without fear of not enough.

In the midst of all God's laws about agriculture and rest and caring for widows, God tells the Israelites who have land that they must not attempt to get every last grain of rice to market.

Instead, they are required by God to leave crops behind so that poor people and foreigners can eat.

Not: "you be good and I'll give you everything" but "being good is about leaving enough for others."

If you've ever been the recipient of life-sustaining food, if you've ever been that hungry, you know that prosperity can look like an abandoned crust of bread.

And if you have control over more than you need, you have probably noticed that the ability and the inclination to give away is its own form of prosperity.

—EOR

How do you exercise your prosperity?

COMMON 181

Come near to God and he will come near to you. Humble yourselves before the Lord, and he will lift you up. —James 4:8a & 10

I love hearing from my kids. They aren't actually kids anymore—my oldest son got married this summer, my middle son is an engineer (not the train kind), and my daughter (the youngest) is no longer a teenager. But that's beside the point: Getting a random text or call from any of them instantly becomes the highlight of my day.

Of course, I can reach out to them, and I do. But when they reach out to me, it's because they are thinking of me. Nothing is better than that.

God feels that way too. When we drop in on God, our Divine Parent drops everything.

Going to God with humility—not because we're wretched, but because God is truly awesome— opens us up to receive whatever God has for us in response to our desire and need. God already knows what we're seeking, but our choosing to bring that as a prayer is an act of trust. It says we believe that God can take care of us, and wants to.

Whether what you need is a listening ear when you're upset, some clarity when you're confused, a cheerleader when you're facing something big, a healthy dose of perspective when your world seems out-of-control, or hope when things don't look so hopeful, God is most willing to meet you where you are.

Bottom line: Nothing matters more to God than you.

—BKS

When have you gone to God with a concern, a dream, or a need to find God ready and willing to listen and help? Is now a good time?

COMMON 182

I am the living bread that came down from heaven. Whoever eats of this bread will live forever, and the bread that I will give for the life of the world is my flesh. —John 6:51

Apparently some of Jesus' listeners assumed he was suggesting cannibalism: literal eating of his fleshly, earthly body.

He wasn't being literal, though. Jesus is comparing himself to the highly perishable manna-bread that fell from the heavens, sustaining the Israelites a day at a time.

Manna was for a day but "eating" Jesus is forever.

Manna was a physical thing so it was perishable. Even if you ate enough manna to feel Thanksgiving-full, you'd be hungry again. That's the nature of material things: they go in and out of existence, and the pleasure (or pain) they provide eventually ends.

We aren't just physically hungry. We are spiritually hungry. But physical and mental cravings are so loud they can drown out all the rest of our needs. We try to satisfy ourselves with perishable "manna"—food, drink, sex, tv, books, work—rather than attending to the needs of our eternal souls.

We have access to the experience of eternity and the companionship of God right now. Call it *the present kingdom* or *an eternal kind of life*. That experience of satisfaction comes when you listen to the very quiet voice of your soul and give it what it's hungry for.

Soul food, to Jesus' listeners, was time with him. Maybe it's yours, too.

When I finally listen to my soul, it usually tells me it needs me to shut out other voices and stop doing other things. I need time to be alone, in the presence of God (whether I acknowledge that Presence or not).

Sometimes I look at a crucifix and contemplate Jesus' experience. Sometimes I read a book or brain-dump write. Sometimes I sleep or walk outside. All these things feed my eternal soul in a way that bread (even really good sourdough) never could.

—EOR

What is one form of soul food for you? What do you tend to consume instead?

COMMON 183

When I came to you, I did not come with eloquence or human wisdom as I proclaimed to you the testimony about God. My message and my preaching were not with wise and persuasive words, but with a demonstration of the Spirit's power, so that your faith might not rest on human wisdom, but on God's power. —1 Corinthians 2:1b, 4-5

Have you ever heard a preacher who was so concerned about sounding smart that his sermon got mired down in big words? I've literally had to google words I didn't know in the middle of a sermon just so I could keep up, and I'm a pretty smart guy.

I've also been in group prayer with people who use a whole different vocabulary when praying than when they're talking with people who aren't God. Like King James and Christian-ese are the only languages God understands. It probably doesn't bother God, but I find it distracting.

Sometimes words get in the way. Especially if you really want to be understood.

Paul was a great wordsmith. I can imagine him editing and re-editing his letters before sending them because he knew that being understood was the most important thing. He considered who would be reading them when choosing both what he would say and how he would say it.

Here in his letter to the Corinthians, he says the point of sharing a testimony isn't the delivery, but the opportunity it creates for God's Spirit to do Her thing.

When we get too concerned about sounding wise and eloquent, it's like we're an emcee whose introduction leaves no time for the star of the show.

The point Paul is making for us is really just this: Live your faith so the Spirit has room to move. When necessary, use (appropriate) words.

—BKS

When have you found words to be especially effective in a sermon or a conversation about God? When have they really gotten in the way?

COMMON 184

Yet among the mature we do speak wisdom, though it is not a wisdom of this age or of the rulers of this age, who are being destroyed. —1 Corinthians 2:6

All the members of my family have snapped at me, "That's not what I need to hear right now!" And given my propensity for using the zoom-in, zoom-out feature of my brain, they were probably right. Whatever "wisdom" I had to share wasn't what they needed.

It doesn't matter how many pearls of Truth you have to give, if you're not speaking to people where they are, you're just dumping manure on their heads.

It's equally useless to offer an unsolicited "Here's what I would do..." unless you and your advisee are at the same place in your life journeys. And maybe not then, either.

Wisdom comes from living, learning from the living, processing what you've learned, passing it through the lens of Jesus, and then, usually, keeping it to yourself, because most of the time when we share our wisdom what we're really doing is trying to *seem* wise or to *be right*.

Beware the desire to say a silent "I told you so." It's never, ever helpful.

Most people, most of the time, need deep listening, empathy, and a good open question. That's usually the best wisdom we can provide, which is probably why it feels like so many prayers go unanswered: God knows when to shut up.

Save your Truth pearls, to spend them on yourself during those days when the world is falling apart and your inner demons are shrieking.

The one who will need to hear them is you.

—EOR

Think of one piece of wisdom you've gleaned from living. Pass it through the Jesus lens of love and eternity. Write it down and put it where you can find it when you need a reminder.

COMMON 185

On the appointed day Herod, wearing his royal robes, sat on his throne and delivered a public address to the people. They shouted, "This is the voice of a god, not of a man." Immediately, because Herod did not give praise to God, an angel of the Lord struck him down, and he was eaten by worms and died. —Acts 12:21-23

At a church I used to attend, I had a friend named Spencer who had a beautiful singing voice. He would sing solos from time to time that brought the congregation to their feet. Whenever someone complimented him for a performance, instead of saying "thank you" he would say "all glory to God" or something like that. He would redirect the praise every time.

King Herod was the polar opposite of my singer-friend. He was an egomaniac, like many kings and world leaders throughout history have been. When the people proclaimed him a god, he didn't say, "No, no, there's only one God." Instead, he soaked in the adoration to the point where an angel of the Lord couldn't take it anymore. That's when Herod was taken down, left for worm food.

Herod's story is a cautionary tale for any wannabe messiahs out there.

I don't know any Herods personally, but they show up in my news feed every day. They live for attention, believe they're always right, refuse to be corrected, and use people to get what they want. The Herods, unfortunately, won't ever go away, even when angels decide it's time for them to be humbled.

I want to be among the Spencers.

In Matthew 23:12, Jesus said, "All who exalt themselves will be humbled, and all who humble themselves will be exalted." And he practiced what he preached. He modeled humility for us by washing his disciples' dirty feet, refused to demand justice from those who wronged him, and ultimately, chose to die when he could've saved himself.

I would rather be humble than humbled. Wouldn't you?

—BKS

What are some ways you could practice humility?

COMMON 186

All were baptized into Moses in the cloud and in the sea, and all ate the same spiritual food, and all drank the same spiritual drink. For they drank from the spiritual rock that followed them, and the rock was Christ. —1 Corinthians 10:2-4

Jesus is not Christ.

I don't mean that Jesus isn't the Messiah or isn't the Son of God. I mean that Jesus of Nazareth—the historical reality who shows up in the books that are scripture to Christians—is not identical to Christ, who is the eternal reality and who shows up all through the Bible as well as in plenty of other writings and in our daily lives.

That's why reading Jesus backward into the Hebrew Scriptures is a mistake. If Isaiah was prophesying about a Messiah apart from his own king, it wasn't *Jesus of Nazareth* he was talking about. He was talking about *Christ*, who showed up in Jesus, and possibly in others.

Why does this matter? Because much of the anti-Semitism and general arrogance Christians display is founded on the idea that the Hebrew prophets were predicting Jesus of Nazareth, which would make any Jewish person who doesn't claim Jesus as their messiah an ignoramus deserving of much proselytizing and condemnation.

Which is an attitude that is about as antichrist as you can get.

When the Jewish Christian Paul says that Christ sustained the Israelites in the desert, he's not talking about Jesus. He's acknowledging the eternal person of God we know through Jesus, and whom the Israelites knew through their spiritual and physical survival.

Follow Jesus. Make him your model and your Lord. Watch him to learn how to know God in Christ, because he was really good at it: Greatest Of All Time, even.

And remember that the same Spirit that sustained the Israelites is the One you know, too.

—EOR

When have you drunk the same spiritual drink as the Israelites? Where were you lost? How did it feel to be led out of the wilderness by God?

COMMON 187

The Lord said to him, "Who gave human beings their mouths? Is it not I, the Lord? Now go; I will help you speak and will teach you what to say." —Exodus 4:11-12

I'm gonna go ahead and say it: People are awkward. We say the wrong thing. We laugh at the wrong time. We trip over nothing—or maybe that's just me.

Moses was awkward too. He didn't think he had what it took to capture the attention and imagination of the Israelites. His public speaking skills were lacking; his brother, Aaron, was the eloquent one. He never dreamed he could be God's megaphone. I'm sure he surprised himself many times with the words that came out of his mouth.

But he didn't surprise God. And surprisingly, neither do we.

God uses awkward people like us to spread hope and light all the time. In conversations, in social media, in blogs and podcasts, poems and song lyrics. All it requires of us is being willing, being open, and being ourselves.

I wrote a song several years ago called *All Right To Be Okay*. In it, I talk transparently about feelings I had a year or so after my divorce. The song asks the question, "When's it all right to be okay?" In other words, when can I/will I finally be ready to move on?

A woman came up to me after I'd sung the song at a concert and thanked me for writing it. She shared that she was a therapist and had used the song with patients who had lost loved ones to suicide. She said many told her they'd found comfort in their grief from the words in my song. I was floored, and grateful.

Like Moses, when God speaks through us, we may be surprised at the outcome. We can't possibly know how our words will impact someone who needs to hear (or read) them. But they can't hear them if we don't say them.

—BKS

Who needs to be encouraged, enlightened, or emboldened by your words today?

COMMON 188

No testing has overtaken you that is not common to everyone. God is faithful, and he will not let you be tested beyond your strength, but with the testing he will also provide the way out so that you may be able to endure it. —1 Corinthians 10:13

I have a friend who hears "you're not able" as "prove it to me" and responds with "hold my beer." She's deeply competitive. She's never met a mountain she didn't want to conquer, or a critique she didn't want to prove wrong.

I'm not like that. I'd rather save my strength for something I have some hope of doing well.

You see the problem, right? My friend gains the strength she needs to go forward. I'm afraid of not having the strength to get through. We both experience what we expect: she makes the game-winning catch; I leave the field rested.

The reality is that we all have mountains to conquer, games to win, days to slog through. That's all testing is: facing obstacles, persisting, enduring, getting creative in our solutions.

The testing we face isn't pass/fail. It's more like load-testing: how much can we take before we get reinforcement?

There's no failure in needing reinforcement. My friend plays team sports, uses climbing equipment, consults mentors. Fear of failure makes me think that the result is all on me, rather than leaning on the ones or the One who can give me the insight, strength, or companionship to get through.

God has never let me down. Ever. Imagine what would be possible if I ran into my imaginary fire and let Them pull me out.

—EOR

How about you? Are you more of a go-it-alone-er, scared of feeling incompetent or needy? Or are you willing to ask for help, accept it when given, making you ready to climb whatever peak life puts in your path?

COMMON 189

Though you have not seen him, you love him; and even though you do not see him now, you believe in him and are filled with an inexpressible and glorious joy, for you are receiving the end result of your faith, the salvation of your souls. —1 Peter 1:8-9

At a church camp in Dickson, Tennessee, I went to an altar with several of my closest friends and made a profession of faith. It felt important and consequential, sure, but as a ten-year-old, I didn't fully know what I was doing. I couldn't possibly have understood all the implications of choosing to follow Jesus, especially at such a young age.

My church-camp profession of faith wasn't the completion of anything. Instead, it marked the beginning of a spiritual journey that has required making the choice to follow Jesus again and again.

Salvation is a present-tense kind of thing. In his first epistle, the Apostle Peter says we are *receiving* the end result of our faith, not that we have received it. We keep being saved as we learn to trust God through falling, failing, getting up, getting lost, and being found.

Peter says that because we love and believe in God we are being filled with an irrepressible joy, a result of our faith and an undeniable symptom of our ongoing salvation. A saved soul doesn't live a joyless life while waiting in line for the reward of a blissful afterlife. Instead, we saved souls trust God, even though neither God nor the outcome we face can be seen. We learn to follow in the way of Jesus by living as he did. As we do those things, our confidence grows, our faith deepens, and our joy blossoms. That's salvation.

All these years later, I am glad I went forward with my friends to begin this lifelong journey. My faith has guided me through trying times, has strengthened my resolve and built my character, has helped me recover from loss and grief, and has recalibrated my compass when I've wondered off-course. I know I am being saved as I continue to trust God.

—BKS

What is your salvation story? Where did it begin and where are you in your journey today?

COMMON 190

As Jesus was walking along, he saw a man called Matthew sitting at the tax-collection station, and he said to him, "Follow me." And he got up and followed him.
—Matthew 9:9

When the tax collector Matthew got up from the treasure he was collecting for Caesar, what made him do it?

This isn't a mystical question. Asked another way: When have you stopped doing one thing and started doing another? Broken up with a partner? Quit a financially sufficient job?

The only thing that motivates big change is pain + vision. (This is why New Year's resolutions don't tend to stick: they tend to lack both.)

The pain that motivates change could be almost anything: physical pain, fear, secrets, sorrow, frustration. The vision might be sexual attraction, possibility of a better job, a sense of the possibility of freedom, health that allows you to romp with your children.

I usually can't name my pain until I've acted on it. The fall I told my first husband I wanted a divorce followed a summer when I unintentionally lost thirty pounds and he got his first real job. I didn't know I was depressed and hopeless (*pain*) until I caught a glimpse of his potential financial freedom (*vision*). And: I couldn't name either of those things until I'd said "divorce" out loud (*big change*).

Something about Jesus gave Matthew a vision of a different reality, a better way of being in the world. Maybe it was Jesus' personal charisma. Maybe it was the Spirit poking Matthew into action. But if Matthew had been satisfied with his life as an extortionist-for-Caesar, he wouldn't have listened to Jesus' "follow me."

—EOR

When have you made a big and lasting change? Name the pain that finally pushed you into action and the vision that pulled you toward a new life.

COMMON 191

Lead me, Lord, in your righteousness because of my enemies. Declare them guilty, O God! Let their intrigues be their downfall. Banish them for their many sins, for they have rebelled against you. But let all who take refuge in you be glad; let them ever sing for joy. Spread your protection over them, that those who love your name may rejoice in you. Surely, Lord, you bless the righteous; you surround them with your favor as with a shield. —Psalm 5:8a, 10-12

When I first started reading comic books at eight years old, *Superboy and the Legion of Super-Heroes* was my favorite title. The stories took place in the 30th Century where a young Kal-El (Superman, for the uninitiated) traveled forward in time to help a small army of super-powered, interplanetary teenagers keep the universe safe. Every month, when a new issue came out, I knew who the good guys would be, and I knew the bad guys would go down in flames. Justice prevailed every time.

If only real life were like that.

In the Psalms, David often pleaded with God to end the injustice in his world. He believed that God was the ultimate Arbiter Of Justice, whose favor was like a shield. So he prayed for God to protect and prosper his allies and to make his foes answer for their many sins. He prayed for gladness, singing, and joy among God's people. He prayed for the good guys to win.

We live in a world that's saturated with injustice. Even though it's hard for me to see it now, I do believe that one day, God's justice—which isn't necessarily our justice—will prevail. Jesus talks about that in Matthew 5:3-11 (aka *The Beatitudes*), where he says, among other things, that the meek will inherit the earth (5:5), and that the Kingdom of God belongs to those who are persecuted because of their righteousness (5:10).

Until that day comes, it is up to us to work toward righting the wrongs we see around us, even (especially) in the face of persistent and powerful opposition. Even without capes. After all, that's what Jesus did.

—BKS

Name an injustice you see in the world around you. How can you help?

COMMON 192

A disciple is not above the teacher nor a slave above the master; it is enough for the disciple to be like the teacher and the slave like the master. If they have called the master of the house Beelzebul, how much more will they malign those of his household! —Matthew 10:24-25

How do you prepare a child for the dangers of the world without scaring them half to death?

When children are young, you carefully pad table corners, lock toilet seats, take knobs off stoves, and hold their hands. That's not hard, though it does take attention.

What about when they need some room to move? Or when they are called to step up and take responsibility for something beyond their wisdom and years? The padding comes off the table corners and, ready or not, they're pitched into the potential for danger.

That's the tricky balance Jesus is trying to strike with his immature disciples. He knows the real and present danger of sending them out: since he's not liked, they won't be either. It's not going to matter whether they are meek and kind, like innocent children, they will be targets of anger and arrogance.

Look at Rev. Dr. Martin Luther King, Jr or Mohandas Gandhi: when you face evil with goodness, you are likely to suffer. They followed the ways of a loving God, as did their followers, and were martyred for their efforts.

That's not to say that choosing martyrdom proves your saintliness. You can be a jerk and get run over by a truck.

It's as true now as it was when Jesus warned his friends: if you're going to actually follow Jesus, live as he did instead of how the day's loudest influencers do. Don't expect prosperity and ease. Students don't get off easier than their teachers.

If your role model is called evil or a heretic, chances are good you will be too.

That's why, after his death, so many of Jesus' apprentices scattered.

That's why, after their baptism, so many Christians go back to their old ways.

Are you scared yet?

—EOR

When you have consequential choices to make, how do you decide what to do?

COMMON 193

And if your eye causes you to stumble, gouge it out and throw it away. It is better for you to enter life with one eye than to have two eyes and be thrown into the fire of hell. —Matthew 18:9

Sometimes it's hard to know when to say goodbye. To a sweater that doesn't really fit anymore, but that reminds you of that amazing trip to Seattle ten years ago. To a job you hate because you're not sure where you'll go next, and because: bills. To a relationship that used to be fun and fulfilling, but now leaves you feeling lonely most of the time.

Most of us aren't good at cutting our losses and moving on, even when staying is hurting us. Same goes for unhealthy habits.

I love carbs. Bread is the one food I'd want on a deserted island. I survived on pop tarts and cereal and chips and sandwiches and sodas when I was younger. If I'm being honest, I still consume three of those things now, at least a couple times a week. But I'm not the carb-metabolizing machine I was in my teens and twenties.

Now I'm not going to hell for eating carbs. But I do pay a price if I eat like a teenager as a middle-aged guy. And we pay a price when we hang onto life-destroying habits, lifestyles, relationships, and attitudes, even those that weren't always life-destroying.

Taking stock of what we're doing in our lives—and why—can be difficult, even painful. But so can the consequences of living an unexamined life: consequences for ourselves and for those who love us.

—BKS

What in your life has passed its expiration date? What will you get in exchange once you let it go?

COMMON 194

Those who find their life will lose it, and those who lose their life for my sake will find it. —Matthew 10:39

Let's get this over with: Jesus isn't talking about bodily death. He's not extolling martyrdom as a sign that you're Really his disciple. Suffering doesn't have moral value in itself.

Sure, there are those who think that continuing a marathon after you break your leg is more laudable than not breaking your leg at all. And you may have been brought up to believe that keeping your needs to yourself and "manning up" is proof of your faithfulness.

That's not Jesus, and it sure as heck isn't God.

Jesus' point is simple: if you value the things of the world—fame, wealth, security, ease, power over others—more than you value the things of God, you won't experience the unshakable hope, the deep peace of communion with Eternity. The things of the world are just too alluring. They're the pastries of spiritual food: tasty, but addictive and not nourishing.

God is not an either/or kind of person. If you wind up famous or secure as you develop connection with God, great. But if you pursue fame, security, or whatever is your personal symbol of success, you're likely to miss out on the other stuff, the eternally life-giving reality.

That's what "losing your life" means: setting aside the common successes, as needed, to pursue the greater ones.

For me, it's shutting off my phone and its constant distractions in order to read deeper words. Or reminding myself that stepping away from tv with my family is actually okay.

That's what laying down my life looks like today: hushing the voices of guilt, envy, or distraction to do what draws me nearer to my deepest self. Which is God.

—EOR

What is your "life"—the most powerful voices, distractions, or successes—that pulls you from your deepest good? How can you lay it down from time to time?

COMMON 195

So the law was our guardian until Christ came that we might be justified by faith. Now that this faith has come, we are no longer under a guardian. —Galatians 3:24-25

Early Christians in Galatia (and everywhere else) were mostly Law-abiding Jews. They didn't stop being Jews even though they were also Jesus-followers. They continued to live according to the customs and commandments in the written Torah as well as those passed down verbally through generations, like all good Jews did. Like Jesus did.

The problem that started to arise within the Galatian church (and in every other church), was what to do with non-Jews, aka Gentiles. The Apostle Paul explains in his letter to the Galatians that following Mosaic Law is not required for Gentiles to become Christians. That, in fact, the Law doesn't apply to Jesus-followers at all. Faith is what defines a Christian.

I'll admit that I have felt like a First Century Jewish Christian.

I grew up in a church with some pretty strict requirements for being a Christian. First, I had to decide that I wanted to dedicate my life to following Jesus and profess it publicly. Then, there were rules to follow, against dancing, going to movies, drinking, smoking, and playing cards, as well as the big obvious ones. After that, I had to invite the Holy Spirit into my life (the concept of *entire sanctification*). And even after all of that, I had to always be on my toes because if I sinned it could sully me in the eyes of God, taking away any security I had in my relationship status with God.

Now I didn't have an issue with Christians who didn't follow the same rules as me. I just had a hard time accepting that following the rules wasn't a critical part of my Christian identity. I had to learn what it meant to let my faith guide my actions, not the doctrine of a church.

The Law isn't bad. Neither are rules if they help you live within healthy boundaries. But following rules doesn't save us, nor does it justify us. Faith, and living it, does.

—BKS

What are the rules you abide by as you live a faith-guided life? Why are they important to you? How do they help you?

COMMON 196

Let the little children come to me; do not stop them; for it is to such as these that the kingdom of God belongs. Truly I tell you, whoever does not receive the kingdom of God as a little child will never enter it. —Mark 10:14b-15

Little kids don't wrestle with whether unicorns are real. They also don't lose sleep over the stock market or wonder why reforming gun laws is so hard to do. Their imaginations are free to roam. Their hearts and spirits haven't been broken. They are trusting, idealistic, simple creatures.

I know I can't go back to being a little kid, though sometimes I really wish I could. Like you, I get weighed down with the worries of the world. I read too much news, consume too much social media, and get lost in the shadowy corners of my own adult mind.

Jesus knows we are grown-up citizens of a world that, at face value, doesn't resemble the kingdom of God. He knows we make good decisions and bad, motivated by both the desire to be good and the fear of losing everything. He understands the trappings of a human experience, because he was human too.

When he says that to enter the Kingdom of God we must have childlike faith, he isn't asking us to forget our sorrows or leave our doubts at the door. He knows we bring our histories, heartbreaks, and questions with us. But he does ask us to believe that God might be bigger than all of that—much like a child believes her dad can vanquish monsters from under the bed.

If I am living with a childlike faith, I don't get too hung up on whether I'm doing everything the right way. I don't have to have all the answers. Instead, I rely on God, whose arms are always open to me, and live accordingly.

—BKS

What does living with a childlike faith look like to you?
How would your life be different if you allowed your inner child to trust in someone, especially God?

COMMON 197

And they came and said to [Jesus], "Teacher, we know that you are sincere and show deference to no one, for you do not regard people with partiality but teach the way of God in accordance with truth. Is it lawful to pay taxes to Caesar or not? Should we pay them, or should we not?" But knowing their hypocrisy, he said to them, "Why are you putting me to the test? Bring me a denarius and let me see it." And they brought one. Then he said to them, "Whose head is this and whose title?" They answered, "Caesar's." Jesus said to them, "Give to Caesar the things that are Caesar's and to God the things that are God's." And they were utterly amazed at him. —Mark 12:14-17

Raise your hand if you've been told this passage is about how everything belongs to God and so you owe God everything, especially all your money, preferably as a check made out to The Church You Belong To.

I've heard that sermon. Heck, I've considered preaching it when the accounts got low. But even if it all belongs to God, it doesn't seem to be in God's nature to demand rent or repayment. God isn't demanding or withholding.

Perhaps all of this—our lives, the planet, the cosmos, love—isn't listed on a bill somewhere, waiting to be paid. (If there had been a bill, which I deeply doubt, Jesus paid it for everyone and for all time.) God is the very best parent possible, which means that what God wants for us is love, wellbeing, and peace. What God wants from us is love, affection, and tender care for all the things we've been given, like the trees and the oceans and each other.

Caesar and church may want your time and treasure. God desires your love.

—EOR

When do you think more in terms of paying your debts than expressing love?

446

COMMON 198

Tim McGraw, the country star, had a song out many years ago called *Live Like You Were Dying*. In it, Tim sings about a conversation he had with a friend who had been told he was dying. When Tim asked him what he did after the diagnosis, the friend said:

> I went skydiving
>
> I went Rocky Mountain climbing
>
> I went 2.7 seconds on a bull named Fumanchu
>
> And I loved deeper
>
> And I spoke sweeter
>
> And I gave forgiveness I'd been denying.

The chorus ends with the friend saying, "Someday I hope you get the chance to live like you were dying."

I've thought about what I would do if I were told I had only six months left to live. I'm sure you have too. Me, I'd ride more roller coasters, eat more barbeque, spend tons of time with all my favorite people, make a whole lot of music, and care a lot less about how I look. I wouldn't squander a minute.

The Psalmist says living like our days are numbered results in wisdom. Notice that the Psalmist doesn't say we gain a *brain* of wisdom, but a *heart* of wisdom, which says to me wisdom is about more than just what you know, but what you've experienced and felt. Wisdom comes from being observant, engaged, and invested in everything going on inside and around you.

So it seems to me that over a lifetime, regardless of how long that is, one can become wise just by living life to its fullest.

—BKS

What would you do if you knew you were dying? What on that list could you do today?

COMMON 199

He is God not of the dead but of the living; you are quite wrong. —Mark 12:27

When my husband and I married we bought tiny life insurance policies, basically enough to pay burial expenses. When our child was born, we bumped up the life insurance payout. When my husband started having health problems, we got another policy to help cover the financial costs of long-term care.

We didn't get married for those life insurance policies. Our relationship is built on mutual love *now*, not avoiding financial ruin later. The policies are symbols of that love.

Of course, there are those who marry to gain money after their spouse's death. Do we value their vows the same way? Do we call that relationship *love*?

Yet we're told to "marry" Jesus in order to inherit streets of gold from his Dad.

That's not a relationship of love. That's an afterlife-insurance policy.

Trusting Jesus isn't about gaining something later, after you die. Jesus was clear: relationship with God is for the living. Relationship with God is based on loving *now*, not avoiding eternal ruin later.

Sometimes I realize I'm feeling distant from my husband. When that happens, I reach out to him. Tell him about my day. Listen to him talk about his. Scoot in closer when we're hanging out together. Doing that helps me overcome my distance and reminds him that I love him.

It's the same with God, you know? When you feel distant from God, you can reach out, tell Them about your day, listen to whatever They have to say to you. Scoot in closer when you're hanging out together.

That's what builds a relationship of mutual love. Eternal insurance is just a happy extra, tagged on as a symbol of that love.

—EOR

Why did you connect with God to begin with? Are your reasons for nurturing connection the same now?

COMMON 200

Observe the Sabbath day by keeping it holy, as the Lord your God has commanded you.
—Deuteronomy 5:12

Even though it's one of the Big Ten, observing Sabbath isn't something Christians (myself included) do well. Most Christians I know don't even attempt such a counter-cultural practice as being deliberately unproductive and intentionally God-focused for 24 consecutive hours every week. It seems extreme. Some might say even Jesus found it extreme since he healed sick people on the Sabbath.

But I digress.

Now I am not claiming to be an expert on this subject. I am terrible at slowing down, let alone halting most everything I do in my daily life, for the sake of observing a holy day. So what I'm about to write is for me as well as you.

Orthodox and other observant Jews follow strict guidelines for Sabbath (Shabbat) from sundown Friday to an hour past sundown on Saturday. That means they choose not to earn or spend money. They limit their activities and their consumption. Some don't cook meals or use electricity. Some don't drive. What they choose to do instead is worship together, and then rest, trusting God to take care of everything while they do.

I've worked in churches for most of the last 13 years, so Sundays have not been a day of rest for me. I've also worked at least one additional job, usually two, to make ends meet. So taking a day during the week to rest has felt costly. Plus, the desire to get out of debt, to meet other people's expectations, and to talk back to self-condemning voices ("You're lazy!") has driven me to stay busy seven days a week.

So Sabbath for me, when I've tried to practice it, has come less in the form of a whole day, and more in the form of moments. Like taking time to pray, take a bath, or go for a walk, especially when I feel compelled to check my emails or the news for the tenth time of the day. Or like maybe devoting an hour to write at my piano instead of watching Disney+ or scrolling Instagram to disengage.

If practicing Sabbath is new to you—or hard for you, as it is for me—maybe try starting small. It helps to understand that it is an invitation for us to trust God, and to rest in God's provision for us. It isn't another thing we have to do, but something we get to do.

—BKS

Have you ever tried to observe Sabbath? What did you do, and abstain from doing, and how did it feel? What would observing Sabbath look like for you now?

COMMON 201

Then the scribe said to [Jesus], "You are right, Teacher; you have truly said that 'he is one, and besides him there is no other'; and 'to love him with all the heart and with all the understanding and with all the strength' and 'to love one's neighbor as oneself'— this is much more important than all whole burnt offerings and sacrifices."
When Jesus saw that he answered wisely, he said to him, "You are not far from the kingdom of God." After that no one dared to ask him any question.—Mark 12:32-34

You don't have to grovel.

You don't have to beg.

You don't have to fast, or tithe, or go to the temple every week.

None of those things gets you any closer to the kingdom of God.

What does get you closer?

Knowing God, loving God, loving neighbor, loving self.

Jesus wasn't letting the scribe off easy. Loving is a lot harder than begging, fasting, tithing, and showing up at a designated place.

God's love is the foundation of the kingdom, so the more you love, the closer you are.

While you practice loving, you may find that fasting and tithing and churching weekly help. Rhythms of self-restraint and giving and worship reinforce the practice of love, but they're not the point.

Any questions?

—EOR

What is one activity that you do (or could do) regularly that would help reinforce your practice of loving God, or neighbor, or yourself?

COMMON 202

For I know how many are your transgressions and how great are your sins—you who afflict the righteous, who take a bribe, and push aside the needy in the gate. Therefore the prudent will keep silent in such a time; for it is an evil time. Seek good and not evil, that you may live. —Amos 5:12-14a

For Jesus-followers, it seems as though seeking good and avoiding evil would be an obvious baseline expectation. I mean, shouldn't we always be leading the charge against injustice, corruption, and obvious malevolence? Some of us are, to be sure. But some of us, well, aren't.

I read in the news every day about self-professing Christians working diligently to weaken or even take away the rights of women, immigrants, minorities, and LGBTQ+ citizens. I see them exert their privilege over others while calling themselves victims. They are loud, angry, and determined—and they are getting their way.

These Christians actively perpetuate and promote evil in the name of Jesus. (Sit with that for a minute.)

I think about how much could be accomplished if those same Christians used their influence for good. What if Christians of every stripe—heck, let's include Jews, Muslims, Buddhists, Hindus, and other spiritually guided citizens—decided the most important thing we can do today is speak out against oppression, right the societal wrongs we see in our own backyards, and just love our neighbor?

What if those Christians who are shouting about how mistreated they are just stopped talking?

All it really takes to fall into evil is setting our sights on something or someone other than Jesus. Once our desire to be good is replaced with a desire to be powerful, that's when we should know we're in trouble.

And change that desire. Again.

—BKS

What is one action you could take today in the pursuit of good and the defeat of evil?

COMMON 203

As he taught, [Jesus] said, "Beware of the scribes, who like to walk around in long robes and to be greeted with respect in the marketplaces and to have the best seats in the synagogues and places of honor at banquets! They devour widows' houses and for the sake of appearance say long prayers. They will receive the greater condemnation." —Mark 12:38-40

I'm going to be honest with you: I like being treated well. I enjoy a warm welcome and a comfortable chair. My ego is stroked when listeners stay through my whole message. When someone I admire wants me to sit next to them, my heart flutters a little and I feel a flush of pride.

Is Jesus condemning me for that?

More honesty: I'm not sure. I'm not the target of his overall teaching in this part of Mark—he's focusing on arrogance and stealing from the poor—but what about my desire for acclamation? For acceptance by my "betters"?

How much energy that could be spent on God and goodness is taken up by my ego's assertions? How much more willing-the-good-of-others could be achieved if I weren't willing-the-comfort-of-me?

I don't believe God condemns anyone permanently, but I expect God is more pleased (on multiple levels) when I am not satisfying my own insecurity. I know for certain that when my ego isn't in the way I *see* and *hear* others better. Self-centeredness becomes habitual; loving less does too.

The only question is whether I choose to do anything about it. Honestly.

—EOR

What is blocking you from the full expression of love?

COMMON 204

> For we do not have a high priest who is unable to sympathize with our weaknesses, but we have one who in every respect has been tested as we are, yet without sin. Let us therefore approach the throne of grace with boldness, so that we may receive mercy and find grace to help in time of need. —Hebrews 4:15-16

The letter to the Hebrews is unlike the other epistles: it is written in a decidedly Jewish voice for Jewish-Christian readers. In other words, it explains Christian ideas in a way that would've made sense to Jewish followers of Jesus. For example: comparing Jesus to a high priest.

Here's a bit of background on high priests. They were all descendants of Aaron (the brother of Moses), at least to begin with. In addition to their genealogy, they had to meet some exemplary standards, including things like having never touched a corpse. Then, once elevated to their position, they wielded a great deal of political power.

High priests lived in something like a bubble. That's because a high priest's sins were regarded as sins of the people: if he committed a sin, it was as if everyone had committed that sin. So high priests had to always live above reproach and away from anything that might defile them.

On Yom Kippur, the highest of the Jewish Holy Days, the high priest would carry out his most solemn duty. He would enter the Holy of Holies, which was the inner sanctuary of the Tabernacle where God's presence was said to appear. He would go in alone and make sacrifices on behalf of himself, his house, the priests, and all the people. Atonement for everyone's sins relied on him.

Jewish Christians understood well the role of a high priest. So when the writer of Hebrews compares Jesus to a high priest, they get it. But unlike a high priest who lived apart from the people and away from degradation, Jesus lived among the people, and was well-acquainted with their struggles, even facing struggles of his own.

Yet, because he was regarded by God as sinless, he was uniquely prepared to bear the sins of the people before God, and then act as an Advocate for us all. That's why we can approach God boldly: Jesus is there to speak on our behalf.

—BKS

How's your boldness before God doing? Why do you resist?

COMMON 205

For now they will say: "We have no king, for we do not fear the LORD, and a king—what could he do for us?" They utter mere words; with empty oaths they make covenants; so litigation springs up like poisonous weeds in the furrows of the field.
—Hosea 10:3a-4

Kings are rough trade. Whether they're emperors fiddling while their city burns, or titans of industry underpaying their workers, or tyrannical presidents marching their slaves into war: extreme power doesn't look good on humans.

But we long for kings. There's something about the promise of order and charisma that tugs at our imaginations. We cheer them on, bragging on their behalf when they best those they consider lesser, sneering at those who lack the influence to decree, "I wore it better."

The Israelites ran out of kings from time to time, so smattered throughout the Hebrew Scriptures are scenes of them wailing to God to send one along. In fact, when the throne was empty, they assumed that God was deliberately withholding out of spite or disappointment.

But in the book of Hosea, the problem with kings is named: they abound in false promises that do nothing but spread rancor, destroying the tender roots of providence and peace.

Rather than rewarding us for our goodness and faithfulness, maybe God puts idols and kings in place to punish us for our indifference and arrogance.

Maybe the purpose of earthly rulers is not to lead us but to teach us that the only good king is the King of kings: God Themselves.

When we are leaderless, maybe we really *don't* deserve a king. Maybe we're being rewarded with the possibility of strength under the guidance of the only Sovereign we really need.

—EOR

Have you ever handed over your personal sovereignty—to a job or a marriage or an addiction? How did you (or will you) right-size that ruler in your own mind?

COMMON 206

> As [Jesus] was setting out on a journey, a man ran up and knelt before him, and asked him, "Good Teacher, what must I do to inherit eternal life?" Jesus said to him... "You know the commandments." [The man] said to him, "Teacher, I have kept all these since my youth." Jesus, looking at him, loved him and said, "You lack one thing: go, sell what you own, and give the money to the poor, and you will have treasure in heaven; then come, follow me." When (the man) heard this, he was shocked and went away grieving, for he had many possessions. —Mark 10:17-18a, 19a, 20-22

I don't have all that many possessions. I don't own a house. My car is a (paid-for) 2015 Hyundai. I don't have a flush retirement account, or a lot of cash stuffed in a shoebox under my bed.

The things I value most are things most people wouldn't consider very valuable. Like my comic book collection (DC, dating back to the mid-1960s), my vintage Converse All-Star sneakers (I bought them new), my passport (so I can go anywhere I want), my aforementioned Hyundai (affectionately called Sparky), and my MacBook and iPhone (so I can write, create, take photos, and stay connected to the world).

I would be sad to give up any of those things. I get why the rich young man was sad too.

We attach to things to feel secure. Our identities are wrapped up in what we have, what we do, and who we love. If you're rich and you give away all your money, what are you left with? How will the world see you, and treat you? How will you survive without wealth? How will you survive with no money at all?

Sometimes Jesus asks us to let go of the thing we are holding the tightest so that we can grab hold of the amazing thing the Divine has for us. It's a risk we take—a leap of faith—because we can't see precisely how it's gonna play out for us. But our faith isn't living until we act on it.

In this story, Jesus wasn't condemning the man for having riches. Money and possessions are not bad. But the rich man couldn't have the life he was asking Jesus for until he laid down the one he had a death grip on.

And neither can we.

—BKS

What do you hold onto the tightest? What would happen if you loosened your grip? How would it change your life?

COMMON 207

But as for you, return to your God; hold fast to love and justice, and wait continually for your God. —Hosea 12:6

Idols and influencers captivate. Kings and wanna-be rulers lie. And you will get caught in their traps. You will, at some point in your life, realize you're ensnared and not know how to break free.

Whether you're an addict, an apologist, or apparently optionless, the first step to breaking away from life-destroying ideas and people is to realize that something needs to change.

The problem is that while we don't tend to make real changes until we're desperate, it's a lot harder to climb out of a pit when you're at the bottom.

In those fleeting moments that you're feeling okay, notice where you're spending your time and focusing your attention. Does what you're doing make you anxious? Envious? Cynical? Impatient? Angry? Consider that a clue that idols and liars and plain old bad habits are cutting away at your wellbeing.

The second step is to turn toward what is Eternal, True, and Good. Whether it's named God or Allah or Atman, if it is eternal *and* true *and* good, that's where your focus needs to be.

How can you tell what's really eternal *and* true *and* good? It will be all about love, which is willing and enabling others' best life, and justice, which is equity interlaced with mercy.

The third (and fourth and fifth and...) step is to hang on tight. The lure of the immediate and the power of fear will try to regain your attention. Keep returning to God, trusting that They are already at work in your life.

Waiting is not a passive activity. That's despair. Waiting is doing the part that is yours to do while anticipating the participation of others. Even when they take longer than you'd like.

God is always engaged and active in the world God has made. That's God's part.

As for you, your part is to change your ideas and take all those little life-giving actions when needed, and to keep returning to love and justice: the most noticeable attributes of God.

—EOR

Is there something in your life that you're paying more attention to than you should? Something that's not contributing to love, peace, justice, and hope? What changes do you need to make in your thinking and habits to deal with that?

COMMON 208

For the Lamb at the center of the throne will be their shepherd; he will lead them to springs of living water. And God will wipe away every tear from their eyes.
—Revelation 7:17

I used to be afraid of death. More specifically, I used to be afraid of facing God. Even though I was always asking forgiveness for sins I'd committed (the ones that I knew of), I was not at all sure I'd named them all. I mean, what if I'd sinned and didn't know it? Would God give me a pass? In my old way of thinking: not a chance.

So death for me equaled judgment. And judgment equaled hell. Maybe.

These days, I don't worry so much about dying with unconfessed sin in my heart. I know God loves and accepts me, even though I'm imperfect. I also feel confident that God isn't keeping a spreadsheet on me and my choices.

As for the afterlife, I don't often think about it. To be honest, golden streets, gates of pearl, and hilltop estates don't really excite me. And sitting on a cloud strumming a harp? I'll pass.

But here's something I do look forward to: "God will wipe away every tear from their eyes."

I believe that I will be with God, which means I'll be without fear, pain, grief, worry, anxiety, and depression. The rest is gravy.

So while I'm in no hurry to leave this earthly plain, I'm also not living in dread of the day when I do. Because what I will have there is peace. Just peace. And that sounds pretty great to me.

—BKS

When God wipes the tears from your eyes, what will you be leaving behind?

COMMON 209

He said, "To you it has been given to know the secrets of the kingdom of God, but to others I speak in parables, so that 'looking they may not perceive and hearing they may not understand.'" —Luke 8:10

Here's my idea of a great long-car-drive game: give my then eight-year-old daughter a multiplication problem to do. Something like 323 x 761. Without paper and pencil.

Once the problem was issued the air would fill with her questions and thinking-throughs as she kept the numbers in alignment, logically and visually processing the steps.

Sometimes.

I don't think she can multiply like that anymore; pens and computers have replaced the rigid mental columns that made it possible.

But accurate multiplication—getting the right answer—was never the purpose of the game. (Well, not the whole purpose.) The point was to engage her in creative thinking. I wanted her to break out of her current brain drone, visualize the answer, and then figure out how to get there.

Jesus teaching in parables seemed to drive his closest disciples a little crazy, mainly because they were terrible at understanding them. They wanted clear answers and direct instructions. Laws, if you will, that they could just obey and be done with it.

But Jesus taught in parables to help his listeners break out of the brain drone of legalism, visualize the present Kingdom of God, and then figure out how to live there.

Jesus taught in parables because he respected the ability of his followers (if not his closest friends) to break out of the boxes that constrained their spirits and get to know his Dad intimately, life-givingly.

Looking and not perceiving, listening and not understanding, can inspire us to think and eventually to know, as long as we can be comfortable with mystery for a while and stop looking up the answers.

—EOR

What life-mysteries make you uncomfortable and crave quick & simple answers?

COMMON 210

"See, I will make you small among the nations; you will be utterly despised. The pride of your heart has deceived you, you who live in the clefts of the rocks and make your home on the heights, you who say to yourself, 'Who can bring me down to the ground?' Though you soar like the eagle and make your nest among the stars, from there I will bring you down," declares the Lord. —Obadiah 1:2-4

God has infinite patience. But I'm convinced that if there's one thing can try God's patience, it's pride.

The people of Edom were descendants of Esau, the impulsive son of Isaac who lost his father's birthright (that's leadership of the family and judicial authority over the people of Judah) to his younger brother, Jacob. Even though Edom was a brother-nation to Judah, controlled by Jerusalem, the Edomites were arrogant because their nation was situated in the mountains of Seir. Their location had gone to their heads.

Obadiah, the prophet, warned Edom that God would take them down a notch if they didn't dial back their pride. That's because God had revealed to Obadiah that Babylon, led by Nebuchadnezzar, would sack Jerusalem and take the people of Judah captive. And as if that weren't bad enough, the Edomites would help the Babylonians cart off the wealth Judah left behind.

The Edomites were not only prideful, they were opportunistic and self-serving. And like their forefather, Esau, they didn't think things through. Ultimately, turning their backs on Judah would lead to their demise— their perch in the mountains would be overtaken by Egypt, and the Edomites would cease to be a people.

Obadiah's warning is for all of us, of course. Makes me wonder: What am I prideful about? Do I look down on others from a place of self-importance? Am I capable of taking what isn't mine if I want it and the opportunity presents itself, even if the opportunity comes at the expense of someone I care about?

—BKS

What are you prideful about?

COMMON 211

> He said to them, "Take nothing for your journey: no staff, nor bag, nor bread, nor money—not even an extra tunic." —Luke 9:3

"I'm not ready."

"When the kids leave home, then our marriage will be better."

"I'll be there as soon as I'm completely done with this over here."

"Once I lose the weight then I'll ... [fill in any unrelated wish here]."

If you are waiting for the right time to do the next right thing, you'll never get it done.

If you're preparing for change when you could be doing the changing, the status will continue to be quo.

We are never fully ready for the big game, the raise request, the new child, the escape to safety. Truth is that overpreparing and delaying are usually nothing more than fear's loud shouts.

Most of the choices in our lives, from the mundane to the monumental, come down to one simple truth: do or don't do. (*Thanks, Yoda.*)

Forward movement is less the result of preparation than of trust: trust in yourself, trust in others, trust in God.

When Jesus sends the disciples out on their first gospel-spreading mission, he tells them to take nothing with them. It's not that he wants them to be poor. He wants them to trust in themselves, in others, and in God.

Change reveals our vulnerability, which is why real change always begins with an act of trust. (Change never stops being just one act of trust after another, though whom you are trusting at any particular juncture can shift.)

Love is an expression of trust. You cannot fully will the good of another without trusting that you are fundamentally okay and that God (or someone) has your back.

You are. And God does.

—EOR

What small step forward are you postponing out of fear?

COMMON 212

[Jesus] said to him, "If they do not listen to Moses and the Prophets, they will not be convinced even if someone rises from the dead." —Luke 16:31

Ever heard the conspiracy theories about the 1969 moon landing of Apollo 11?

Seems there are people who still believe that Neil Armstrong and Buzz Aldren never stepped onto the moon. That the whole Apollo mission was staged, completely fake, even though all those theories can be easily disproven.

Apollo deniers claim that the shadows of Neil Armstrong and the US flag on the moon's surface in one of Armstrong's famous photos were created using stage lighting. They say that the Apollo astronauts could not have survived the radiation belt that surrounds the Earth's atmosphere. They cite the absence of stars in the photos taken on the moon. They point out that a flag can't wave where there is no wind. And lastly, they ask, "If Apollo was a success, why haven't we sent more astronauts to the moon?"

All of these theories have been repeatedly debunked, but that doesn't stop people from believing them. The truth is that people believe what they want to believe. Our minds aren't easily changed by science, persuasion, a sermon, or even common sense.

But being rigid in our thinking leaves no room for revelation. If Moses couldn't believe that God could speak to him from a burning bush, then he would've never led the Israelites out of Egypt. Sometimes being a person of faith requires imagination.

There are beliefs I hold to wholeheartedly. But I pray that I'll always leave room for the possibility that I could be wrong, because I'd never want to miss something that God wants to show me in a way that I wouldn't expect.

—BKS

Think of a time when you changed your mind about something. What did it take to convince you? How did it affect your views on other things?

COMMON 213

They went to him and woke him up, shouting, "Master, Master, we are perishing!" And waking up, he rebuked the wind and the raging waves; they ceased, and there was a calm. —Luke 8:24

Sometimes circumstances freak me out that seem to have no effect on others. My co-conspirator Benton enjoys socializing with groups of people, whereas I can enjoy everyone involved and still have my anxiety shoot through the roof.

Usually I can remind myself of the reality outside my responses and endure. Even enjoy!

Sometimes, though, no amount of looking at my abilities and experience and external reality calms me down. At that point I have three choices: skip the event; grind my teeth and get through it (breaking down in the bathroom when needed); or ask for God's help.

Yes, I know that I should pray first, and I do, but I don't depend upon God until my own strength isn't enough.

When the waves of anxiety and the fear-filled winds cast me out to sea, and I accept that I'm panicking and unable to deal and finally plead for help, God calms the storm.

The event is the same, right? It's still multiple people I think expect individual attention and engaging stories (whether they do or not is irrelevant). And I'm still not equipped to do what I think they expect. But the storm inside me loses its destructive power.

God's presence, and my awareness of God's presence, makes it possible to steer my emotional boat to safety.

—EOR

When has God calmed your storm and tempered the waves? When did you notice that was happening?

COMMON 214

"Because he loves me," says the Lord, "I will rescue him; I will protect him, for he acknowledges my name. He will call on me, and I will answer him; I will be with him in trouble, I will deliver him and honor him. With long life I will satisfy him and show him my salvation." —Psalm 91:14-16

God doesn't care if you dance. Playing cards is fine too. You can wear your hair however you want. If God has opinions on such things, you'll probably never know what they are.

Wear what you want (within reason). Self-respect and self-expression are both important. God is mum on tattoos, but I'll say this: please check your spelling first.

Your alcohol consumption doesn't have eternal consequences, but it might have earthly ones if you do it irresponsibly. Same with food.

The gender and skin color of the person you love are not Divine concerns either. Nor are: the thing you do for a career, what zip code you live in, who your favorite band is, or whether you're a Marvel or a DC person.

In fact, there really are only two things that matter a whole lot to God. Jesus was pretty clear on this, and Moses points out one of them beautifully in Psalm 91.

God wants our love. Our wholehearted, deeply devoted, fully intentional love.

And when we love God, our life's choices will reflect that. We will behave in ways that are in sync with God's hopes and dreams for us. And we will more naturally do the second thing God cares most about: we will love (*will the good of*) our neighbor.

One caveat: If any of the things I mentioned above are things you take issue with—e.g. if you think drinking is something you shouldn't do— then by all means, don't do them. Just don't let your motivation be fear, guilt, or shame. God would never want that.

—BKS

How do you feel when you consider that God's only explicit mandate for us is to love? Liberated? Afraid? Concerned? Something else?

COMMON 215

Those who trust in their own wits are fools, but those who walk in wisdom come through safely. —Proverbs 28:26

Not too long ago I decided to put together a DIY furniture kit at 5 a.m. I didn't want to wake anybody by rifling through cabinets and drawers to find the tools I needed, and since I've done a lot of manual labor in my life I said a mental "forget it" and figured I'd figure it out.

The butter knife managed the screws until it didn't. Then one evil wood screw wouldn't pierce the plywood, so I grabbed a nail to get a hole started, using the cork side of a tile coaster as a hammer.

Go ahead and laugh as you picture me slamming both my thumb and finger with the "hammer", biting my tongue to silence my groans, and continuing this fool's errand until the tile broke.

Actually, I think Benton came out and stared at me before the tile broke but I didn't notice.

Me (holding my swelling thumb and looked for super glue): "Oh, I'm sorry. Did I wake you? What time is it?"

Benton:

(Yeah, that's about all he said.)

Had I decided to heed the wisdom of the enclosed instructions and gathered the correct tools, my thumb would have one less scar and Benton might've slept until daylight.

Hubris is not my friend. Or yours. Or Benton's, obviously.

I'm hoping I've learned from this. And that my words here will serve as your wisdom, and you will too.

—EOR

When have you ignored others' wisdom, giving you the opportunity to learn painful lessons?

COMMON 216

Accept one another, then, just as Christ accepted you, in order to bring praise to God.
—Romans 15:7

We've all heard the terrible adage "Hate the sin, but love the sinner." (Some people believe Jesus said that. He didn't.)

We know that sin is any life-destroying act or attitude that impacts ourselves or other people. By that definition, sin includes spreading rumors, harboring resentment, being short-tempered, and a host of other things both Christians and non-Christians do. But the adage isn't really about those things.

The Greek word Paul used in Romans 15:7 that was translated as "accept" also means "welcome." As Christians, when we chose to follow Jesus, we were welcomed with open arms, without conditions. Repentance—turning the other way, making different choices—was the result of that welcome, not a condition of it. Jesus' acceptance of us didn't—and still doesn't—require us to be perfect.

By the same token, accepting someone as Jesus accepts us means welcoming them into our churches, our communities, our families, and our lives. We may not like the way they dress, how they vote, who they love, or what is in their past. But none of those things are sin in and of themselves. And even if they were, if we accept someone as Christ accepts us, then there is no hating the sin, only loving the person.

One more thing: When we welcome someone into our lives as they are, we don't see the things about them we would change if we could. We only see the beautiful person God created and dearly loves. And that puts a smile on God's face.

—BKS

Why do you think it is hard for us to accept people as Jesus accepts us? What can we do to change that in ourselves?

COMMON 217

Let the sea roar and all that fills it, the world and those who live in it.
Let the floods clap their hands; let the hills sing together for joy at the presence of the LORD, for he is coming to judge the earth.
He will judge the world with righteousness and the peoples with equity.
—Psalm 98:7-9

How do you picture Judgment Day? Jesus coming from the sky, surrounded by dark clouds, eyes flaming? If God's predilection toward punishment was used as a threatening behavior-motivator, your image of the day of The Lord's Coming might not be all unicorns and rainbows.

Judgment Day is when God exerts justice, sending the wicked to hell and the good to heaven, right? Which would be great if you're one of the good, but not so great if you're unknowingly among the wicked.

That's the scary part: that you might have destroyed something precious, as if God were a parent who comes across a broken heirloom and somehow knows you're the naughty child, finds you hiding in the closet, and withholds their kindness forever.

That's not biblical, and it's not God.

Look at how the Psalmist describes the day of judgment: nature claps its hands and sings for joy.

Look at how God is described: with righteousness and equity. God may be a judge, but God isn't judgmental.

Judgment is the discernment of truth, the application of mercy, and the setting-right of all that's gone wrong.

Judgment Day is about God's determination to restore direction, beauty, and goodness to a world that's gone off-course and gotten ugly and mean.

How does God do that? I don't know, but it seems to me that if God created everything and loves all that They created, Their focus isn't on punishing Their children, but on mending what's been broken.

You don't have to hide in a closet, afraid of God's punishment. God's got the design skills and the glue to put anything broken back together.

Even you.

—EOR

Are you afraid of God's judgment, or think Hell's for others but not for you? Close your eyes and mentally scan your body. When you think on the idea that God is judgmental and vengeful, what do you feel in your shoulders, stomach, butt?

COMMON 218

The Lord makes firm the steps of the one who delights in him; though he may stumble, he will not fall, for the Lord upholds him with his hand. —Psalm 37:23-24

We don't use the word "delight" nearly enough these days. I'm not even sure I understood exactly what the phrase "delights in" meant until I consulted Webster's Dictionary. Turns out that to delight in something is to enjoy it very much.

I delight in roller coasters. I can be spotted wearing the goofiest grin you've ever seen when I get strapped into a coaster, especially one that is super-tall and super-fast. (Lookin' at you, Millennium Force!)

I also delight in singing songs I've written for an audience. Getting the immediate positive feedback of people nodding to a poignant lyric, or dancing in (or out of) their seats to a beat I made makes me giddy with joy.

I also delight in my kids. They make me laugh hysterically. Watching them have fun makes me tremendously happy. Seeing them thrive brings me outrageous joy. I enjoy them very much.

The question is: do I delight in God?

I do enjoy spending time with God, especially when I'm driving or taking a walk. That's when I do my best pondering and praying. I do experience God's presence in the aforementioned riding of roller coasters and singing of songs. I also know that God is with my kids and me when we're doing whatever we're doing.

I can also testify that God has upheld me many times when I've stumbled. There were times when I should've fallen, hard. But I didn't because God held me in bigger, safer hands than mine.

So yes, I delight in God and amazingly, God delights in me. And in you. How about that?!

—BKS

What do you delight in? Where do you find joy? When has God held you up when you could've (should've) fallen?

COMMON 219

For thus says the high and lofty one who inhabits eternity, whose name is Holy: "I dwell in the high and holy place and also with those who are contrite and humble in spirit, to revive the spirit of the humble and to revive the heart of the contrite."
—Isaiah 57:15

It's hard for me to picture God without thinking *up*. I understand God is everywhere and nowhere (because *where* is a description of physical reality), and I experience God's presence within and around me, but when I imagine that unique divine being, it's always *up there*.

Isaiah talks about God as "the high and lofty one" which sounds like *up there* to me. How far up did Isaiah think God was? Did the sky seem closer before we had cameras in space? If God is simply above the sky, or beyond the firmament, and the sky isn't that far away, then God wouldn't have to be that far away either.

Isaiah also writes that God dwells not only in the high and holy place, but with human beings too. Wrap your heavens-focused mind around that for a minute. Isaiah's not talking about Jesus of Nazareth, that flesh-and-blood person who ate and drank and died. Jesus wasn't even around at that point.

Isaiah is saying that *God* is all at once high and holy, and here. Right here with me as I type these words. Right where you are as you read them.

Let your mind linger on that reality for a moment. Can you grab hold of the there-and-here, then-and-now of God?

Unless you're a character in some multiverse scenario, you can't be in two places at once. But God is up there and down here, no matter where down here happens to be.

God is actually, for real, where you are right now. If your hand were non-material you might be able to reach out and touch God, whatever *reaching* and *touching* would mean in that case.

God isn't distant at all. When you are bored, God is right there with you. When you are distracted, God is right there with you. When you are joyous or despairing, God isn't *up there* somewhere. God is right there with you.

And why does God hang around with you, physical and right-here creature that you are? To revive that eternal part of you—the god-ish soul and spirit of you—when you need it.

My soul and spirit don't have the same imagination problems I have. They're always part of God's eternity. Right here.

—EOR

Try picturing God sitting right next to you, looking over your shoulder as you read. If you could impress that image in your mind, how might that change your experience of the rest of reality?

COMMON 220

For the sake of his great name the Lord will not reject his people, because the Lord was pleased to make you his own. —1 Samuel 12:22

God doesn't reject us. Ever.

It took a long time for that to get into my brain and my heart. As a young Christian, I thought that surely I annoyed God with my persistent sin and my near-constant penitence. I was taught that I could lose my place at God's table if I was disobedient, even unknowingly so. I was always afraid that I was one misstep from a hellish eternity. So my nagging guilt drove me to my knees multiple times a day.

Much of that guilt came from the idea that I was damned to begin with thanks to sin I was born with. Yes, I know that doesn't at all square with the idea that God was "pleased to make (me) his own." That was a conundrum I spent years grappling with. Maybe you did too.

But here is the truth (brace yourself): God was indeed pleased when you were born. God claimed you even before that. You were never cursed, never a disappointment to God. When you took your first step, read your first book, scored your first home run, danced in your first recital, God grinned from ear to ear.

God has always been happy to say, "That's my kid!" No matter what you've been told.

Many misfit Christians I've talked with over the years have been taught to believe that they are outside of what God could ever be pleased with. I felt that way too. But it is simply untrue.

Always remember this: God loves and accepts you, as you are, where you are. It is not in God's nature to turn you away for any reason ever. God is pleased with you.

—BKS

Do you worry that God is not pleased with you? When does that fear creep up on you? What are the voices telling you that you aren't good enough for God?

COMMON 221

Rend your hearts and not your clothing. Return to the LORD your God, for he is gracious and merciful, slow to anger, abounding in steadfast love, and relenting from punishment. —Joel 2:13

When you mess up, how do you prove that you see what you did wrong and that you regret doing it?

Once I was at an acquaintance's home for dinner and knocked over a wine glass, shattering it. Though I apologized profusely and helped clean up, I didn't feel like I'd done enough to warrant their forgiveness. So the next day I bought a package of four identical glasses and trudged through the rain to deliver them. (The rain was a happy accident since it added to my sense of appropriate suffering.)

While the glasses were a nice gift, the giving of them had very little to do with the recipient and nearly everything to do with my wanting to prove I was contrite. And thoughtful. And honorable. And I don't know what else.

When I was a professor I developed a crush on a student 5 years my junior. Let's call him "Ross." We were friends, part of a larger group, but I blurred lines I shouldn't have as his teacher. When I realized what I'd done, the guilt was horrible. For 20 years I couldn't think of it without crying, sometimes for hours.

Then "Ross" came to speak at a local bookstore. I went to apologize, not to excuse or explain, but to say that I saw what I'd done wrong and that I regretted doing it.

After the talk he was inundated with questions and fans. I waited until the last person had left the store. Shaking, I apologized to his smiling, confused face for something he didn't remember and wouldn't have been upset by even if he had.

God is kind of like "Ross." When you do something wrong, God isn't looking for you to beat yourself up. And God isn't looking for some divine version of wine glasses with which you fix the relationship. Any brokenness in your relationship with God is just in *your* head and heart. God's fine.

Here's what God wants, and what Ross wanted, and what my hosts got immediately after the glass crashed to the floor: you. That's it.

God doesn't carry grudges or want revenge.

God wants you, in all your messy, broken, confused, gloriousness. You are God's cherished child and creation.

Does that mean you shouldn't accept responsibility and apologize? Of course not.

Does God's forgiving nature mean that you shouldn't try to make amends when you sin? No, because making amends is how we humans begin to heal.

—EOR

What guilt are you still carrying around? How can you accept your fault, make amends, and let go?

COMMON 222

When [Jesus] had finished washing their feet, he put on his clothes and returned to his place. "Do you understand what I have done for you?" he asked them. "You call me 'Teacher' and 'Lord,' and rightly so, for that is what I am. Now that I, your Lord and Teacher, have washed your feet, you also should wash one another's feet. I have set you an example that you should do as I have done for you. Very truly I tell you, no servant is greater than his master, nor is a messenger greater than the one who sent him. Now that you know these things, you will be blessed if you do them."
—John 13:12-17

When Jesus knelt before each of his disciples and washed their dirty, naked feet, it was awkward and uncomfortable for them. It was also counter-cultural. Hosts at a Passover meal didn't wash their guests' feet. Not even Jewish servants washed anyone's feet.

Here, Jesus modeled servanthood in its purest sense for his disciples. Emptying himself of the dignity afforded practically anyone, he demonstrated what it means to serve someone else. And then he told his disciples to go and do likewise.

The last few years in the US have shown Americans to be fearful, suspicious, prideful, and self-centered. As a society, we don't value serving others as generations before us did. In fact, many see it as a sign of weakness. Instead, we admire those who take more for themselves, usually at the expense of others.

God must grieve over the lack of care we show for each other, especially those of us who call ourselves people of faith. We've strayed so far from the teachings and example of Jesus.

How can we reverse the direction we're moving in? By meeting the challenge Jesus put before his disciples to care for others. In big and small ways. Consistently.

—BKS

What are some ways that you can put others first?

COMMON 223

So I tell you, whatever you ask for in prayer, believe that you have received it, and it will be yours. —Mark 11:24

Dear God—please give me musical talent and an accordion. Thank you.

Even if I pray this prayer really hard for many days, I'm not likely to open my eyes and see an accordion or suddenly have musical talent. I'm okay with that, mostly.

Oh, heavenly Father, I beg you to give my hungry child food.

Papa, I've been sick for so long. Please release me from this pain.

If these were my prayers, and my child starved or I kept suffering, I would not be okay with that. I would be angry and despairing.

I know that God answers all prayers, and sometimes the answer is "no."

I know that loving parents don't always give their kids everything they ask for.

"No" isn't good enough if my child is hungry and I can't figure out how to feed them. So what could Jesus possibly mean by *believe that you have received it and it will be yours*?

I don't know. I can't explain this passage without giving a canned answer.

I do know this: God has never stopped being with me, comforting me, guiding me, even in the worst of times. Even when I've been pissed off and no one else was there, God was. Even when I knew my world was collapsing and that I wasn't safe, God helped me through.

I know this too: when I remind myself of God's persistent presence and of my own resourcefulness—that is, *believe* that God and I are working together—I'm much more likely to find a solution or to reconsider one that I'd rejected.

That's enough, for now.

—EOR

What would you do next if you believed you had what you needed?

COMMON 224

The Lord said to him, "Who gave human beings their mouths? Who makes them deaf or mute? Who gives them sight or makes them blind? Is it not I, the Lord? Now go; I will help you speak and will teach you what to say." —Exodus 4:11-12

I've talked myself out of doing many things throughout my life because I didn't think I was good enough.

I didn't pitch my song. I didn't pursue that job. I didn't speak up in that meeting. I didn't defend myself. I didn't get that cute guy's number. The list goes on.

Sure, there's the fear of rejection. Also a lack of self-confidence. But sometimes, I feel the nudge of the Spirit to do something and I ignore it or defy it. Because I don't think I'm good enough.

Moses didn't think he was the man for the job. God was telling him to go to Pharoah and demand that he free the Israelites. Yes, that's a tall order and yes, I'm sure I would've responded the same way Moses did. He said to God, "I'm not special. I'm not smart. I'm not eloquent." And God said, "Who are you to tell me you're not capable when I'm telling you that you are?"

God sees the things in us we don't see. God sees the landscape in front of us, the opportunities and the pitfalls. God knows all the variables and has no intention of watching us fail. So at the end of the day, I can trust God, as scary as that might feel, or I can listen to my own self-doubt and miss whatever God is offering me.

What if God knew my song was exactly what Carrie Underwood's producer was looking for at that very moment? Who am I to say my song isn't good enough when God says it is?

—BKS

When have you talked yourself out of doing something because you thought you weren't good enough?

COMMON 225

> And the Lord said to me: "The prophets are prophesying lies in my name; I did not send them, nor did I command them or speak to them. They are prophesying to you a lying vision, worthless divination, and the deceit of their own minds."
> —Jeremiah 14:14

Prophets are truthtellers. Inspired, nudged, or led by God, they see what others do not and share their sights with the world.

Actual prophecies are always in line with general truths such as cause/effect and the fact of God's unbreaking love for every one of God's creations.

Prophets do not claim God's favor, nor do they accept titles like "Chosen" or "God-ordained" because they don't need to.

Someone who is actually prophesying cannot be lying: "prophesy" like "fact" implies truth. A false prophet is someone who claims to be uniquely chosen by God to share some "truth", some secret, that is unsupported by general truths.

A false prophet is not a prophet, but a liar and, often, a swindler playing a long con.

When a government or religious or business leader positions himself (*usually it's a "him" but not always)* as a prophet, his arrogant lies are especially dangerous. His claims to unique and hidden knowledge, along with the rabid devotion of his followers or employees, allow him to create an alternate universe—a dangerous world that only they can see and from which only he can save you.

Know anyone like that?

When God shows someone truth that others don't seem to see, it's not that the truth has been held secret. God is giving the prophet an eternal perspective. Actual prophets tend to be humble, and they always point beyond themselves to the greater Reality, from which hope springs.

I hope you know someone like that, too.

—EOR

Whether you understand Jesus to be the only son of God, the incarnation of the Second Person of the Trinity, or not, he's clearly a prophet. Get to know Jesus, and see the greater Reality.

COMMON 226

Now faith is the assurance of things hoped for, the conviction of things not seen.
—Hebrews 11:1

Your phone rings before the sun is up. You groggily answer: "hello?"

It's a close friend: "I can't get out of bed!"

You're jolted awake: "What happened? Are you okay? Have you called 911?"

The friend: "I'm afraid to put my feet on the floor. What if it's not there? What if it gives way and I crash through?!"

At which point your concern for your friend's health moves from the physical to the mental, because, as a rule, floors that were present before they went to sleep are present when they wake up.

Now imagine that your friend lived in a house under construction, with big holes in the wooden floor. Suddenly not being certain of the safety of the ground under their feet makes a lot more sense.

Rolling out of bed, putting your feet on the floor, then putting weight onto your feet is an act of faith: that the floor is solid, your legs are strong, and your balance is sufficient. Even if you can see the floor—examine it, test it—and feel your legs, back, and balance, moving takes faith.

Everyone has faith in something. The only difference among us is what we have faith *in*.

And here's the scary part: faith is always in something unseen and unproven, because we are incapable of knowing what will happen in the next moment.

Faith is being confident that what you hope is true, is in fact true. Faith is trust in what cannot be fully determined.

Faith is not blind. Faith is not irrational. Faith is the trust on which all human action depends.

Personally, I have more faith in God than in any human being because God is the only one who has consistently proven Themselves. And, having lived in earthquake country, I have seen the results of the ground giving way, so am inclined to trust God even more than I trust the floor.

Does that mean I have to get stuck in bed? No. You can, and must, have faith in more than one thing, one person, one situation. It's the only way to live.

My faith is big enough to includes both floors and God.

—EOR

When push comes to shove, where do you invest your faith? The news? Democracy? Math? Your partner?

COMMON 227

Thus says the Lord: "Cursed are those who trust in mere mortals and make mere flesh their strength, whose hearts turn away from the LORD." —Jeremiah 17:5

I don't think I've ever been cursed. Cursed *at*, sure. But cursed? Been the object of a vengeful or capricious decree that supernaturally destined me to pain, failure, or humiliation?

Well, when you put it that way...nope.

I *have* experienced painful and humiliating (and predictable) consequences of my (and others') actions. I didn't predict those outcomes, of course, and I *think* I would have chosen different actions if I had. But maybe not.

My pride can get me into trouble. Ditto my self-dependence.

And if I expected authorities or celebrities to satisfy my needs and wants, I'd be disappointed, all the time. Maybe feel cursed, even scream "Why ME?!!" at the sky.

The only person who has never let me down is God. Because God is the only one who can actually hold me up.

That's what *trusting in mere mortals* means: expecting a human being, including yourself, to be flawless, or at least powerful enough to do something that matters without assistance.

Lately I've been practicing asking people, including God, for help, and aiming to not be hurt if they say "no" or don't follow through as I'd like. Just asking for help—whether I receive it or not—is a spiritual practice that gradually shapes me to be more humble and forgiving. Asking for help, especially when I don't receive it, also trains me to be more patient with myself and others...and more persistent.

Becoming more humble, forgiving, patient, and persistent doesn't sound like a curse to me, but the joyful (and predictable) consequences of my (and God's) actions.

—EOR

Have you turned an unpleasant or hurtful outcome into something good? How did you and God do it?

COMMON 228

The vessel he was making of clay was spoiled in the potter's hand, and he reworked it into another vessel, as seemed good to him. —Jeremiah 18:4

I used to be a potter. I studied ceramics for years, with good teachers, learning correct techniques and practicing faithfully. I made my own clay, more or less well, and bought better clay than I could make.

I'd knead the clay, slap it onto the throwing surface, then gently (but firmly) use my hands and tools to shape it as it whirled round and round.

Sometimes making something beautiful would happen on the first attempt. More often than not, the clay would wobble off its center, or its rim would flop down all around it, or I'd just decide it wasn't as good as it could be.

When whatever I was shaping fell apart I'd scoop it up, take it to a dry table, and knead the clay from failure into pure potential.

It wasn't like I was mad at the clay or blamed it for not becoming as beautiful and useful as I imagined. Yet every preacher I've ever heard expound on the God-as-potter verses has made "being reworked" sound like a threat.

"You, Clay, had better shape up or The Potter will knock you down, beat you up, and start all over again. Or He'll just drop you into the dustbin or an awful bucket of slop."

Wow. I wasn't even a good potter, yet I wouldn't have blamed the clay for not becoming the exact bowl I had in mind. And I sure as heck wouldn't have put it through the fire, then pulled it out and smashed it.

When I started over, the clay was still the same clay, made of the same dust and water, but I would change my approach, being more gentle or more firm as needed. I'd nudge an area differently or leave it alone and let the rotation and the environment do their thing.

When the clay and the wheel and I worked together, what emerged was beautiful, every single time.

—EOR

A spiritual practice to try: Remind yourself that you are pure potential, held gently by the Potter and meant to be beautiful in Their eyes.

COMMON 229

Come to me, all you who are weary and are carrying heavy burdens, and I will give you rest. Take my yoke upon you, and learn from me, for I am gentle and humble in heart, and you will find rest for your souls. For my yoke is easy, and my burden is light.
—Matthew 11:28-30

Kitchen floor mopped? Done.

Laundry folded? Done.

Cat picked up from vet? Done.

Checking items off my to-do list is really satisfying.

Until it's not.

Like when my to-do list is longer than the amount of time I have to complete it, or when preparing to complete Task 1 uncovers Tasks 1a through 1z that have to be done before Task 2 can be.

Then my to-do list is just a burden that gets heavier until I want to give up.

Spiritual to-do lists can be burdens too, especially when they determine whether you are Good or Bad, heaven-bound or hell-condemned.

Tithe? Check.

Bible chapter read? Check.

Straight, white, cisgender, married, successful kids? No?

Uh oh.

Wherever those spiritual checklists come from, it's not God. And Jesus isn't Santa, checking his list to find out whether you're naughty or nice. Jesus is kind of the anti-Santa. Jesus gently removes the list from your clutching fingers, saying "Follow me."

"Follow me" can be a lot harder than "do this" if you think "follow me" means "be perfect, but without rules." How do you know how well you're doing if there's no checklist?

How well you're doing? You're not getting graded. There's no shame in not keeping up, because there's no keeping up involved.

Jesus isn't keeping score. He's inviting you into a loving, learning relationship.

The rest he's already done.

—EOR

What is the spiritual burden you're carrying around? How might you cross a few things off that checklist, for good?

COMMON 230

Before [Josiah] there was no king like him who turned to the Lord with all his heart, with all his soul, and with all his might, according to all the law of Moses, nor did any like him arise after him. — 2 Kings 23:25

If you were brought up in a church that emphasized the connection between King David and Jesus, or if you learned that David was "after God's own heart", you may have thought that David was The Righteous King before Jesus.

Um, no. David was the umpteenth-great-grandfather of Jesus, but he himself was kind of awful, at least in the beginning. While the prophet Isaiah talked about a future king from David's lineage he wasn't saying that David was such a great guy that the savior of the Jews would have to be descended from him.

King Josiah, who ruled a few hundred years after David, was the first king to obey what Jesus called the Greatest Commandment: Love the Lord your God with all your heart, soul, and might.

And, the Bible says, "nor did any [king who obeyed the greatest commandment] arise after him."

None? Zero?

We shouldn't be surprised. Human kings tend to not be pinnacles of virtue. Kings of media, kings of industry are not likely to love God with all their heart, soul, and might, if with any at all.

Any king who arises from royal blood or popular acclamation isn't going to be all that great. We love our kings, but we don't choose well.

The only ones worthy of our adoration and obedience are those who love the Lord their God with all they are, their entire being, because if someone does love the immortal God that way they're going to love mortal beings too.

Only that kind of king is worthy of your trust and devotion.

Josiah may have been the only one who was fully human and fully devoted to God.

Thank God for Jesus: human, divine, loving, and worthy of trust.
Literally. Thank God.

—EOR

A spiritual practice to try: Thank God for the fallibility of human kings and the dependability of Jesus. See where that prayer takes you.

COMMON 231

Although [Jesus] was a Son, he learned obedience through what he suffered.
—Hebrews 5:8

If you've known any addicts, alcoholics, or compulsive anythings, you know that suffering doesn't make you change those actions that caused it.

Or if you've had a heart attack and the doctor has told you to lay off the smoking and the bacon, do you do what you've been told?

Can't say I know many people who change their ways because their suffering woke them up. We're stubborn, and every one of us sees ourselves as different from the other 2 billion people who have the same problem.

Your heart attack that would have killed you if someone else hadn't called an ambulance? Genetics. Obviously.

Your horrible, day-long, not-the-first-time hangover? You shoulda just eaten something, right?

If we obeyed the natural law of actions & consequences, our lives would probably be better. Our climate sure would.

And our kids are just like us, because they're human too, and sometimes it doesn't matter what we say: they're not going to do what they're told.

Jesus was different. Oh, not in that kid-ignoring-what-the-parent-says kind of way. According to the Bible, he wasn't always obedient (check out Luke 2:41-52 if you don't believe me); he ignored his parents too.

What's unusual is that he learned from his suffering. He learned to obey his parents, and his Parent. He learned to be open, to listen closely, to question, to trust, and to obey.

To be fair: Jesus' heavenly Dad proved His trustworthiness a whole lot of times, even before His kid was born. But we are perfectly capable of ignoring perfectly trustworthy Persons, aren't we?

Maybe following Jesus has something to do with getting close enough to God to eventually trust that what God has told us is true. And then obeying, instead of denying our own suffering, its clear causes, and the suffering of those around us.

Jesus had to learn it. Maybe we can too.

—EOR

Have you learned something from the pain in your life? What did it take to get you to change?

COMMON 232

Thus says the Lord: Act with justice and righteousness and deliver from the hand of the oppressor anyone who has been robbed. And do no wrong or violence to the alien, the orphan, and the widow, or shed innocent blood in this place. —Jeremiah 22:3

Kids ask questions. When my daughter was very little she asked her dad why he had no hair on his head. He told her that his hair had uprooted, crawled down onto his back, and settled there. She gasped and nightmare. He earned the wifely chiding he got.

As God's kid the only question I've ever really asked was "how, then, shall we live?"

(Really. Started asking it when I was around 8. I was a weird kid.)

Over the many intervening years I've received a lot of answers from politics and the pulpit. Most of them have been some version of "the way I (*the answer-giver*) think is right."

That response tends to contain 1) a condemnation of someone else, alongside 2) an exaltation of the speaker. Who, he himself tells us, has a uniquely insightful relationship with Truth or God.

(By the way, if someone says they are a prophet or have a gift of prophecy, back up slowly and get out of there. Prophets—God-inspired truthtellers—don't need to announce themselves. Con artists and condemners do.)

It takes no special insight to discover how God wants us to live. Throughout the Bible the writers are clear:

> Do justice, love kindness, and walk humbly with God. (Micah 6:8)

> Love God with all your heart, soul, and might; and your neighbor as much as yourself. (Deuteronomy 6:5; Matthew 22:37)

> Act with justice and righteousness and deliver from the hand of the oppressor anyone who has been robbed. And do no wrong or violence to the alien, the orphan, and the widow, or shed innocent blood in this place. (Jeremiah 22:3)

"How, then, shall we live?" is the easiest question a kid has ever asked, because it's been answered time and time again, by Someone who in fact has a uniquely insightful relationship with Themselves.

—EOR

What is your real-life response to "how shall I live?" What other questions do you need answered?

COMMON 233

Why in the world is Noah's Ark a children's story?

Sure, the image of animals trotting up a gangplank is pairs is pretty cute. Two waddling penguins. Two trumpeting elephants. Two languid tigers, housed far from the white-tailed deer and the antelope.

The unicorns were too busy playing to heed the rising waters, I hear.

Then rain falls and seas swell and everyone not on the little boat drowns.

This is our idea of a tale for toddlers?

It is, because it is the story of a Creator grieving the broken masterpiece. It is the extent a Parent will go to save what's left of their child.

So destroyed is God by the evil that people wreak on one another that God does the only thing They can think of: rescue what's left of beauty and truth, let the rest slip down into the grey sea, trusting that what little is left is somehow enough to begin again.

Come to think of it, maybe Noah's Ark *is* a story for children. It speaks to God's rescue, not just a single family or a breeding pair of mosquitoes, but of the entire Creation Project.

Though humankind goes terribly, horribly wrong, God sees the potential and keeps it alive.

Keeps us, as a species, as a work of God's hands, alive.

That's hope.

Perhaps Noah's Ark isn't a story of cuteness, or of the only family worthy of saving.

Perhaps it's a story of how God saves every tiny shred of goodness and life, even when the world is coming apart and light is hard to find.

Even at our worst, the Ark tells us, we are worthy of rescue and care.

And having sworn that They would never allow the world to be wiped out again, the next time a rescue was needed God came to us, so that we all could learn, and do better, and live.

—EOR

How far would you go to save your child? And what does "save your child" mean to you today?

COMMON 234

Justice is far from us, and deliverance does not reach us;
we wait for light but there is only darkness and for brightness but we walk in gloom.
—Isaiah 59:9

I deal with lifelong chronic biochemical non-situational depression which sometimes can knock me down even when I'm doing everything right. When that tsunami washes over me, it doesn't matter what uplifting mantras I repeat or what silly movies I watch: whirling, chaotic, feverish darkness wins while words fail.

I recognize those now-rare times in moments between verses of the Bible, as well as in slave narratives and the sound of Billie Holiday songs.

Real despair lacks language. But we try to explain or at least express, and to hold on until the world slows down and gets quiet enough for us to hear the wordless voice of Hope.

I think that's what Isaiah is doing here—trying to find words for the deep anguish that his people felt as they suffered under oppression. For him, justice and hope are far away, beyond the water and the sky, far too far to rescue his people. They've waited, and waited, in the darkness of pain and suffering until their feet drag and their eyes cannot make sense of an outline of hope in the shadows.

Light buried under the weight of pain and hopelessness emits only silence.

These waning days of autumn can feel like that, as the days grow shorter and midnight crowds out the light of the sun. Add in the busyness and loneliness of holidays and it may not matter what inspiring quotes are in your Instagram feed: sometimes shadow wins.

But in a few short weeks the light of a star will pierce the darkness, the cry of a long-expected savior taking his first breath will echo through the emptiness.

Hold on. The light of the world is coming.

Again.

—EOR

LAST SATURDAY BEFORE ADVENT

**But be doers of the word, and not merely hearers who deceive themselves. For if any are hearers of the word and not doers, they are like those who look at themselves in a mirror; for they look at themselves and, on going away, immediately forget what they were like. But those who look into the perfect law, the law of liberty, and persevere, being not hearers who forget but doers who act —they will be blessed in their doing.
—James 1:22-25**

My bathroom mirror doesn't lie. It points out my blemishes and wrinkles and weight gain. It reminds me I look more like my mother's father the older I get. Sometimes I like what I see. Sometimes it pisses me off.

I have other mirrors too. My (now-grown) kids. The people I live with. The lyrics I wrote last decade and last night. When I'm paying attention, it's hard to unsee what I see in my mirrors, even the good things.

James says being a doer of the Word is what makes the Word a part of us. I believe that is true. Practice does make (closer to) perfect. He also says that when we merely hear the Word and don't act on what we hear, it's like we forget our own faces.

Truth is, the Word is itself a mirror. It reminds us we are beautiful and flawed and sacred and made-from-mud and fragile and eternal. That is, if we're paying attention.

When I started writing these devotional thoughts back in 2021, I had no idea the practice would become such a window into my own spirit, soul, and mind. I reconnected with truths from my youth and experienced anew a whole lot of Scripture that I read completely differently now. Once the Word gets into your bones, it shows you who you really, truly are.

Like a mirror.

—BKS

What and who are the mirrors in your life? What are they showing you?

ABOUT US

Benton Stokes is a songwriter, a recording artist, an author, a worship leader, a podcaster, a collector of comic books, a lover of roller coasters, a dad, a friend, and (with ministry partner Elane O'Rourke) half of *School For Seekers*, the nonprofit powerhouse behind this book.

Benton has a passion for helping post-Evangelicals, particularly queer men, find their way to healthy theology and healing perspectives. He also loves communicating hope in his songs — his third album, Streams, releases in February 2023.

Benton co-hosts (with Elane) *Cocktail Theology* — a podcast that tackles topics such as defining what an abomination actually is, exploring why Christians and science are at odds all the time, and reclaiming Christian-ese language like "born again." All while sipping tasty libations.

Benton happily offers a prayer, an ear, or a song whenever warranted.

Rev. Dr. Elane O'Rourke is a spiritual director, lifelong teacher, theologian, mom, contemplative, Enneagram 1, and a bunch of the other things Benton wrote. She was a professor of philosophy for a decade, a pastor for another decade, and the instigator of *School For Seekers* since 2014.

Elane's first book was *A Dallas Willard Dictionary*, written to explain the difficult words of Christian philosopher Dallas Willard, which may explain a lot of her role in the podcast she co-hosts with Benton, *Cocktail Theology*.

Elane's deepest desire, and life's work, is for you to believe that you are God's cherished and beloved child, worthy of care and respect.

School For Seekers is a 501c3 nonprofit dedicated to your spiritual growth, utilizing classes, counsel, and community designed to help you rethink your faith and re-establish your relationship with God, yourself, and others.

Contact us at info@schoolforseekers.com

Made in the USA
Coppell, TX
22 November 2022

86805992R00273